Advance Praise for *Dreams of the Overworked*

"This marvelous book captures the contemporary experience of nine families, allowing them to speak for themselves about their dreams and how they cope with everyday life. Uniquely, it celebrates the fact that it is the dense web of social connections, or scaffolding, that enables family life to thrive in the digital age."
—Judy Wajcman, London School of Economics

"Beckman and Mazmanian capture timeless and essential truths about blending parenting and employment. This is a book about cooperation and dependence—dependence on both earning an income and being an involved parent; dependence on our children for their cooperation in the shared endeavor; dependence on our family and friends for their engagement and care; dependence on caregivers who provide the scaffolding that makes each unique work–family blend possible."
—Kathleen L. McGinn, Harvard Business School

"In their excellent new book, Beckman and Mazmanian explore the Herculean task today's families face as they strive to live up to the unrealistic expectation of doing everything perfectly while also being bombarded by 'helpful technologies.' Their in-depth look at different family configurations frames the challenges—and potential solutions—that today's unique families need to understand in order to thrive in these changing times."
—Brad Harrington, lead author of *The New Dad* research series

"This wonderfully intriguing book reveals how invisible and undervalued support from extended family members, friends, neighbors, and communities is the scaffolding that makes survival and success possible. The example-rich writing is delightful and the informative endnotes fully cover a wide range of literature. This book is eye-opening and a must-read for all."
—Lotte Bailyn, MIT Sloan School of Management

"What makes this book unique is its tough love message. Left to its own devices, technology makes us more likely to buy into myths of our perfectibility. The way out begins with our deep understanding of our vulnerability. From there, these savvy and humanistic researchers can help you design a customized plan for individuals and organizations. But it's going to be a *plan*, not a gimmick."
—Sherry Turkle, author of *Alone Together*

"Beckman and Mazmanian show the stakes in everyday life as we pursue perfection. Whether being the best parent and worker or having a perfect body, we try achieving the unattainable by working hard and efficiently to do more and do it better. *Dreams of the Overworked* explores the internal work that fills our days as we navigate life, simultaneously alone and in a crowd."
—Chuck Darrah, co-author of *Busier Than Ever!*

DREAMS OF THE OVERWORKED

DREAMS

OF THE

OVERWORKED

Christine M. Beckman

LIVING, WORKING, AND PARENTING IN THE DIGITAL AGE

and Melissa Mazmanian

STANFORD UNIVERSITY PRESS
Stanford, California

STANFORD UNIVERSITY PRESS
Stanford, California

All artwork courtesy of Vera Khovanskaya.

Printed in the United States of America on acid-free, archival-quality paper

Library of Congress Cataloging-in-Publication Data
Names: Beckman, Christine M., author. | Mazmanian, Melissa, author.
Title: Dreams of the overworked : living, working, and parenting in the
    digital age / Christine M. Beckman and Melissa Mazmanian.
Description: Stanford, California : Stanford University Press, [2020] |
    Includes bibliographical references and index.
Identifiers: LCCN 2019051227 (print) | LCCN 2019051228 (ebook) |
    ISBN 9781503602557 (cloth) | ISBN 9781503612334 (ebook)
Subjects: LCSH: Mental fatigue. | Quality of life. | Families.
Classification: LCC BF482 .B43 2020 (print) | LCC BF482 (ebook) |
    DDC 155.9/2—dc23
LC record available at https://lccn.loc.gov/2019051227
LC ebook record available at https://lccn.loc.gov/2019051228
Book design by Kevin Barrett Kane
Typeset at Stanford University Press in 10/14 Mercury Text G1

to Kim and Mary,

who scaffold our dreams

CONTENTS

PREFACE

AMERICANS ARE WORKING HARDER, parenting with more anxiety, and living more and more frenzied lives. The mental checklist is long: Did you finish the report? Remember to text the acting coach? Sign the kids up for camp? Get to the gym? Professionals are expected to be at-the-ready, parents are told to be ever-present, and everyone hears the message to exercise and eat well. Do you live in world where work is endless, family is all consuming, and exhaustion is the norm? You are not alone.

Technologies promise to help. You can respond to an important work email while at a child's baseball game; you can monitor your kids while at work; and you can count your steps and track your sleep rhythms. All true. But at the same time technologies make you *more* available, *more* accountable, *more* frazzled. Changing expectations about accessibility make it all the more difficult to be the kind of colleague, parent, and person you want to be.

While you may know in your heart of hearts that perfection is unattainable, do you still flush with pride in those brief and fleeting moments of having it all under control? Is there an insistent voice in your head measuring yourself against unrealistic expectations about what it means to work, parent, and live in the digital age? It is hard not to.

But these expectations miss a lot. Do you also give yourself credit for being a good friend? Are you proud of your ability to find and offer help?

With all the demands of work, parenthood, and taking care of yourself, you know that you don't do it alone—but do you see those around you who make your daily life possible?

Take this morning. You probably accomplished, or tried to accomplish, a series of tasks: getting to work on time, eating, seeing children off to school, squeezing in some exercise. How did you do it? While struggling through a hectic morning, it's easy to feel alone, the center of a bad movie in which nothing is going right for the protagonist. But, most likely, you were supported, enabled, and empowered by others—what we'll call *scaffolding* in this book—in numerous ways: someone else may have purchased the coffee beans, packed the kid's lunches (or yours!), cleaned your house, signed your child's permission slip, or got the kids to school so you could get to work on time or fit in some exercise.

Current obsessions with individual triumphs in work, parenting, and self-improvement obscure the unsung yet equally essential need for community, collectivity, and help. In an age of increasing isolation, when technology seems to be pulling people apart from each other, this book shows how—in spite of the increasing obstacles of modern life—you are actually using technology to build connections with others. In truth, your reliance on others (and their reliance upon you) is the basis of everyday accomplishments. The emotional and practical moments associated with collective engagement deserve to be celebrated.

DREAMS OF THE OVERWORKED

PART I

STRIVING FOR IMPOSSIBLE DREAMS

CHAPTER I

INTRODUCING THE DREAM(S)

Waking at 5:30 a.m., Nancy Huron drags herself out of bed to take a shower. After weeks of trying (with some success) to get up at 4:30 to walk on her treadmill in the garage, she has finally given up and let herself "sleep in." Work email kept her up the night before. The treadmill will have to wait. By 5:45 she is showered and wrapped in a thick bathrobe. Wandering down the hall to the kids' rooms she gently shakes her sleeping six-year-old daughter, Melody, and eight-year-old son, Dylan, murmuring, "It's time to get up. You get to see all your friends at school!" As she dries her hair and gets dressed, Nancy walks back into each of their rooms. She repeats various encouragements with increasing firmness: "Come on. It's time to get up. Time to get up now. You can do it. I know you can. Your clean clothes are folded outside your door. Pick out something to wear." The kids slowly emerge and get dressed. Dylan bounces into her room smiling and says, "I'm ready mom. I even have my socks on."

Making their way downstairs at 6:17, Nancy sets breakfast on the table: Kix cereal, vitamins, and a banana. She reminds them to stay focused. At 6:26 she repeats, "Okay, no playing with your napkins. Eat your food. No paper airplanes. Come on." Frustration mounts as she glances at the digital clock on the microwave. Somehow in the next twenty minutes she braids Melody's hair, clears the breakfast dishes, and puts on a necklace and a touch of lipstick. Nancy wears her daily outfit of slacks, pumps, and a sweater set. A single working mom, she doesn't have time to shop. She stocks up once a year at the Ann Taylor outlet store.

Nancy reminds each kid to put on shoes and makes sure they each have their backpack, sweatshirt, and homework as they file out the kitchen into the garage. She remembers to grab the kids' snacks waiting on the kitchen counter and makes her way out the door. She is vigilant about packing snacks at night before she goes to bed. "I have to push through and pack them even if I'm tired . . . because otherwise it doesn't get done." They are all out the door at 6:46. The morning went relatively smoothly with the kids, and Nancy breathes a sigh of relief. Although school doesn't start until almost 9:00, Nancy drops her children off at early care as soon as it opens at 7:00. "It's just one of those things that breaks your heart," she says.

After dropping off her kids, Nancy heads to Starbucks for a skinny vanilla latte before hitting the road. It's a regular stop: "I don't care if I'm late. I have to. I'm completely addicted." Today she is driving sixty minutes to corporate headquarters. As a senior director at Silver Lake Hospitality (SLH), Nancy splits her time between corporate headquarters and the multiple hotels for which she is responsible. Her closest property is about forty-five minutes from her suburban home.

While she is in line for coffee, her fingers fly over her company-provided smartphone. Head down, inching forward, Nancy spends the time in line replying to emails. She answers a question about finding a lost contract and accepts several meeting requests. Her smartphone is key to a successful day: "I have all these people that need something. But they're all things that I don't need my computer to do; stuff I can get off my plate so when I'm sitting down to work I can actually work. Otherwise I'd be up until 2:00 a.m. every night just answering emails." A typical day might find Nancy dealing with over a hundred emails and numerous text messages. Back on the road, she glances down and taps a quick response while at a red light: "I would not be able to do the job if I didn't text and drive."

Fast forward to the evening. Today is one of the two days a week that Nancy leaves work at 4:00 p.m. so she can have dinner with her children. She picks up the kids from after-school care, and they are home by 5:00. She leaves her smartphone on the kitchen counter, changes into her pajamas, and makes dinner. By 6:15 one child has showered and the three of them are enjoying leftover cupcakes after a meal of chicken nuggets, tater tots, green beans, and watermelon. Nancy desperately needs a trip to the grocery store. Thankfully, before rushing out the door this morning she looked in the freezer and realized she could pull together some dinner. Finding time to stock up on groceries is always a challenge and, really, after work she just wants to go straight home.

After Nancy shepherds the kids upstairs to finish showering and brush their teeth, the three of them make their way back downstairs. It is 6:46 p.m. Nancy confirms that each finished their homework in after-school care, and Dylan takes this as an opening to beg for some time on Nancy's tablet to play "Angry Birds." She firmly says no, but offers to let him play tomorrow when they meet the neighbors for dinner. Dylan reluctantly pulls out a giant box of mismatched Lego pieces. Melody puts on a CD of her favorite dance hits and starts wheedling Nancy (who is now splayed out on the couch) to dance with her. Making silly gestures she dances around her mom, teasing, "Don't be a party pooper. Don't poop on the party. Come be a good sport." Sighing with a wan smile, Nancy eventually gets up, and a full-on dance party ensues—complete with jazzercise moves and floor spins. Even Dylan gets involved. The kids pull out a box of musical instruments, and everyone plays along to Kidz Bop. At 7:16 Nancy flops back on the couch. Soon after she takes a quick phone call in the kitchen with her long-distance boyfriend, Ken, while the kids continue to play.

At 7:50 Nancy declares, "Okay, it's time to start cleaning up." They begin to pick up the cars, Legos, and instruments that are strewn around the living room. By 7:59 they are cuddled together on a futon in the upstairs landing, reading bedtime books. By 8:15 the kids are in bed and Nancy is back downstairs checking her phone. She sighs and says, "I could do so much tonight. I really should, but I just can't." Nancy could be working on the property budgets, finishing a contract for one of her hotels, or answering emails. She received twenty-two emails since leaving work at 4:00 p.m. and has been checking them subtly throughout the evening (glancing as she ducks into the laundry room or while the kids are in the shower). But she is tapped out. After putting two Tupperware containers on the counter to remind herself to pack snacks before she goes to bed, Nancy pours herself a glass of wine, tucks her feet up on the couch, and flips open a People magazine. A moment for herself.

FIGURE 1.1. Nancy Huron Braiding Melody's Hair in the Morning

NANCY HURON'S DAY includes moments of joy, stress, productivity, and exhaustion. Nancy has a good job, happy children, close friends. At a fundamental level, she is privileged—and she knows it. Nancy feels like she "has it all." And along almost any metric, she does. But her life is still a nonstop and intense grind.

Nancy's life is driven by love for her children and her pride in her work. She tries to exercise and eat healthy food while maintaining a home. She craves downtime with friends, family, or occasionally just a People magazine. Nancy's desires don't seem unreasonable: work, parent, stay healthy, with a little bit of time to relax or socialize. So why does her life feel relentless (to her and us)?

The answer is that Nancy's life feels relentless because impossible dreams—shaped by the particular place and time in which she lives—leave Nancy and her colleagues, neighbors, and friends all living with unreasonable aspirations. In this book we tease apart the different and compounding expectations that motivate Nancy (and others like her) to strive for the impossibility of perfection. We examine what helps her get through the day—from the mobile devices that keep her in the loop, to the caregivers who watch her children so she can work a full-time job. The expectations—or myths—of perfection that haunt Nancy pervade current U.S. society, and create an image of the kind of person we all should strive to be.

The threads of expectation that anchor Nancy's life in cycles of satisfaction and guilt, and tie her to others, emerge from the overriding narrative of three dominant cultural myths[1]—the Ideal Worker, the Perfect Parent, and the Ultimate Body.[2] Striving to be an Ideal Worker, Nancy drops off her kids at 7:00 a.m. every morning so that she can grab a coffee, catch up on email, and get to work prepared and on time. Nancy's phone and laptop are her conduits to work during her "off hours," and she uses them to show her colleagues that she is dependable, accessible, and at-the-ready. For example, when her boss emails her on a Sunday afternoon asking about the status of a project, she uses her phone to immediately tap out a quick reply—commenting wryly, "Well, good thing I got that done this morning." Her devices allow her to keep up with incoming emails, stay on top of tasks, and maintain a sense of competency and control.

Nancy carries the satisfaction of acting like an Ideal Worker alongside the guilt of not being a Perfect Parent. A single mother, she adores her children and constantly asks herself how to give them the childhood she feels they deserve—comparing their lives to the "great" childhood she had with her mother, who stayed home. She makes a conscious effort to put down her phone and play with or read to the kids in the evenings. She monitors how much TV and iPad time they get and makes sure their homework is done. With the help of babysitters for transport, both kids engage in after-school enrichment activities. Several nights a week a babysitter will pick the kids up from school and take them to karate or gymnastics. Nancy usually checks the refrigerator before running out the door in the morning and texts the babysitter about what to do for dinner during a break in her schedule of back-to-back meetings. Nancy expects the babysitter on duty to monitor homework, feed the kids dinner, and try to get them bathed before she gets home between 7:00 and 7:30 p.m. Some sitters are better than others, and she works hard to stay in the good graces of those who can keep her children on schedule. Nancy measures herself against the ideals of the Perfect Parent, and she pieces together what she can.

After experiencing a major health scare, Nancy struggles to fit in regular exercise. When she responds to requests from colleagues in late-night emails, her hopes for early morning exercise are dashed. She has to decide whether to trade off sleep for exercise. Whichever she chooses, the result is a feeling of guilt. Nancy also works hard to provide healthy meals for herself and her children. Once a week she gets together with her neighbor to prepare a home-cooked meal. These nights are about more than a healthy dinner. Both families look forward to these nights as a time to relax and socialize. But such nights take planning—and rely on the neighbor being a stay-at-home mom who can make the last-minute run to the grocery store. For Nancy it is hard to find time to shop, much less cook. She wants to care for her body but simply cannot fit any more into the day. The myth of the Ultimate Body is often a reminder to Nancy of where she's falling short.

Nancy's life is hectic. The pressures are constant. At multiple points over the three years we spent with her, Nancy declared that *this* was the most stressful time she had ever experienced. If she could just get through the next two days, or two weeks, or two months, things would calm down. Like the conductor of an unruly orchestra, Nancy is forever trying to bring into synch the yearly rhythms of work (quarters, annual budgets, the holiday sales season), school (summer camps, new teachers, holidays, standardized testing), and her body (sleep patterns, medical treatments, hunger, pressure to exercise) with the inevitable and unexpected snafus of everyday life (an unhappy client, a child breaking an arm, the supermarket reorganizing where they keep the cereal).

How does Nancy strive for these three myths of perfection? She relies on her phone, tablet, and laptop to get through the impossible days. With the help of her devices, Nancy expects to do *more* than a day's worth of work, be available to *more* people than those she is with physically, and handle *more* demands than one person reasonably can. She expects this of herself and others expect it of her. And while technology might help in the moment, over the course of weeks, months, and years of using it to do *more*, it only intensifies the pressures.

The real answer as to how Nancy manages can be found in the people that she is connected to *through* her devices. We can see it in the time and energy she spends fostering supportive relationships with babysitters and teachers. We can see it in the relationship she has with her neighbor, who texts her multiple times a day: saying "hi," offering to pick up something at the store, or sharing a recipe. This network of human support is often masked by technology's emphasis on individually managed lives, but it is the thing that keeps people going, no less striving.

Nancy's colleagues and counterparts in this book have similar dreams of perfection: from single parents to families with a stay-at-home parent and dual working couples. Each family does their best to manage the complications of everyday life, and each feels incredibly lucky. But nearly everyone is bone tired, overwhelmed, and frequently stressed. They rarely feel like they have done enough. The idealized expectations for work, parenting, and the body are unrelenting and always in the background. The real story in this book is the ways in which they rely on the support, or scaffolding, of others, so that they may get up each morning ready to do it all again.

The specific contours of a myth are different depending on one's background or location. Take being a Perfect Parent. In lower-income households this ideal may be lived through everyday challenges such as getting enough healthy food to make home-cooked meals. For higher-income households, it may be breastfeeding children and buying local organic food at the farmers market.[3] We focus on the myths as represented in nine middle- to upper-income families in Southern California. But the act of striving is not unique, and the reach of these myths extends to many different types of families in the United States.[4] Even when a person rejects aspects of these myths of perfection, everyone lives *in terms* of these ideals. The myths manifest as expectations that shape everyday actions. Nancy and other working parents across the country may not ever feel they have achieved the status of Ideal Worker, Perfect Parent, or Ultimate Body. But still, people's inadequacy according to the myths is likely to bleed into their sense of self.[5] The feelings of guilt, responsibility, and rationalization that run through their heads at night suggest that even when such myths aren't upheld, they wield power. These myths are so ingrained in the conversations of middle- and upper-class Americans that it is difficult to imagine work, parenting, and health in any other light.[6]

Nancy's colleague Teresa Davies pokes fun at the fundamental impossibility of the myths, posting an article on Facebook about invisible work[7] and commenting, "If you add this to our shift at work, and the fact that we're also trying to care for our health and bodies, it's really a miracle we're not in the looney bin . . . or are we?" While recognizing that the myths make her crazy, Teresa does not attempt to stop following them. Like those around her, she feels pride and joy in the moments when she is, in fact, living her dreams.

IMPOSSIBLE MYTHS

In this book we explore the specific injunctions of these myths of perfection: Ideal Worker, Perfect Parent, and Ultimate Body. Through the experience of nine families with school-age children living in Southern California between 2012 and 2015, we show how these myths play into everyday life. The myths give shape to hopes and aspirations, and define success or failure. They provide a roadmap for the striving to accomplish their dreams.

These myths are everywhere in U.S. society: assumed in movies and TV shows; perpetuated by jokes and stories; and valorized in the massive number of self-help books and magazines that promise to instruct people on getting ahead at work, raising perfect children, and sculpting their bodies. The myths gain power through exposure and prevalence—making social media an especially potent tool for amplifying them. The myths are not inherently bad. There is real value and satisfaction in being a dependable colleague, an engaged parent, and a healthy person. But the intensity of the myths, and the craziness of trying to live them all, makes them impossible.

People believe in these myths and believe that they can achieve them because of a long-standing faith in personal responsibility and the power of individuals to shape their own destiny.[8] This has been true since the founding of U.S. democracy and, thanks to the prevalence of information and communication technologies, holds special resonance today.[9]

It is 9:36 a.m. on a Saturday. Roger and Linda Waldo slam the door to their minivan and trudge through the large parking lot of a Southern California high school. Their twelve-year-old son, Ryan, has disappeared ahead of them, a large lacrosse bag slung over his shoulder. Linda exclaims with some consternation, "What? He's not waiting for us?" Roger laughingly replies, "Well, would you want to walk with your dorky parents?"

Roger and Linda lug foldup chairs and carry travel mugs of coffee. They make their way across fields of brightly colored team jerseys, milling parents, and young siblings running after balls or glued to iPads. Roger wears a white baseball cap, a bright blue hoodie, and athletic pants. Linda is comfortable in a red sweatshirt and jeans They are ready for a long day. The three have driven over an hour to attend a lacrosse tournament. Roger and Linda eagerly discuss how Ryan is doing on the team and whether the team has a chance of winning today. Making their way to the sidelines they find a spot to unfold their chairs. Plopping down in her seat Linda pulls out her iPhone. Roger glances at her and says nonchalantly, "Don't post on Facebook that we're here. Okay?"

"Why not?," she asks, looking a bit taken aback.

He laughs. "There's that karate tournament today and I don't want the guys to know I'm here." She looks at him quizzically. Roger shrugs his shoulders and says, "I told them that I had a work thing today." He pauses, then adds, "It was just easier. . . . "

As an SLH manager, it is not unusual for Roger to work on a Saturday. So Linda just raises her eyebrows, shrugs, and mumbles, "Okay." She looks down to respond to a text from their teenage daughter, Sadie. When the game begins, they both turn their attention to it.

ROGER WALDO'S FIB that he is at work and not the lacrosse game is both instinctive and revealing. Even if he could have told his karate buddies that he was going to the lacrosse game with his wife and son—and even if they would have likely accepted his actions (perhaps after a bit of good-natured ribbing)—"it was just easier" to lie and say he had a work retreat (as long as social media didn't give him away). He is spending his Satur-

FIGURE 1.2   Roger and Linda Waldo at Ryan's Lacrosse Tournament

day as a Perfect Parent at lacrosse. But in so doing, he is missing the karate tournament and an opportunity to demonstrate that he is an Ultimate Body.[10] And he is calling on the Ideal Worker to help smooth his choice and provide a justifiable reason to ditch his friends.

Roger's fib also reveals that there is a general hierarchy of these myths in daily life. The myths are pitted against each other, but the primacy of the Ideal Worker myth is hard to deny.[11] That said, the fact that the myths seem to be in competition with each other masks a deeper truth. It is fundamentally impossible to achieve even one of these myths, no less all three.[12]

One does not reach the status of Ideal Worker, Perfect Parent, or Ultimate Body. Success is not an end state. Instead, people experience elusive moments of success: checking email on a Sunday and knowing the project someone is waiting for has been sent off; looking around the table during family dinner when everyone is laughing and chatting; enjoying the endorphins after a run. So people keep striving, knowing that it will never be enough. Not only is life always moving (jobs changing, kids growing, health failing) but the myths themselves are also shifting and intensifying, so that they remain just out of reach.

INESCAPABLE TECHNOLOGY

Technology is one of the culprits.[13] Smartphones, laptops, tablets, apps, and Fitbits suggest it is possible to "do it all" and live according to the myths.[14] But when people use these tools to be productive, vigilant, and at-the-ready, they only allow the myths deeper into their lives, so that the myths change what it means to be a good colleague, parent, or self.

Technology ties people closer to those around them: work colleagues, friends, and family. Roger can, and does, answer work emails during lacrosse (during halftime). Linda keeps in touch with their older daughter, who is several hours away at a college visit. She even texts her son from the front seat of their minivan, while he is a passenger in the back! People take connectivity for granted. Nearly everyone has a smartphone and assumes that messages are immediately received. People respond quickly, as the strings connecting them to others tighten, and it changes expectations of what it means to be available, productive, caring, and healthy.[15] As these expectations shift, so do shared understandings of what it means to be an Ideal Worker, a Perfect Parent, or an Ultimate Body. Technology is making it harder, not easier, to enact the myths.

Undoubtedly, technology has become an important component of how people manage their day-to-day tasks. But it also increases the pressure and expectations. So how do people actually get through the day? No one strives for these dreams on their own.

NECESSARY CONNECTIONS

People rely on each other. People live connected lives. The connection may be mediated by technology, but the connection is between people; formal paid help in the form of babysitters, summer camps, and house cleaners, and informal help from grandparents, neighbors, co-workers, and friends. This help may be motivated by love and support. It may be paid for. It is often a combination of both. Regardless, *it is other people who provide the critical scaffolding that bolsters people's efforts to work, parent and care for their bodies in certain ways.* The more people embrace and live in terms of the myths of perfection, the more they need the scaffolding of others to get through the day.[16] At its core, this book takes on the task of exposing (and celebrating) the collective effort that goes into any one person's ability to live up to one, no less multiple, myths.

Striving for the myths requires various forms of invisible work, and families rely on various structures of scaffolding to help with that work. We show how scaffolding others is made easier *and* harder by the capacities of technology. In ignoring the invisible work of others, individuals perpetuate the myths—allowing them to appear achievable and possible. The "mythic" qualities of the dreams are key—making people feel like failures when they inevitably fall short. This book helps open the door to new forms of seeing, valuing, and accounting for time, choices, and interdependencies.[17]

REAL PEOPLE, REAL LIVES

Everyone in this book attempted to enact some version of these myths— some in a wholesale manner, others in a more piecemeal way. In our time with these nine families we witnessed their daily frustrations, triumphs, and joys. We observed bedtime rituals, last-minute trips to the grocery store, and people fitting in a quick run or walk during a child's sports practice. We watched people, tied by their shared relationship to one company, navigate overlapping kids' activities, incessant emails, and late-night requests for a work report. We had a front-seat view of how they use technology to do an impressive amount of coordinating and communicating, and of the role of scaffolding in making it all (mostly!) work.

At the end of the book, we provide a full description of the project and our research methods. We spent about eighty hours with each family, and they all had at least one young child. We were interested in how they used technology in their everyday lives as busy parents, and how this intersected with the myths of perfection. Others strive for many of these myths as well (such as nonparents and parents of both older and younger children), but by looking at this group of families—all within a single company and with children of a similar age—we can see the variety of ways by which families in similar circumstances handled competing demands. We were not focused on relationships between spouses or romantic partners.[18] The families are white, Asian, and Hispanic, and their household incomes placed them in the middle- to upper-class income bracket in the counties

Nancy Huron is a senior director at SLH; her days are spent traveling to different hotels or at the corporate headquarters. Nancy has been divorced for four years, and her ex-husband does very little to help with Melody (6) and Dylan (8)—often cancelling his monthly visits at the last minute.

Roger and Linda Waldo moved to their house ten years ago, choosing stability and good schools over frequent moves to Roger's property assignments. Roger is a director at SLH, and Linda works at the local middle school. Linda manages the daily duties of raising Sadie (17) and Ryan (12).

Tim Andrews is an executive at SLH. His ex-wife watches their girls after school, Chloe (5), Olive (8), and Hannah (9), while she looks for a full-time job. Tim picks the kids up on his way home two to three days a week and has them every other weekend.

Teresa and Chip Davies rent a studio apartment close to both of their workplaces and commute to a larger home sixty miles away on the weekends. Teresa is a director at SLH, and Chip is an engineer for a contractor. Teresa's mother often watches their son Max (7) either at the apartment or at their house.

Franco and Katrina Garcia recently moved into their suburban dream house. Franco is a director at SLH, and Katrina is a manager for a restaurant chain. They stagger their work schedules to minimize childcare, and Katrina's half-sister lives with them to watch Matt (2) and Charlotte (4) four days a week.

Brenda and Cory Finchley are looking to buy a house in their neighborhood where the local elementary school is walking distance from home. Brenda is a director at SLH, and Cory stays home with their three children, Bobby (7), Kyle (4), and Tabitha (2).

Sanjay (Jay) and Olivia Shah have remodeled the home they bought when they first married. Jay is an executive at SLH, and Olivia runs a small travel agency out of their home. Olivia's parents help with the cooking and transporting of their two daughters, Tessa (9) and Neelam (13), to various activities.

Nick and Rebecca Stewart moved from out of state a couple years ago and are looking to buy a home. Nick is an executive at SLH, and Rebecca has put her job as a social worker on hold to care full-time for Brittany (8), Peter (6), Eric (5), and Frankie (3).

Dave and Lisa Phillips live in the community where Lisa grew up. Dave is a director at SLH, and Lisa teaches at a middle school forty minutes away. Lisa's mother lives nearby and helps manage the daily activities of Danielle (13), Lauren (12), and Harry (7).

TABLE 1.1 Description of the Families

in which they live. None struggled economically; they were comfortable but most kept a close eye on expenses.[19] While one parent in each family worked for the same private hotel management firm (Silver Lake Hospitality), they did not necessarily work in the same location, or even the same county as each other. While some are friends, others don't know each other at all. Table 1.1 provides a brief introduction to the families in the order they appear in upcoming chapters (see Reflections on the Project for a table with the demographics of each family).

Through the everyday experience of these families we explore the realities of working, parenting, and living in today's digital age. Every example, detail, and story presented in this book came from these families (although on occasion we were not there in the moment but heard the story recounted after the fact). Every illustration is from a moment in their lives. They are real people.[20] And while their lives are unique and entirely their own, as a group they provide a compelling portrait of the daily lives, pressures, aspirations, and dreams of working professional families in the United States.

Tim Andrews awakes with a jolt. It is 7:00 a.m. and the alarm on his phone is beeping. Snatching up the device and stopping the alarm, he grabs his Clark Kent glasses and opens his email. The most recent message was sent at 6:44; it is a note from his boss, Noah, asking why his financial reports are not yet online. Tim groans inwardly and, bleary eyed, taps out a short reply: "I will post as soon as I get to the office." He takes a deep breath and swings his feet out of bed.

Showered and dressed in jeans and a crisp button-down shirt, Tim calls to his three daughters as he makes his way downstairs. His phone stuck firmly in his back pocket— he is vigilant about not checking with the children around—Tim focuses on the morning routine: pouring cereal, packing each girl a lunch, finding shoes, and joking with them about the day to come. As for Noah's request, Tim shrugs his shoulders and flashes an easy smile: "That is Noah; he's an early riser. It's just one of the things that I hadn't gotten around to."

At 8:15 Tim shepherds his girls to the car, dropping the two oldest at school and the youngest at his ex-wife's house. He makes it to work just after 9:00, sheepish that he has missed the soothing music that is played across headquarters every morning—a quiet time for people to focus and plan their day. But he's known his plan for hours by then: getting the financial reports online is clearly the first thing on his agenda.

LIKE MANY COMPANIES, SLH tacitly prioritizes Ideal Worker behaviors. Employees describe SLH as filled with hard workers who are on "24/7." These SLH employees generally spend at least eleven hours a day away from home: working and commuting to and from work.[21] Noah's morning email is par for the course, but this doesn't diminish Tim's loyalty to the firm or appreciation of his job. Nancy Huron was grateful to have kept her job during the last recession when many competitors were shedding managers. In an industry with high levels of turnover, SLH employees appreciate the relative stability of their employment (even if it means long commutes as they move from property to property as needed).[22]

That said, the infiltration of work-related communication into every moment of the day has an effect. Noah wakes up thinking about the financial reports and, unlike a time before the advent of smartphones, has the capacity to dash off a quick message to Tim. Tim wakes up and, unlike before the advent of smartphones, has the capacity to check his email and learns that his boss is waiting on him. Tim sees the message and writes back, immediately assuring his boss that he will get on it. He begins his day with an unmet expectation, and, even though he has the wherewithal to set his worry aside during breakfast with his girls, he'll operate as if he has some ground to make up until the reports are online. Noah may have just wanted to get the thought off his mental plate, but now Tim has the reports on his. All before 7:00 a.m. This technologically enabled Ideal Worker behavior is typical of SLH, but also of many other firms across industries and around the country and the world.

However, as counterbalance to this culture of hard work and commitment, SLH explicitly promotes family and health. Tim Andrews appreciates that SLH encourages him to commit to both work *and* family. In his words, "[SLH] is really focused on building everybody's foundation; making sure each individual is the best individual they can be, and knowing that that's going to yield the result of having the best company we can." This means, "work and family are extremely integrated and the line is blurred between the two."

People talk about their children, and colleagues visit with each other's families at SLH gatherings. The corporate office holds a monthly wellness meeting at which people discuss their exercise and eating habits. The CEO regularly sends out emails with stories about the latest trends in healthy eating. The company culture encompasses professional achievement, family satisfaction, and personal wellness. Nick Stewart recalls a recent performance review when the CEO told him, "Be a good parent. Travel well. Dress well." Employees feel supported and committed to the organization because of the multiple ideals it supports.

While SLH honors each of the myths in their corporate culture, they're not immune to the tension of upholding these ideals in the context of a growing for-profit firm. Top executives expect hard work and long hours from each other and those below them. The company provides laptops and phones to help make it possible. The integration is not seamless. Tim explains,

> But when it comes to the home front—I don't know that we really walk the talk as far as having a work-life balance when we are home or we're on trips or we're with our families. There's still an expectation and a need to be connected. You can separate [work and life]. But if you totally separated, I mean, you would end up being very behind. Or I would be. If I never did any work at night and only tried to do work during work hours, it wouldn't work out.

Even though the organization values family and health, the needs of the workplace remain a priority. There is always more work to do, and people generally assume that technology will make everything more doable. Therefore, SLH is a perfect organization in which to explore how employees experience the dominant, and often conflicting, myths of Ideal Worker, Perfect Parent, and Ultimate Body. From this perch, we observe how these myths are experienced in everyday life.

TOUR OF THE BOOK

In Part I, "Striving for Impossible Dreams," we dive into the myths that tantalize, inspire, and define so many Americans. In Chapters 2 through 4 we examine each myth in turn, describing in full the elements of each and how they play out in these families. These chapters locate the myths of perfection in popular culture and reveal how these external ideals invade everyday life. We delineate the behaviors expected by each myth and explore how the individuals we studied enact, reject, and make sense of these tenets in daily life. These chapters are full of stories, details, and the complexity of what it entails to attempt to *be* any one of these ideals in an era of smartphones and constant connectivity. And like Nancy Huron, Roger and Linda Waldo, and Tim Andrews, whom you've already met, you'll find that the lives of these subjects appear and reappear organically throughout these chapters.

The myths themselves are gendered ideals; the Ideal Worker is a masculine model, the Perfect Parent is a feminine ideal, and the Ultimate Body is both strong (masculine) and thin (feminine). While the myths themselves are gendered, the individuals who inhabit them may or may not identify with the gender attached to the role. More and more, people who identify as women are full-time professionals enacting the qualities of the Ideal Worker, and people who identify as men take on Perfect Parent aspirations.[23] In each chapter, we explore how gendered expectations shape what it is to live within a particular role.

Next, in Part II, "Why It Is Getting Harder," we show how technology transforms not only individual lives, but the ways in which individuals access and aspire to the three myths of perfection. In Chapter 5 we discuss the promises attached to digital technologies. Technologies that promise constant availability and accessibility have become a fixture of everyday life.[24] In Chapter 6 we outline how the use of technology subtly changes and intensifies the myths through a spiral of expectations. The Ideal Worker has to be *more* available in order to simply perform his or her role. The Perfect Parent has to coordinate *more* enrichment activities and monitor *more* behavior. The Ultimate Body has to be *more* aware of daily habits and attend to the number of steps walked in a day. Technologies are the strings that tie people to each other—devices serve as connections to others, and by themselves they are not the salve for (or the cause of) excessive demands.

Finally, in Part III, "How People Survive and Thrive," we explore the core idea of the book: *scaffolding*. Here we focus on a plethora of invisible work that needs to get done in order for some people to strive for the myths, and the structures of support that families rely upon to do some or all of this work. The Ideal Worker must have someone on the home front to watch the children and take care of the house. The Perfect Parent cannot be everywhere at once, simultaneously driving kids to numerous activities, monitoring behavior, and cooking healthy meals. The Ultimate Body requires someone who facilitates time away from work and family in order to focus on the project of the self.

In Chapter 7 we spell out the various forms of invisible work that suffuse daily life—*Physical Work, Mental Work, Coordinating Work,* and *Emotional Work*.[25] Physical Work involves the innumerable tasks that go into running a household (for example, cooking, cleaning, and shopping).

Mental Work is the time and energy that goes into planning, organizing, and remembering (such as making shopping lists and organizing doctor appointments). Coordinating Work entails orchestrating the labor of various helpers and schedules. Emotional Work includes managing relationships and accommodating the feelings of those helping with the household.

As technology expands the myths, and connects people more tightly to those around them, the amount of invisible work required to manage daily life increases. And the more that people ascribe to the myths of perfection, the more they need someone to do the invisible work that supports their dreams. But who is actually doing and managing the invisible work? Invisible work is generally seen as "women's work."[26] This is true regardless of the fact that we see men doing this work as well.[27]

In Chapter 8 we describe the different structures of scaffolding that people craft, build, and maintain: *Single Scaffolding, Modular Scaffolding, Double Scaffolding, and Needle Scaffolding.* Single Scaffolding is the first model, when one spouse focuses on his or her career and the other spouse takes on principal responsibility for parenting and the lion's share of invisible work.

In Modular Scaffolding the primary worker can continue to focus on his or her career while the other spouse becomes the hub and crafts additional layers of support to help with the invisible work. The hub often calls upon substantial external support: paid help in the form of before- and after-school care, summer camps, nannies, and housecleaners, and informal help through the efforts of grandparents, neighbors, and friends. This enables the hub to work, develop another interest, and/or engage in activities aligned with being a Perfect Parent. In both Single Scaffolding and Modular Scaffolding the spouse can deploy the primary worker to scaffold them and help with invisible work—just as they might hire a babysitter or ask a friend.

In Double Scaffolding two adults attempt to prioritize their respective careers *and* share the invisible work that goes along with running their household and finding, crafting, and hiring the supports necessary to make it all happen. Needle Scaffolding, on the other hand, is the structure of support crafted by single parents and those who cannot rely on their spouse for help with any invisible work (perhaps the spouse is deployed overseas, is incarcerated, or has significant physical limitations).

In all these structures of support, scaffolding is fundamental to supporting the people enacting the myths of perfection. Reliance on others to scaffold people's lives is the *real* way that individuals are able to get through the day, no less come close to achieving their dreams. Male or female, but often female, those who provide scaffolding are the saviors of everyday life. The collective failure to notice this critical infrastructure promulgates an individualistic narrative that hides the role of co-workers, families, and communities in enabling individual success.

The intense individualism perpetuated by each of the myths directs shared attention *away* from community and governmental solutions to address what are shared problems of overwork, childcare, and health. Throughout the book we connect these insights (and many others) to academic and popular conversations in our extensive endnotes.

The myths keep the conversation focused on individuals rather than communities, so people blame themselves for falling short.[28] And if these families struggle, who have well-paying and stable jobs, what about those who lack predictable schedules and financial security?[29]

The book concludes with Chapter 9, in which we highlight the challenges of building scaffolding but also the joy and connection it brings. We outline two broad strategies to reduce the exhaustion and stress that so many people experience everyday: making scaffolding visible and valued, and rethinking how scaffolding fits into our daily lives. The first asks that people value caregiving and domestic work and see it as real work. The second encourages families, employees, and organizations to re-envision their workplaces, build new forms of community, and support redesigning the infrastructures that they rely on to get through the day.

We then summarize steps people can take as individuals and families: reevaluate their attachment to the myths; communicate differently about invisible work; use technology in new ways; engage more with local communities; reshape the workplace; and support policies that advance critical changes in society. Given the variety of circumstances in which families find themselves, and the importance of individual choice to the American psyche, we offer a range of suggestions that are not one size fits all.[30] We do not expect all of the suggestions to be useful to everyone—every family is under different pressures and has different resources. Each has its own values and concerns (many of which change as children grow). Still, we offer these ideas in the hope some will resonate. Our goal is to make people's dreams a little more realistic and attainable.

CHAPTER 2

ASPIRING TO BE THE IDEAL WORKER

A director at SLH, Teresa Davies needs to send out paychecks by the end of the day. While Teresa often works ten to twelve hours in the office, this afternoon she is stationed in the basement of a medical building, waiting for her seven-year-old son, Max, to finish his regular therapy appointment. Teresa and her husband, Chip, have been trading off taking Max to his biweekly visits.

Settled into one of the green plastic chairs that circle the waiting room, Teresa connects her phone to wifi, plugs her laptop into her phone, and tethers to the internet in order to access SLH's internal network. A TV high in the corner plays a daytime soap opera. As she begins digitally cutting checks (which are then physically printed at each hotel), her boss, Eleanor, calls with a friendly but pointed inquiry: "So, I'm just wondering if you did this check." Teresa is able to say definitively, with her infectious smile, "Oh yes, I'm working on it now." Teresa congratulates herself for being one step ahead.

However, after struggling to maintain the VPN internet connection, her pride turns into frustration. Teresa gets through five checks before the slow connection in the hospital basement gets the better of her. She gives up and turns to Facebook on her phone. She likes a friend's post and, giggling to herself, reposts an image: "Good things come to those who wait WORK their asses off and never give up."

Teresa and Max arrive home a little after 5:00 p.m. Teresa hands her son his Nintendo DS and the two curl up on the couch next to each other. After quickly twisting her long dark hair into a bun, Teresa logs on again to SLH to cut the rest of the checks. A call from a colleague who is going on vacation interrupts her. He needs a new employee added to the system. Employee added, then checks finished, she begins looking up details for a labor report she needs to pull together before tomorrow. At 6:00, Max looks up from his DS and asks to use the iTouch to play a different game. Teresa puts down her laptop and the two search the small studio apartment for a few minutes—no iTouch to be found. Max satisfies himself with the DS and moves onto the bed. Teresa settles back into her spot on the couch.

Chip Davies gets home just before 7:00, having stopped for groceries on his way home from work. Teresa keeps her computer in her lap, checking Facebook, replying to work emails, and running the labor report while chatting with Chip as he puts away the groceries. When Chip moves to the bed, where he helps Max navigate a tricky level on his game, Teresa settles again on the couch with her phone to respond to a text. Then she continues both working (and not working) on her laptop for the rest of the night.

WHILE SHE MIGHT JOKE on Facebook about the demands of the workplace, Teresa Davies is deeply committed to SLH. She cares about being seen as a valued colleague and competent professional. Teresa willingly puts in long hours at work. While she and her husband both have full-time jobs, Chip is no stranger to the last-minute text alerting him that she is going to be a little (or more than a little) later than expected. At home, Chip wryly notes that Teresa's laptop "lives" on her lap as she runs reports and checks email and Facebook. She is ready and available for requests, demands, or just friendly updates from colleagues and friends. Te-

FIGURE 2.1 The Davies Family at Home in the Evening

resa's actions reflect her desire to be an Ideal Worker. She recognizes the impossibility of fully achieving the myth and laughs at the idea of "catching up." She wonders aloud what would that even mean. But Teresa is doing a pretty darn good job of acting the part.

WHAT IS THE MYTH OF THE IDEAL WORKER?

The Ideal Worker puts in long hours at the office, works from home in the evenings and on the weekends, and is regularly available to respond to incoming texts and emails. Last-minute extensions of the workday, regular work trips away from home, and a willingness to relocate for a job demonstrate how someone prioritizes work.[1] The Ideal Worker projects the desire to be a loyal, competent colleague, and expects to achieve professional success.[2] Broadly conceived, the Ideal Worker is a masculine role, and "he" has no competing obligations that might get in the way of total devotion to the workplace.[3] This expectation of total dedication to work makes this identity valuable and sought-after by employers.[4] Busyness is a marker of elite status and a demonstration of efficiency and worth.[5]

This myth, however, rubs up against the realities of daily life. People simply cannot be 100 percent devoted to the workplace and, at the same time, maintain a home, keep up with friends, stay fit, and (Crazy as it sounds!) raise a family. Yet this reality—that the myth of the Ideal Worker is impossible to achieve—has not fundamentally shifted what is actually expected from a career-focused worker. Not only do individuals fail to live up to the ideal, but colleagues, superiors, and friends employ the ideal to assess one another. These assumptions shape how people work, and how workers relate to one another.

The image of the Ideal Worker influences how people imagine they *should* orient to work—elevating things such as face time in the office, availability, and prioritization of work tasks to the top of the to-do list. It's not wrong to want to be a good worker, or to achieve professional success. Work, after all, is one of the ways people find meaning and financial security. The danger isn't the desire, but the standards to which people measure their desires. Because right now, people are accountable to the myth of the Ideal Worker, whether or not it is practically possible or emotionally sustainable to do so.

This image pervades popular culture. Movies, television shows, blogs, magazine articles, and comic strips capitalize on the cultural figure of the workaholic—willing to sacrifice everything to succeed at work. The premise of these plotlines builds on people's familiarity with and shared expectations of what it means to be focused on a career. And while the protagonist often has an epiphany or life change that pulls him or her out of this mode, the baseline assumption remains an implied and unquestioned sacrifice: work or life.

Companies celebrate employees who dedicate long hours and are responsive to work requests. People know that intense efforts and dedication are expected and rewarded. Even while some of the families in this book might chafe at these expectations—especially single parents for whom enacting the myths is especially challenging—they don't question them. Work at SLH remains the central frame around which all of these families organize their lives.

Franco Garcia, a director at a large SLH property, sits in his small office in the basement. In the "backstage" of the hotel (with its flimsy walls and tight quarters). Salespeople, catering managers, and event coordinators buzz about, everyone focused on making the next sale or putting out the latest fire. Looking crisp in his white button-down and designer jeans, Franco is reviewing the weekly catering report. Out of the blue, his boss, Maria, barges in. Leaning over his desk with an exaggerated grimace, Maria punches the air in frustration. She looks at Franco and declares, "Just listen. I'm going to call my husband, and you're going to hear what's going on. That way I kill two birds with one stone." She picks up the office phone and makes a call on speakerphone. Her husband answers and Maria tells him, "I'm gonna be late tonight because Caleb [a valued manager] is gonna quit." Franco listens as her husband asks, "How do you know?" Maria replies, "Just call it woman's intuition. I can tell. And it's gonna be a rush, a big old rush, and a paper chase, and I'm going to have to deal with all this shit."

Maria is right. Caleb quits that very afternoon. Franco ends up staying late too, working with Maria to figure out how to divide Caleb's accounts and keep everything up and running.

Even though Franco jumps in to help, he can't stem the tide of work. Before he leaves around 7:00 p.m., Franco pokes his head into Maria's office to say goodnight. She is on the phone with her boss, Harry, brainstorming about how to fill the vacancy and trying to convince Harry to let Caleb stay on for two more days. The next morning Maria tells Franco she was there until 11:00 p.m. Showing him the pimple on her chin, she declares that her husband jokingly named it "Harry" because he stresses her out so much. Franco thinks this is hilarious, laughing about it all afternoon.

MARIA AND FRANCO make a great team. They are committed to the job, SLH, and their friendship. According to Franco, "Maria and I have a lot in common in the way we were raised, and I think it's probably because we are both Hispanic. We both had working families. We're both first generation here. Her family came from Mexico as well. So, we just get each other." Asked what they "get" about each other, Franco is unequivocal, "We're extremely hard workers. We both have the expectation that you have to perform."

Franco is committed to his career. He works long hours (usually away from home ten to twelve hours each day). Even when his plate is overflowing, Franco admits, "I never want my bosses to question my commitment." Franco feels "100 percent vested" and doesn't want to be one of those managers that "don't respond on their days off." Watching Maria deal with the Caleb crisis only serves to reinforce his belief that when something unexpected happens, a valued SLH employee will drop everything, call his or her spouse, and stay as long as needed to repair the damage.

Franco's sense of self is founded on the Ideal Worker myth. Franco shares, "By nature I'm a workaholic. That's just who I am. I'll never change that about myself. I've accepted it. I have to manage it now that I have a family. And I'm okay with that." And his wife, Katrina, understands his commitment and ambition: "He has always been an overachiever and always needs to be challenged, acquiring the next title, moving forward with his career."

Franco's willingness to put in the time and energy has given him a reputation as someone who can be counted on to go the extra mile. Recently, Franco jumped at the opportunity to be on an SLH task force. Task forces are a key part of SLH's growth strategy. When the firm takes on a new property to manage, they send a cross-functional team of top performers to help get the new property up and running: training new employees in SLH's IT systems; setting up sales processes and budgeting practices; and simultaneously infusing the new property with the goals, values, and culture of SLH. SLH needs to either retrain the staff of the hotel that they are now managing or bring in new people. Usually it's a mix of both. Franco will work with the sales and catering teams—employees who schedule large events and groups coming to the hotel for a meeting or conference. Being on a task force means leaving home and living in the new hotel for a couple of weeks or sometimes for over a month (without an increase in salary or a major reduction in other responsibilities). Even if his home property picks up some of the slack, Franco essentially takes on two full-time jobs for the duration of the task force.

In other organizations, an Ideal Worker reputation might be cemented by all-nighters in the office or near-instant response times by email. These might be the expected-but-not-required activities that signal dedication and commitment. But at SLH, task forces are a "signature" work practice that is critical to "onboarding" new properties. Despite the extra work and time away from family, Franco sees it as an honor to be one of the "A players" that they pull onto the task force. He is not alone in framing these task forces as a "golden opportunity" to prove himself, gain visibility, and show his strengths. Task forces serve to celebrate Ideal Worker behavior at SLH.

Despite these extra work demands, Franco sees SLH as unique because the firm is "like a family" and employees are treated as "whole people." Co-workers go to lunch together, talk about their hobbies and families, attend to personal obligations during the workday (recall how Teresa is able to take her son to regular afternoon doctor appointments), and socialize outside of work. He recognizes hospitality as a "brutal industry" that "eats people up and spits them out." People feel they would work just as hard in another firm in this industry, but without the camaraderie, recognition, and loyalty they get at SLH. Franco passionately describes the company as follows:

> They understand that it's important for people to have time with their family and it's important for people to be afforded that time. And not to be viewed differently or frowned upon if you need a three-day weekend or you need some time off to go spend with your family. All the companies in the past that I've worked for it's like, work, work, work. Work comes first and then if you have time left over—well, then maybe you can spend it with your family.

While Franco believes that SLH wants him to spend time with his family, he nevertheless still works long hours and regularly works at home on his days off. The firm also operates under a mandate to grow aggressively. Franco is not blind to this tension:

> Maria and I talk about the sacrifices. We talk about the sacrifices that we have to make with our kids and, you know . . . we don't have all the time

that we want with them. But we're a good temperature check for each other, and we pinky promised at the beginning of this year that we're going to push each other out the door when we see the opportunity.

Months after this promise, neither is doing a good job of getting out the door to spend time with their children. While Franco's "pinky promise" with Maria might make him feel like he can be a "good" parent and work at SLH, it also serves to make him feel closer to his colleague and committed to their joint endeavors at work. Franco and Maria dive in, work hard, and go the extra mile for each other and the company. And while it is common for people to talk about their families, they don't let that get in the way of their performance.

SLH employees find long hours at work more pleasant because their colleagues are their friends. The back offices in hotels are lively, irreverent, and fast-paced environments. The well-appointed corporate headquarters house energetic executives, easy laughter, and an oft-used ping-pong table. SLH employees love to say, "None of us is as good as all of us." The firm has consistently grown in the face of unpredictable markets and daily crises. They feel camaraderie and a sense of pride, alongside long work hours and constant connectivity.

Employees do not fundamentally question the expectations of long hours and total dedication and do their best to display the traits of the Ideal Worker. They do so not just to be good colleagues, or successful at SLH, but because they cannot imagine doing otherwise.

THE IDEAL WORKER: LONG HOURS AT THE OFFICE

Nancy Huron has driven forty-five minutes to corporate headquarters this morning for a joint meeting between senior directors and executives across different functional areas. After she arrives, Nancy makes herself comfortable in the glass-walled conference room off the main lobby. She is joined by two executives and other senior directors. Following some friendly banter they get down to business.

Harry, an executive and Nancy's boss (the same Harry that inspired Maria's pimple-naming), kicks off the meeting. He expresses concern that sales are down and several properties aren't hitting their numbers. He urges directors to ensure their teams are getting to work early and are focused on sales and making deals with new groups. "Everyone should be getting the urgent stuff out of the way first, then prospecting [for new business] second. Wait on paperwork until the end of the day." The message is that paperwork shouldn't be happening until after 5:00 p.m., when most potential clients have gone home. Harry insists, "I'm not trying to get people to work extra hours. But we have limited time to get to clients, and we need people at their desks earlier." Despite his assurance to the contrary, it is clear that Harry would like employees to spend more hours in the office.

Part of the problem, according to Harry, is the timing of the daily morning meeting. At the start of the day, each hotel brings together the sales and revenue management teams to do a quick check-in on the status of the property relative to their forecasted numbers. They discuss new leads and special rates, and make sure their actions are in line with overall hotel goals. These cross-functional meetings are another "signature" practice of the company. Harry wants to start the meetings earlier. "We need to talk about the timing. I want live body coverage on the phones from 8:00 a.m. to 6:00 p.m. But if the morning meeting is at 8:30 or 9:00 a.m., people aren't getting to their desks until later. I'm thinking that it needs to be 7:30 or 8:00 at the latest."

Harry goes on, "We're still coming out of the recession. This is not the time to shorten the workday. We're managing a portfolio here. I don't mean to be rude, but we are in a position where we want positive tension until numbers are up." He pauses, "I mean, am I being too old school here?"

Nancy has been sitting quietly while Harry laid out his argument. But with this, she can't help but say something. She speaks calmly but firmly, "Actually, I think you are. We say 'family this' and 'family that' but are we really doing it? As a single mom, I get it. It's really hard for people to get in that early. We preach the balance of family and life ... but ... " Nancy lets her words hang.

A moment of silence descends on the room. Not everyone, it is clear, would have spoken up like Nancy.

After the pause, Nancy's colleagues begin to respond, throwing out comments that both support and undermine her statement. Another director asserts that people should be preparing for the morning meeting the night before—presumably so the meeting is shorter and they can get to their desks earlier. No one asks whether that preparation is supposed to happen after 5:00 p.m. along with the aforementioned "paperwork." Harry emphasizes that they are in a transition year and things are supposed to be improving but they're not. An executive asks whether or not shifting the time would be a "strategic move." Another director notes that he has a single mom on his team with a hard start time of 8:00 a.m., no earlier.

After going back and forth for a bit, Harry interjects, "Okay, I don't want to be a hardass. Let's keep it at 8:30 for the older properties and do PS and QA at 8:00 a.m. because they are new [properties], so it will be easier to get started with better habits there."

THE MESSAGE FROM THE MEETING is clear: putting in face time (both at the morning meeting and at one's desk) is expected at SLH. In a small way Nancy Huron is pushing back. She is not questioning whether or not people should show their face predictably and spend long chunks of time in the office. But we feel the passion in her voice and admire her willingness to put herself out there. It would have been easier to stay quiet.

Nancy's comment is brave because, of course, an Ideal Worker simply doesn't have obligations outside of work. Full-time U.S. workers spend an average of forty-two hours a week in the office and more than three additional hours working at home. Many work considerably more.[6] Directors and executives at SLH work more than average, generally around forty-seven hours a week in the office with another eight hours at home.[7] The fact that the workday is expected to start earlier, and end later, than public school suggests that school is clearly designed for a child whose parents have predictable schedules and often a dedicated parent who stays home. It presents nearly insurmountable challenges for households in which either or both are not the case.

It is certainly a challenge for Nancy. Despite her efforts to cobble together formal childcare, babysitters, and summer camps, Nancy spends less time physically in the office than many of her colleagues (even though she works an identical number of total hours). Thankful for the ability to leave at 4:00 p.m. a couple of days a week, Nancy works more than most in the evenings to make sure she is pulling her weight. Yet given her commute, even the "short" days involve ten hours away from home.

Unlike those who have family members to help, Nancy pays for every moment of the time she is away from home. Expensive and predictable, such care is also inflexible (try being an hour late to pick up a child from after-school care or summer camp). These limits are at odds with what is expected of an Ideal Worker.

Months after Nancy tried to push back against the timing of the morning sales meeting, Harry begins to feel the tension himself. Going through a divorce, Harry is having a hard time getting out the door at 4:00 p.m. once a week in time to pick up his girls from his ex-wife. Harry exclaims, "I don't know how you do it!" Nancy responds (with only slight exasperation), "You know, you just have to leave. When I have to leave, I have to leave. There is no question to it. You have to be in that mode. You have to think of it differently. It's not a choice."

This necessity of leaving at a particular time makes symbolic displays of dependability and commitment difficult for Nancy. Even with IT-enabled access and a willingness to work from home, physically being in the office is a palpable signal: one that people use to assess others. That's because visibly spending time in the office is a classic measure of dedication and a long-standing signal of Ideal Worker status.[8] Managers strategically schedule early morning meetings (like the morning sales meeting at SLH) to get people into work, and meetings late in the day to keep them in place.[9] But employees also bring their dedication home from work—and work on the weekends or in the evening.

THE IDEAL WORKER: WORKING AT HOME

Brenda Finchley, a rising star and director at SLH, opens the front door to her home at 6:12 p.m. She is pleased that she made it home before dinner on a Friday. She had texted her husband, Cory, at 5:30 from the office, and again a few minutes later as she walked out the door. Brenda gives a warm hello to her kids playing in the living room. Her seven-year-old son, Bobby, sits at the family desktop computer reading digital books, and the two younger kids watch the Nick Jr. channel on television. She walks to the back of the house to change out of her work suit and quickly returns in sweatpants and a sweatshirt. Brenda chats with Cory in the kitchen as he finishes dinner. She catches him up on her day, and, with a sigh, tells him that she needs to work on two forecasts this weekend. She couldn't fit them in today.

Fast forward to 7:35 Brenda and Cory stand up from the table. Cory does the dishes while Brenda orchestrates the bedtime routine. With minimal grumbling, the kids pick up toys from the living room floor, parade to their rooms, put on pajamas, and brush their teeth. Water, milk, good night kisses, and lights out ensue, all before eight o'clock.

The kids in bed, Brenda and Cory both make their way into the living room and ease onto the couch next to each other. Cory has poured them each a glass of red wine. Brenda pulls out her phone from the purse on the floor to glance at email. She is waiting for a message from a colleague, Sam, confirming when the forecasts need to be done. Nothing yet. She checks again just before bed. This time she finds an email from Sam asking her to complete at least one of the property forecasts over the weekend so he can do his part first thing Monday morning. That's a relief.

The laptop stays in her bag until the last possible moment: Sunday night after the kids go to bed. The weekend had been relatively quiet. A baseball game for Bobby. Cory bought new tires and got the oil changed for the car. Brenda spent most of Sunday home alone with the kids while Cory was taking photos for a class assignment (he is taking a photography class at the local community college). Once they have the kids tucked into bed, Brenda pulls out her laptop and settles in on the couch. Cory sits at a nearby desk, touching up his photos on the family desktop.

With the television in the background, Brenda works on the forecast numbers. She finishes one property. She gets enough done on the second that she can easily complete it in the morning at work. She emails Sam the first forecast, and Cory joins her on the couch. Cory picks up the remote, moving between a cooking show and something about "wicked tuna" Bluefin fishing on the National Geographic channel. At 11:00 they head to bed. Brenda is pleased that she got most of her "homework" done while still having a good weekend with her family. No last-minute crises or demands threw a wrench in her plans.

BRENDA FINCHLEY TRIES HARD to extract herself from the office at a reasonable hour and spend regular focused time with her husband and her children. She and Cory have an impressive bedtime ritual that allows them to move to adult-oriented evening activities with predictability and speed. As we watched, we found the lack of drama from their three children around bedtime awe-inspiring (of course we did see drama at other times).

As a result, Brenda knows she can pull out the laptop in the evening a few times a week to finish whatever tasks she didn't have time for during the day. She does a good job of saving those tasks until after the kids go to bed. Oftentimes this involves finishing the report she didn't have time for at the office or doing tasks that don't require too much concentration. She may work on proposals for new business, typing out stock text describing the relevant amenities of her hotels to be sent to possible customers. But she has limits. On Mondays Brenda and Cory have a glass of wine and watch one of their favorite TV shows, such as *Bones* or *Grey's Anatomy.* Her work laptop stays tucked away in her briefcase.

Every SLH worker that we observed regularly worked from home. There is simply too much work to fit into the workday. Some worked after the kids went to bed or while older kids were doing homework. Several stayed up later, waiting until after their spouse went to bed before logging in some time on the laptop. Some woke up early and worked in the mornings (often on weekends while the kids were sleeping or watching cartoons). For everyone, the desire to have some dedicated time with kids and spouses, combined with the need to work from home, resulted in regular late nights and chronic exhaustion.

The ability to work remotely means that Teresa Davies can take her son to his doctor's appointment without compromising her ability to be (and project the image of) the Ideal Worker. Her hours on the couch at home allow her to keep up with everyday demands. Similarly, Brenda Finchley knows she can combine a television show, time with her husband, and getting a few things done in the evening, occasionally with a glass of wine in hand. Working from home is an expected and accepted part of their days. It's how one keeps on top of the demands of the job.

THE IDEAL WORKER: ALWAYS ACCESSIBLE

In an effort to enjoy a long holiday weekend, Brenda Finchley has taken Friday off. Bobby joins her for an outing to the grocery store. The two shop and chitchat as they make their way up and down the aisles. As they get back to the car, just after she gets the groceries unloaded, her phone rings. Brenda glances down at the number and answers the call.

It is Ellen, one of her employees. Ellen immediately blurts out, "Okay. I am really sorry to bother you. It's, like, your one day off. But we got this pop-up group for next week and Scott [another manager] wanted me to call and verify rates with you and just make sure you are okay with them." Brenda clarifies, "Okay, wait. You need my what. . . . "The employee reiterates that the other manager wasn't really comfortable quoting a rate without Brenda's approval. Brenda rolls her eyes. She agrees to the number and is just about to hang up when Bobby pipes up from the backseat, "Mommy, are you done working yet? I don't think you are supposed to be working right now." She looks back at him and says, "I'm sorry honey. Almost done!" When the call finishes, she takes a quick look at her email to see the numbers Ellen was referring to, then puts the phone in her purse.

IN HER CAR IN THE PARKING LOT, with minimal details about the customer, no spreadsheets to confirm whether the proposed prices are in line with property goals, no computer to see what other business is confirmed for that week, Brenda Finchley is asked to sign off on the room rate. So she does. Given her reaction to the call, Brenda clearly didn't think her input was necessary. But, like all SLH employees, Brenda is accessible. She keeps her SLH-provided smartphone with her, alongside her personal phone. She is generally artful about checking messages when the kids are busy and her husband is doing something else; she doesn't come across as frazzled or distracted.

FIGURE 2.2   Brenda Finchley Headed Home from the Grocery Store with Bobby

Yet Brenda is generally aware of what emails are coming in and will always answer a phone call from work—calls usually mean urgency. Was it really urgent for Brenda to approve the rates on her day off? Maybe. Maybe not. Either way, Brenda trusts her people, and she encourages them to operate without her when her input isn't needed.

But her employees know they can reach her, and accessibility shifts what Brenda and her colleagues think of as "needed." When the boss is easily accessible it feels strange, maybe disrespectful, and definitely a bit daring, to make a decision without her. Thus Brenda's ability (and willingness) to answer calls and check emails during her day off suggests to those around her that they can, and thus should, route decisions through her. When Brenda checks her phone, she's at the ready. Someone may be waiting for her to respond (like Ellen asking about a group booking), or she may be waiting for someone else to respond (like Sam telling her on Friday when he needs the forecast). The result is the same. Cory relays, "She is accessible 24/7 . . . she never seems to be more than a send button away from work."

In the past two decades there has been an explosion of new technologies and channels of communication—and with that a sense that the Ideal Worker can (and should) be available anytime and anywhere to answer work-related queries. Laptops, tablets, and smartphones enable people to work at expanded times and in a variety of locations. Availability and responsiveness are expected at SLH, an organizational environment that has actively positioned itself as the "24/7" hotel management firm.[10]

Nancy Huron suddenly finds herself awake. It is 2:00 a.m. The dark blue throw pillows that decorate her bed are stacked neatly on a side chair; a dull glow from the night light in the hall shines into her room. Nancy is a restless sleeper, sensitive to unusual sounds. She pauses for a second to make sure neither kid is stirring in their bedrooms—Dylan (8) and Melody (6) are generally good sleepers. All is fine. Nancy pushes her hair out of her face and reaches for her phone from the nightstand. She quickly checks her email. Nothing. She rolls over and tries to go back to sleep.

ALMOST EVERY NIGHT Nancy Huron finds herself, half awake, reaching for her phone. Asked why, she pauses and laughs awkwardly.

> I don't know. I just check to see if anything has come in, because sometimes I work at night and I'll send the emails asking questions and so, I guess, I'm looking for responses. But I don't know if it's just that I'm curious? It's not like it's going to make it any better or worse at 2:00 in the morning. I don't really ever respond. But I will check.

Nancy insists that checking her phone in the middle of the night doesn't get in the way of falling back asleep—"unless I am stressed at work." But then again, she is often stressed at work. Pondering further why she checks her phone in the middle of the night, Nancy qualifies,

> Of course, if there's something stressing me out and I see it's taken care of, that helps. Absolutely. And sometimes I'll end up getting up. I'll take my phone into the bathroom and dash out a message. I know when certain people are working. Like, I know Sam, he works first thing in the morning, like 4:30 or 5:00. So, if I need something from him I know I can get an immediate response very early.

Nancy's immediate and instinctive reach for her work phone reveals the degree to which she assumes both her own accessibility and the accessibility of colleagues. Although she knows that it is unlikely that anything noteworthy will come into her phone between 11:00 p.m. and 2:00 a.m., she stays connected, and thus accessible, to work.

Nancy feels that she has control of whether or not she replies to a message or sends something in the wee hours. Such engagement with work through the phone is less about being constantly "on" than never being quite "off." Nancy doesn't think her kids would even notice if she stopped using her work phone; she's not on it every moment. Yet she is accessible. Nancy will know if something major has happened. And her colleagues and direct reports know she will know. Nancy would be there almost any time of day or night, if truly needed.[11]

After hearing numerous comments from people across SLH who describe their lives as "constantly connected," we were initially surprised to find that these SLH employees were *not*, in fact, ignoring their families and spending large chunks of time with their attention focused on a device. Both Nancy and Brenda rarely check their email in the evenings while their kids are awake. Franco keeps his phone on a kitchen counter, checking it once or twice as he walks by in the evening and seldom stopping to answer a message. All three are not likely to work until after their kids (and in Franco Garcia's case, his wife) go to bed.

It became clear that "constantly connected" did not mean that people were continuously working from home, or even responding to emails. Instead people were "at the ready," carrying around with them the expectation that they might be called on. The SLH-provided phone is often used less as a communication tool than a peephole: a window into the work world that allows people to keep an eye on things in a manner that feels fairly unobtrusive. The device allows SLH employees to maintain the accessibility that goes with being a dedicated employee, while still engaging with life outside of work.

Single parents, dual working parents, and primary working parents are all provided the same opportunities and burdens that come with ubiquitous internet access. These two elements of the Ideal Worker (working from home and accessibility) are available to everyone with these devices, but they are not the same. Working from home involves concentrated efforts to do specific tasks that couldn't be completed during business hours—or that came up unexpectedly outside those hours.

Accessibility, on the other hand, is a more passive—and thus less visible—form of work. While checking and being aware of incoming messages might turn into active work at any point (there is nothing worse for Roger than checking messages before falling asleep, and realizing he has to get up to run a report or send someone a needed document), maintaining accessibility is different from working from home. People can work from home for a set period every night, but not make themselves accessible outside that time period. Or, someone can make themselves constantly accessible by checking messages regularly, but wait until the next day to actually do the work the messages might inspire.

Working outside the office and being accessible: together these actions are part and parcel of being an Ideal Worker.

THE IDEAL WORKER: PRIORITIZING WORK

It is 7:30 p.m. on a Tuesday, and Brenda Finchley is alone in her hotel room. The room is dark and she is tired. On the task force for a new property, Brenda is residing in one of the pre-renovated rooms: sagging orange couch, striped brown carpet, and a peeling laminate desk. The heavy rust-colored curtains, open, draw the eye to a sunset view of downtown San Francisco. By the end of the year every inch of the hotel will be renovated: a modern look with plum, gray, and lime green accents.

Tonight, though, Brenda makes herself cozy in the dingy room. With the large TV on and computer open in her lap, Brenda is propped up on the bed. She leaves her husband and three kids every week at 3:30 a.m. on Monday morning and returns after 8:00 p.m. on Friday; this is Brenda's home for the time being.

Today Brenda spent too many hours downstairs in the basement offices of the hotel, working with the staff, building a budget estimate, and sitting in meeting after meeting with the new management team. She retired to her room at 6:30 p.m., changed into her PJs, and ordered room service. She won't step a foot outside of the hotel for days at a time. Brenda nibbles at her dinner and makes a plan for the evening: inputting sales leads into the system, merging and updating documents with the new hotel's logo, catching up on email with her home property.

Brenda looks at the clock and texts her husband, Cory. It's near bedtime for their kids. He texts that it's been a long day and he'll call her after the kids are in bed. It's sometimes hard for the kids to talk on the phone, especially if they are tired. So some nights it's just easier if she doesn't call. He calls a little after 9:00, and the two talk for an hour. Cory tells her about the kids, what he made for dinner, when his parents are arriving to help cover so he can go to his class the following evening. She details the challenges of the new property and how the new director is settling in. After the call, she wraps up her last merge document and a few more emails, then she calls it a night. Brenda gets up to wash her face and brush her teeth. It is 11:00. Another long day.

AS A STAY-AT-HOME SPOUSE, Cory Finchley supports Brenda's work in numerous ways. Caring for the kids and the house, he enables Brenda to prioritize work. These instances are distinct from the near-daily occurrences of Brenda working from home, maintaining her accessibility to colleagues out of the office, or putting in the expected hours of face time. When Brenda travels as part of the task force, and Cory is home alone with their three children, she is prioritizing work. In these moments, the Ideal Worker makes major life decisions in service of a job: moving to a new location for a job, saying yes to increased responsibilities, traveling even if it means days or weeks away from home.[12]

Like a consultant or other project-based professional, Brenda spent Monday through Friday in San Francisco for six weeks. Such intense hours bled into Brenda's meager time at home on the weekends. Early in this task force assignment, Brenda made the mistake of turning off her devices one Saturday after a long week in San Francisco. She woke up Sunday morning, turned on her phone, and discovered over thirty pressing emails about budget negotiations. Disturbed to realize that people were waiting on her to finalize a presentation to the new owners, Brenda spent several hours on Sunday morning reading all of the messages and sent a mea culpa message to the group: "Okay. I'm really sorry. I checked out yesterday. I did not realize you needed me. I should have had my phone on." Now Brenda makes sure to check her email at least every morning and evening on the weekends, "So that I'm not just completely MIA. Because that doesn't look good." Brenda cannot stomach the idea that colleagues would be saying to themselves, or, worse, to each other, "Where'd she go?"

Brenda's willingness to dive into new challenges and prioritize work has likely been part of her success at SLH. Brenda was promoted twice over a two-year period (first from manager to a director of two sister properties, then to a senior director overseeing many more properties). Dedicated to her job, she is recognized for her willingness to work on her day off, stay late if needed, or hop on an airplane to help open a new hotel.

The elements of the Ideal Worker are enacted with great effort by all SLH employees. But there are opportunities that Brenda can say yes to that Nancy simply cannot. For Nancy to make a work trip, she has to plan weeks in advance and worries about whether she can get the one babysitter she trusts implicitly to watch the kids overnight. There is no way she can say yes to weeks away on a task force. Nancy is a valued employee and shows her dedication to SLH in multiple ways, but she is still forced to live in terms of an ideal that will never be within her reach.

WHAT GENDER IS THE IDEAL WORKER?

Despite the fact that Brenda Finchley and Nancy Huron are deeply committed to their work and to SLH,[13] the Ideal Worker myth rests on gendered assumptions. SLH might not assume that only men can be Ideal Workers, but it is those people without other obligations (or with someone else to take care of those obligations) who most align with the myth's definition, and who, consequently, are most rewarded by the company.[14]

For example, SLH valorizes visible dedication to work and 24/7 availability, and management assumes esteemed employees can spend extended periods of time away from home. Brenda has Cory at home, so she can rely on him to support her work efforts. In addition to traveling, she moves across properties at SLH, rising in the ranks and meeting the needs of the growing organization. But this is more difficult for the women who shoulder more of the work of caregiving and domesticity and thus cannot leave for extended periods. And even when they can, research on women in the workplace suggests the women at SLH are in a familiar bind: they are generally viewed as less capable, committed, and likeable than men.[15]

Take Nancy. An incredibly accomplished manager juggling multiple properties, Nancy still struggles with how to appear competent in a masculine environment. Nancy is direct and strong-minded, and can hold her own with her superiors. But she gets emotional when frustrated. Nancy relieves stress by crying. She doesn't let anyone see her cry at work, however, and when she gets frustrated she makes sure to leave the property before

Ideal Worker	Examples
Long Hours at the Office	Franco and his boss, Maria, staying late in the office
Working at Home	Brenda with laptop catching up on evenings and weekends
Always Accessible	Nancy with phone available to colleagues at night
Prioritizing Work	Brenda traveling for long periods

TABLE 2.1   Elements of the Ideal Worker Myth

allowing herself to cry. This helps her to maintain expected profession-alism in front of her colleagues.[16] Signaling competence at SLH requires strength (but not arrogance), and Nancy acts with clarity and authority.

Brenda offers "motherly" advice to some of her younger female staff, but she also views herself as direct and blunt. She accepts with nonchalance that she made a subordinate cry in a performance evaluation. Brenda wears her toughness with pride. She's not a pushover and does not apologize for having high expectations for her employees. Successful women at SLH are strong and assertive, so Brenda and Nancy cover or compensate for their softer traits. And they do so without question. In how they display competence, Brenda and Nancy do not fundamentally challenge the gen-dered assumptions of the ideal.

Brenda, Nancy, and Teresa Davies are all highly committed to SLH, countering the notion that working mothers are less committed than men. Such commitment often requires working late and traveling. This means help on the home front. Nancy has an extensive network of paid help; Brenda has Cory staying home in service of her career; Teresa has Chip's work flexibility (and her mother) to rely on. Yet the commitment of women at SLH was questioned in ways that we did not observe for male employ-ees. Others notice when they leave "early" and muse over what could be pulling them away.[17]

Brenda leaves at 4:00 p.m. one day a week so Cory can take a pho-tography class. On those days, she arrives at 7:00 a.m. and makes up an extra hour or more by working that evening. Her workday is as long if not longer than any other day. Nevertheless, others notice and comment on her absence.

Brenda has learned to react with an artful combination of humor and self-deprecation. She relates how one Tuesday her regional manager, Ned, came looking for her at 4:20 p.m.—after she had already left. The next day, her general manager, Larry, jokingly related to Brenda that he told Ned "you only work half days." So when Larry and Ned are conversing the following week, and motion Brenda to join them, she approaches Ned looking at her watch: "Do you need me? Because, you know, it's almost 2:00 p.m. and I leave at 2:00 p.m. on Monday, Wednesday, and Friday. Larry told you I only work half days, right?" When Ned seems to believe her, she exclaims, "Come on! How could you believe that? I certainly work more than that!"

While Brenda relates this tale as a humorous example of informal collegiality, the underlying message is clear (and is in service of the myth of the Ideal Worker). Brenda may be able to joke, but people note when she leaves early and, as a woman and a mother, her commitment is always under scrutiny.

Larry and Ned regularly tease Brenda about her family obligations (minimal as they are, with Cory home full-time). On a day when Brenda leaves early because Kyle is sick and Cory needs to take Bobby to baseball, Ned jests, "I'm going to have to report you for that. Chooses sick kid over work." The "jokes" about commitment aren't made when Roger Waldo leaves at 4:00 p.m. to go for a run or when Jay Shah leaves to pick up a kid from swimming. In fact, Nick Stewart is respected, not teased, when he leaves early. Like Brenda, Nick has a stay-at-home spouse. In the course of his annual review, the CEO made it explicit that he expected Nick to "be a good father." So Nick is able to pat himself on the back when he leaves work for a Cub Scouts meeting.

Brenda is not the prototypical *male* Ideal Worker (how could she be, she's a woman). The unexamined cause of Larry's joke to Ned about Brenda's half days, and Ned's initial willingness to believe it, is the fact that Brenda is a mom with three young children. People are reminded she is a woman every time she leaves work early.

Would this joke have been as believable or as funny if Brenda was a man? Brenda's humorous expression of shock pushes back on the gendered assumptions of commitment. Ned *knows* Brenda is a dedicated employee who works incredibly hard. In fact, SLH holds Brenda Finchley up as an example of a dedicated employee and a demonstration of the firm's support of women. But Brenda's sex makes it difficult for people to forget that she is also a mother. She must subtly (and regularly) remind her managers that leaving early one day a week does not undermine her commitment.

What about Nancy, who leaves at 4:00 p.m. two days a week in order relieve the babysitter and join her children for dinner? Her dedication is on display through late-night emails and weekend work. The fifteen hours a week she works on the evenings and weekends exceeds what most of the male executives claim to work at home. No one would call Nancy a "slacker." With the company's rapid growth and slow hiring, she currently covers twelve hotels, up from the six SLH initially expected her to cover. She anticipates having twenty properties in the near future.

Given the workload, she cannot help feeling tension regarding her "choice" to leave early and an awareness that others might be noticing and judging her.[18] She modified the signature line on her phone to mask whether her email is coming from her phone or computer. "It sounds kind of sneaky, I guess. . . . I just don't really like people to know where I am. I think it stems from the fact that I have to leave at 4:00 p.m. a couple days a week to get the kids." Nancy pushes back in small ways, such as advocating against moving the morning meeting to 8:00 a.m. (to help other working moms), but she largely buys into the work expectations and displays her commitment by being available and working late into the night.

Another disadvantage women face is a bit more subtle: highly competent women are seen as just a little less likeable.[19] In a vice-president's meeting, Marie, one of two female SLH executives, calls out Tim Andrews when he teases her about getting a vendor to cooperate: "But *you're* the one having dinner with the head of North America who signs all of the contracts," she retorts, implying that it is not her job, as a woman, to get everyone to cooperate. We feel a tension in the room that suggests Marie's response is a little too sharp, too pointed, too feisty, but also what they've come to expect from her. Someone breaks the ice with a "whooaaa . . . that's my Marie"—intimating that she is acting more like an attack dog than an easygoing SLH executive. Single, conservatively dressed, no-nonsense, Marie does not participate in the teasing and casual banter that characterizes interactions among the rest of the executive team.

In trying to be likeable, women face a warmth-competence trade-off in the workplace.[20] As a female executive, Marie (unlike her male counterparts) does not sit with her feet up on a table or wear jeans to the office. She is serious and focused, but this makes her a little less fun and a little less likeable to her colleagues. The male SLH executives, such as Tim Andrews, Nick Stewart, and Jay Shah, likewise display competence and dedication to SLH. But they also project a casual vibe and boyish charm without compromising the masculine Ideal Worker image. They dress down, tease each other, laugh easily, and are always taken seriously. They are men: they fit the role easily. The women of SLH face a narrower range of behaviors that fall within the realm of a professional, capable worker.

Although they don't call it out explicitly, the actions of Brenda, Nancy, and Teresa suggest they know the Ideal Worker is coded as a man. He is a strong, competent figure with complete dedication and focus on work. These women strive for this ideal despite its impossibility.

LATE NIGHTS AND LOYALTY

Every employee has a story like Brenda Finchley's, when they let someone down or missed an important email because their phone was tucked away. Everyone has a story like Teresa Davies's, when their device didn't work as promised or they weren't able to get something done, and they worked late into the night. Everyone has a story like those of Nancy Huron and Franco Garcia, when they struggle to make it to an early meeting or stay late in the office, relying on others to cover at home. The problem is that it's never enough. There is always more work to be done. As Franco reminds us, the company is growing and "the emergencies never stop . . . and everyone is being asked to wear four hats."

Technologies of connectivity exacerbate the pressures to be an Ideal Worker. In fact, phones make it all but impossible *not* to be accessible to work, at least not without missing something important. There is always someone who will respond to email quicker (and SLH employees can tell you who those people are: often the single and childless). Totally committing to work and colleagues often comes at the cost of people's health, producing stress and negative family dynamics.[21] Most troublingly, such commitment may not even benefit the organization.[22]

So why does everyone keep trying? It is for more than financial security. Work serves as a source of pride and identity. It is where they (hopefully) find challenge, stimulation, and triumph. The time and energy dedicated to work are a sign of class, status, and professional success.[23] The need to be (or at least appear to be) an Ideal Worker is stoked by a desire to get promoted and be valued by bosses and co-workers.[24] Not to mention that rejecting these expectations can have negative effects on one's career.[25] And because the myth of the Ideal Worker is inherently impossible to realize, there is always more work to be done.

SLH employees are also motivated by a sense of loyalty. Those that are able to "make it" in this intense environment feel a deep allegiance to SLH.[26] The SLH employees in this book are relatively (and unusually) secure in their positions. Their high performance has protected them against larger economic insecurities in the economy, and in the high-turnover hospitality industry. In return for this "protection," they willingly transfer across properties as needs arise and accept long commutes as well as long hours.[27] Nancy talks about how SLH has "seen her through a lot" in her twelve years with the company. During the recession, SLH found assignments to keep her (even though pay was reduced). The company was supportive during personal crises and health scares. Brenda returned to SLH after working for another company for a few years, even though it meant a longer commute and no pay raise, because she missed the environment and her colleagues. Teresa turned down a job that was significantly closer to home and offered more regular hours because she was worried she'd be bored in the new job. She has "invested so much in this company." For many, knowing the company has, or will, stick by them in moments of crisis (economic downturn, personal traumas, emergency parenting demands) justifies the intensity of daily work efforts. SLH workers like each other, and the collegial atmosphere in the office fosters a sense of loyalty to one another.

THE DARK SIDE TO COLLEGIALITY

Isn't a humane and friendly work environment to be envied? Yes. But this emphasis on family does more than create a friendly environment; it increases the pull of the organization. Integrating family and work, while simultaneously prioritizing work, strengthens the Ideal Worker myth.[28] People don't just feel that they *should* be available and committed to SLH, they *want* to display these traits in order to be a good colleague and friend to those at work.

On the one hand, the close-knit culture encourages people to discuss their personal lives, socialize outside of work, and occasionally bring their children to the office. On the other hand, these activities serve to increase attachment to the firm and the pressure to be available, travel at a moment's notice, and prioritize work when needed. To fall short of these expectations is not only a reflection of the kind of worker one is but a failure of collegiality as well. Nobody wants to be saddled with a reputation for being unreliable and thus be shunned from the company's social life. When people like and want to please those they work with, it becomes all the more difficult to push back on implicit, and often taken-for-granted, Ideal Worker expectations. This explains the downside of work friendships.[29]

Take Nancy Huron. One Tuesday evening she is utterly exhausted from a slew of sixty-hour weeks. She decides to forgo the pile of work that needs to get done in order to get some sleep. She goes to bed immediately after her children, but as soon as she gets under the covers she hears the telltale ping of her phone. It's a text from a female subordinate saying, "I'm super stressed, are you on email?" Nancy immediately texts back, "I could be." After exchanging a few texts, the two end up talking on the phone for over an hour. Her subordinate lost a really big client and needed to vent and brainstorm. Nancy wanted to be there for her. As a manager. As a mentor. As a friend. The two are close. But when Nancy wakes up late the next day—bone tired, with a stomachache, and no time to do her hair—she can't help but ask herself, "Why?!" It is all just too much. Genuine work friendships and collegial environments in the context of substantial work demands can intensify the time and attention spent on work. With technology, even the good aspects of a workplace can become transformed into something that is, frankly, bad.

All this does not negate that SLH executives genuinely care about their workers and their families. We see people pitch in to help when someone has a cancer scare, goes through a difficult divorce, or has a new baby. The organization allows Franco Garcia and his wife to coordinate their days off, in order to use less childcare; Brenda Finchley to leave early to cover for her husband so he can take an evening photography class; and Nancy to depart at 4 p.m. two days a week. Workers are able to plan enough that they can have a life outside of work. These are privileged professional workers with regular salaries and the flexibility and autonomy to navigate regular interruptions to work, not to mention last-minute changes in their schedules.[30]

But we are not confident that intense loyalty to organizations is entirely warranted. Owners and management want continual growth. Companies are attuned to profits and are focused on corporate, not individual, interests.[31] Turnover and growth mean that firms are consistently understaffed and asking people to take on more work. This puts management in a bind even when they legitimately care about the well-being of employees.

It's a bind SLH recognizes, struggles with, and is somewhat abashed about when they fall short. The bottom line looms large in the decision making at most organizations. This tension does not go unnoticed. As one spouse of an executive admits,

> I'm friends with some of the other spouses. And there are times where we just have to laugh. I mean, they say they are so about family, but they

are scheduling conference calls at 8:00 a.m. on a Saturday. It's kind of a double standard because they say they want you to be about family, but at the same time, they want you to be the workhorse that does it all. So you know, like, what do they think that means?

Like many progressive organizations, SLH makes a business case for why happy workers are productive workers: they believe that the company benefits by valuing employees and their whole lives.[32] But the very fact that seeing employees holistically is framed as a business imperative makes clear the problems with entrusting companies to care for employees. It's so easy, in a pinch, for organizational goals to dominate. At the end of the day, although your co-workers may be your friends, the organization cannot love you back.[33] When performance falls short, the organizational needs trump the personal relationship. Even at 8:00 a.m. on a Saturday.

This is not a critique of SLH, or a call for them to abandon their work-life proclamations. It is simply a reminder that it's not reasonable for people to look to organizations, however benevolent, to protect them from the expectations of the Ideal Worker.

The myth of the Ideal Worker may seem strictly personal. It is, after all, closely linked with professional identity. And the myth has a moral valence, one that serves as a marker of elite status for individuals.[34] Moreover, it calls on people to sacrifice, and it is easier to justify these sacrifices when people enjoy those whom they work with. But the myth services the interests of organizations, not the needs of individuals. The company needs to grow and prosper. Therefore, it is up to individual efforts—as dedicated employees—to make it happen.

These intense expectations for Ideal Worker behavior are essentially accepted by all of these SLH employees, but this is not the only myth that shapes their daily experience. They also all have children. For these families, the Perfect Parent myth looms large as well.

CHAPTER 3

PLAYING THE PERFECT PARENT

Having changed out of her work clothes, Brenda Finchley stands at the kitchen counter while her husband, Cory, browns pork chops over the stove. The TV in the front room is on, but only two-year-old Tabitha watches. Four-year-old Kyle has brought an activity kit from his room and says, "Let's play school." Seven-year-old Bobby, the in-charge older brother, says he will be the teacher. Tabitha wanders over and sits down. Bobby hands out small pieces of paper and pencils and instructs them on the assignment: connect the letter with the picture. Tabitha writes all over her paper. Kyle tries to sound out what letter cat starts with. Bobby asks if anyone needs to go to the bathroom. When no one responds, Bobby takes the poster board hall pass and goes himself. The other two kids drift off. Plastic dinosaurs and books are strewn on the carpet. The walls are decorated with Cory's photographs: artistic shots of each of the children. Brightly colored foam blocks with cut-out letters were once jigsawed together on the floor but are now pushed up against the door. Against the backdrop of this activity, Brenda flips through a catalog from the day's mail. She chats companionably with her husband as he finishes dinner. She stops at an advertisement for an "attachment shirt"[1] that extols the benefits of skin-to-skin contact between parent and child. She snorts with a quick laugh, "Oh my gosh, I've caused our babies brain damage." Cory glances up briefly, smiles at his wife, and keeps cooking.

WHILE INTENDED AS A JOKE, Brenda Finchley's comment reveals two things. The first is a fleeting uncertainty about whether she has neglected to give her children something vital. Second is a recognition of the myriad societal expectations around what it means to be a "good" parent:

as she puts on her suit, leaves for work, and *doesn't* wear her child to the office. In their family, Brenda is the primary worker and Cory stays home with their three children. It is Cory who has adopted the traditionally feminine Perfect Parent role.[2] While he appreciates having a relationship with his children similar to what he had with his own mother, who gave him full-time care and attention, living in terms of the Perfect Parent ideal can be exhausting.

WHAT IS THE MYTH OF THE PERFECT PARENT?

The myth of the Perfect Parent is about dedicating one's *entire self* to the project of childrearing. The myth expects parents to put their children's needs before their own and presumes that it is economically feasible for a parent to be at home. This dedicated parent engages in "quality" family time, provides numerous enrichment activities, monitors children's behavior (limiting "screen time" and making sure they are on top of homework), and always puts family first.[3]

Yet this ideal embodies inherent contradictions and innumerable challenges; it includes trade-offs and obstacles that are an implicit aspect of simply raising a child. It is impossible to have family dinner every night *and* make sure children participate in a suite of enrichment activities (many of which involve evening practices). Homework, on the other hand, often gets in the way of both enrichment activities and "family time." And how are parents supposed to keep kids completely off media, when video-based learning games are expected by schools, homework is done online, and one child may need to be pacified while the other gets homework help? Navigating this terrain reveals that, like all myths, one's ability to be the parent that society heralds as ideal is treacherous. But it is also deeply seductive, for who doesn't want to be a good parent?[4]

Injunctions for how—and how not—to parent pervade American culture. For example, experts insist that family dinner is imperative for committed parents to foster "quality time." This image—of the family sharing a meal and discussing their day—evokes 1950s cheer and promises healthy and well-adjusted children.[5] The media campaigns around such efforts are not subtle: the "family dinner challenge" quotes a 2012 study that claims, in no uncertain terms, that more frequent family dinners reduce "emotional and behavioral problems" and ultimately lead to "higher life satisfaction."[6]

Schools also have demands. They expect parents to sign off on homework and monitor their children's academic performance. Many school data-management systems send parents a nightly email with each student's progress: homework, missing assignments, test grades. Parents are regularly reminded by experts that sports, theater, art, and music lessons will create talented, well-rounded human beings, as well as ensure future success.[7] Intense competition for elite colleges feeds parental fears that in addition to grades and test scores, children need to be music prodigies *and* chess club champions *and* captains of the soccer team in order to get into the college of their choice.[8] Facilitating such efforts requires full-time parental devotion.

The expectations of parenting that pervade U.S. society are evident in the families of SLH employees. Everyone attempted some form of "family dinner," even if it only happened occasionally and meant relying on frozen food, parents eating "real food" after their kids went to bed, or having take-out around the table.[9] And every single child over the age of four was in at least one extracurricular activity: even if this meant regularly being late, carting younger siblings to practice, or having a babysitter do the driving.

Parents did actively monitor homework. That often meant giving one child a device in order to focus on spelling or math with another. Technological devices were approached with a mixture of guilt, fear, uncertainty, and (yes) relief. Tired parents and eager children find respite and entertainment in these technologies.

Through these families, we observed the elements of the Perfect Parent myth in action. We saw the myth needle its way into their lives when, for example, Brenda noticed the "attachment shirt" in the catalog. And though new media campaigns encourage and extol fatherhood,[10] the Perfect Parent myth is still largely predicated on a powerful "mommy myth": that the mother should be at home taking care of the children.[11] Abundant media messages imply that Brenda is somehow failing in this world of intensive parenting.

Olive just turned eight. Like all her siblings on their birthdays, she got to spend the day with her dad at work. An executive at SLH and single father of three girls, Tim Andrews works in the company headquarters where such visits are the norm. Bouncing around the kitchen island as Tim pulls together dinner, Olive gushes about the birthday spent at her father's office.

"It was super fun. I was a really big helper." Olive twirls and shows off the SLH plastic lanyard with her name on it. The lanyard string is turquoise just like her new top. It was perfect. The badge looks official, with "Helper" printed below her name in bold letters. What did she do to help? First, she shredded a lot of paper. She actually stood inside of the paper bin to try to crush it down because the paper shredder kept getting jammed. Then she helped design a hotel. And she put labels on a bunch of envelopes. Everyone was super nice—even though she had brought a whole big envelope full of things to do to keep her busy, she ended up not needing to do any of them. Instead, there were plenty of things at SLH to keep her busy.

Later Tim qualifies that it was not a very productive day for him. There were a few "distractions and breaks." But he smiles broadly and laughs about Olive tromping down the paper shreds. He agrees, "It was a good day."

UNLIKE MANY FIRMS, SLH publicly supports and extols the virtues of family. This allows Tim Andrews to talk about and involve his children in his professional life. Family photos are proudly displayed on desks across the firm. "Work-life balance" is a regular topic of conversation. Tim loves that everyone at work knows his girls by name. He and his co-workers talk of their children's activities over lunch, and he does not hide the fact that he needs to get home and cook them dinner.

Even though Tim will take work calls at 8:00 a.m. on a Saturday, he also feels comfortable sending Noah, the CEO, a heads-up email about an upcoming week when he plans to be particularly busy outside of work. Tim is performing in a community theater production of *Annie* with his girls and has final rehearsals and performances that will interfere with his normal work routine. In sending the email, Tim assures Noah that his work will get done, but family will be taking a front seat and will shorten his days in the office. Noah knows Tim's girls: he played ping-pong with Olive's older sister, Hannah, last month on her birthday day with dad in the office.

It is a tricky balance. Although SLH culture encourages employees to aspire to the Perfect Parent, the company still subtly expects and rewards those who adhere to the assumptions of the Ideal Worker myth (assumptions that are by definition not family friendly). So while Tim is able to give his family the "front seat" for the week of *Annie* rehearsals, he will definitely be playing catch-up after the performances are over.

And having kids around while trying to work is not always rewarded. Unlike Tim's experience bringing the girls to work (one at a time) on their birthdays, another executive recalls a performance review when he was called out for once having his "rugrats" in the car while he was on a weekend conference call. The kids, it was made clear, were too loud and distracting. Employees are surely welcome to talk *about* their children, and even occasionally bring them into work for a special occasion. But this is not standard practice. Most important, having a family shouldn't get in the way of being a committed and productive employee. In the hierarchy of ideals, between working and parenting, working comes first.

Navigating the tensions between being the kind of parent that society expects while also upholding Ideal Worker status is made possible by an unexamined assumption at SLH: there is presumably a Perfect Parent, often a woman, who is somewhere, elsewhere, doing the bulk of the work of raising children. This doesn't mean SLH management explicitly expects that a woman's place is in the home. But many SLH executives manage this tension between Ideal Worker and Perfect Parent by specializing: the SLH employee acting as the primary worker, with a "default" or "lead" parent at home.[12]

In fact, even when the parent who doesn't work at SLH has his or her own career, it is still that person—and not the SLH worker—who takes on the bulk of domestic and childcare duties, regardless of whether it is a man or woman. It's not uncommon for these dual-career couples to face questions from co-workers and supervisors about how they prioritize two careers.

Take Franco and Katrina Garcia. They are approximately equal breadwinners. They attempt to divide childcare and family responsibilities equally. But when Franco is offered a better-paying job outside of SLH, two of Franco's superiors encourage him to take the higher-paying job so "Katrina can stay home with the kids." In explaining this advice, one of Franco's supervisors even attributes his own children's success to having a mother at home. Regardless (or perhaps because of) the fact that SLH employees talk about and share their children's accomplishments over lunch, SLH implicitly (and sometimes explicitly) supports the stay-at-home parent model. Even though family life and parenthood itself are exalted in the company, gendered assumptions of parenthood run deep.

THE PERFECT PARENT: "QUALITY TIME"

Dinner is a simple meal at Tim Andrews's house. Tonight they have frozen taquitos, water-melon, three strawberries each, banana, and sliced apple that returned home from some-one's lunchbox. Tim forgot to run the dishwasher before work this morning, so it's "birthday party plate night," with kid-sized plastic flower plates they usually use for birthday parties. At 6:30 p.m., the girls put the plates around the table and pour themselves glasses of water. Nine-year-old Hannah wears roller blades. When they sit down, Tim asks five-year-old Chloe for a prayer. Chloe sings, "Please and thank you. Please and thank you. That is what we do. Please and thank you. Please and thank you." Then she says, "Dear God, Thank you for our friends and our family and our food. Amen." Hannah rolls her eyes at the "long" prayer, and they go around the table sharing the "highs, lows, and mediums" of their days.

Chloe goes first: her high, new clothes from a friend who had a growth spurt. "Oh yeah," she lilts, pointing enthusiastically to the purple "Dance Dance Dance" shirt that sparkles on her chest. Hannah's high is eating taquitos for dinner. For Olive, play prac-tice was definitely her high. Her medium was running into someone in a relay race. She giggles when revealing her clumsiness. Each piece of news is accompanied by a comment or question from Tim or one of the sisters. Chloe can't wait for ice-skating, Olive for the softball game this weekend. Tim's high is a drink with several co-workers after work, his medium a so-so meeting, his low interviewing an unimpressive job candidate. During din-ner, Tim's phone vibrates in his pocket but he doesn't answer it. For forty minutes they are at the table and fully engaged in a spirited dinner conversation.

THIS IS TIM ANDREWS'S VERSION of family dinner. He sits at the table with his girls, with lively conversation and multiple food groups represented. As a single parent, he shares joint custody with his ex-wife. Tim does not have the support of a spouse to help get dinner on the table, but he does have several nights a week when the girls are with their mom. He focuses his attention on spending quality time with his girls on the nights they are together. He tries his absolute best not to work while they are awake and is mindful that his phone can distract him from time with his girls. Tim's assertion that "when I'm on the floor playing with the kids I won't take it [iPhone] out of my pocket" bore up in our time with him. He is an active dad. Fun. Silly. And on his weekday evenings he is fully fo-cused on getting dinner on the table, hearing about their days, and getting everyone ready for bedtime.

Like all aspects of these myths, the local experience of one family—in this case, the particular experience of dinner—is not universal, but instead located in a particular history, place, and economic circumstance.[13] For example, one family's Indian heritage and new-age health inclinations led to hours dedicated to daily home-cooked meals from scratch, while another family's Mexican mother imprinted in them awe for the magic of fast food. Yet the belief in family dinner as a directive was a shared phenomenon, even by those who weren't often able to make it happen. We appreciated the different aspects of what it meant to have family dinner in each family. (In fact, impressed at how well it worked in eliciting conversation with Tim Andrews's family, one of the authors has instigated "highs and lows" at her own dinner table).

That said, family dinner is not always fun or idyllic. The effort involved in getting everyone to the table—with the food prepared, worker home from the office, and kids in their seats—is substantial. Children may be tired and conversation harried.

Brenda and Cory Finchley are also dedicated to family dinner. Cory puts adult and kid-friendly food on the table every night. Brenda does her best to get home in time for them to eat all together. Often it is rewarding. But this Thursday, it is late and a little rushed. The final push toward family dinner begins with a 6:38 p.m. text from Brenda that she's finished her quick stop at BevMo on her way home.

Cory Finchley, quiet and unassuming in a baseball cap and sweatshirt, times his cooking to Brenda's text in order to have dinner ready when she gets home. Their three kids bounce between their bedrooms and the front room. They know not to come into the kitchen. At 6:52 p.m., Brenda arrives home and quickly changes her clothes. She is cutting it close. The family has a well-orchestrated "lights out" routine to have the kids in bed at 8:00. Cory prefers to have dinner on the table at 6:30. At 7:01, the family sits down to dinner. Chicken with rice (and orange sauce for the adults). Plus bananas and milk for the kids. Brenda buckles Tabitha into her high chair and sits down at her end of the table. Cory sits at the other end, nearer the boys. Mom asks each child to recount his or her day, firmly quieting Kyle when he interrupts his brother: "You will get your turn next. I am talking to Bobby right now." When it's his turn, Kyle talks about sharing something that starts with the letter P at preschool tomorrow. He is going to bring a pterodactyl, which is going to be tricky because it doesn't sound like it starts with a P. But it does.

Cory tells Brenda that they went to Target and the kids have been on the verge of "losing it" all day. "We are counting the minutes to bed." Bobby is a slow and picky eater, and his parents take turns trying get him to finish his dinner: "Bobby, five more minutes

until bedtime . . . Bobby, two more minutes until bedtime . . . Better eat . . . Better eat."
Tabitha eats a little chicken and asks for another half of banana. Mom obliges. Bobby
wants another half of a banana too, but he has to eat his chicken first. Kyle hasn't eaten
his banana; he's eaten the chicken and wants more, but Dad relays that there is only
chicken with sauce left. Cory asks Bobby, "Can Kyle have your chicken?" Bobby says no.
"Well, then, are you going to eat it?" Bobby says yes and eats his chicken so Kyle can't
have it. Tabitha and Bobby both want the final half a banana. Dad gives most of it to
Bobby. Bobby asks for dessert and Dad says, "You only have two minutes until bed. There
is no time for dessert." Bobby says, "What about a short dessert? How about girl scout
cookies?" Dad gives each child a girl scout cookie and dinner adjourns. Bedtime quickly
follows, with lights out at 7:47.

CORY HAS COOKED the family dinner and timed it to be ready when
Brenda arrives home from work. As the default parent with a full-time
working spouse, Cory plans, shops, and cooks, while alone with three
young children. Both parents look forward to their family dinner: talking
to each other and their kids around the table, with no electronic devices
or other distractions.

Most families recognize family dinner as an ideal.[14] But the reality
doesn't always live up to the myth. And most do not execute it as often
as Cory and Brenda (who eat together about five times a week). As a full-
time parent, Cory commits to cooking, and Brenda commits to getting
home. "We do it a lot," Cory says. "That is why the kids are pretty good at
dinnertime. They expect to eat at the dinner table." Tonight was pretty
smooth. But when a clogged toilet or cancelled baseball practice unexpectedly changes the schedule, expectations for family dinner are scaled
down and it becomes more challenging, both emotionally and practically.

Other families share hesitantly that they are lucky if they eat together
three . . . ok, really only two nights a week. The acknowledgment is pref-
aced with, "It's so sad." If one, no less two, parents are living within the
limitations of the Ideal Worker myth, the chance of everyone even *being*
home by dinnertime shrinks substantially.

Sometimes the children (or parents) are grumpy and tired. With young
children, there can be bickering, crying, and frustrated attempts to identify
wants and desires: "Is this what you want? This? Is this what you want?"
More than once, we saw children wander away from the dinner table and,
instead of corralling them back, the parents would sit back and enjoy the

moment of quiet. The bottom line is that having family dinner is not only difficult to orchestrate, it is often not very fun.

For those with older children, the kids' busy schedules and activities undermine the ability to have family dinner. Schedules change by the season; on top of that, there are often several activities in full swing at any point in time. With multiple children and multiple activities, the goal is simply to eat, often with no hope of eating together. Even within the boundaries of the Perfect Parent myth itself, family dinner still directly conflicts with the injunction for children to pursue after-school enrichment activities that often run into the evening hours.

THE PERFECT PARENT: PROVIDING ENRICHMENT

Jay and Olivia Shah's two daughters, thirteen-year-old Neelam and nine-year-old Tessa, have carefully orchestrated schedules—both girls swim, manage homework, and participate in several other activities. This Tuesday runs like clockwork. Tessa has fashion camp from 2:50 to 3:50 p.m., Mathnasium from 4:30 to 5:30, and swimming from 6:00 to 7:00. Neelam is on the advanced team and has swim practice from 4:00 to 6:00.

In order to make it all happen Olivia picks Tessa up from school at 2:30. Her dark hair pulled back at the nape of her neck, she greets her daughter with her typical calm smile, listening to Tessa's animated chatter about needing to sell cookies for a school fundraiser as they drive to fashion camp. Olivia then meets Neelam at home—carpool dropped her off at 2:00 and Neelam immediately started on homework. This year's amped-up amount of schoolwork means Neelam has no time to waste before swimming. At 3:25 Olivia makes her way upstairs to tell Neelam that it is time to go. Olivia drops Neelam at swimming a bit early (3:40), so she can pick up Tessa from fashion camp by 4:00.

Back at the house with Tessa, Olivia measures the lentils and puts them on low for dinner as Tessa gathers her things for Mathnasium and swimming. The two get back in the car at 4:20, and Olivia drops Tessa off at 4:30. On the way home she takes a call through her car's Bluetooth system. It is her husband. After a quick update she asks, "Do you think you can pick up Tessa from swimming at 7:00?" Jay responds, "Yeah. I think so. But I will text you." Back at home, Olivia's mom and sister-in-law arrive to help make a traditional Indian meal. Cooking is a communal and regular part of Olivia's afternoon schedule.

Olivia returns to Mathnasium at 5:40 and takes Tessa directly to swimming. Tessa changes into her swimsuit in the car. It is still a little wet from yesterday because she cannot find her other swimsuit. Oh well. At 5:58, Tessa gets out of the car for swim practice. Olivia waits in the car until 6:07 when Neelam runs out and hops into the car. Upon arriving home, Neelam, starving, immediately eats dinner. She is still wearing her big swimming coat and sits at the kitchen island chatting with her grandma.

At 6:35 Olivia receives a text from Jay that he will pick up Tessa on his way home. Olivia exhales a sigh of relief and decides to eat. Olivia's mother rolls her eyes and says, "Oh, all the coordination." But she acknowledges with a chuckle, "We haven't forgotten the girls yet!" Olivia's mother and sister-in-law leave with food to take home to their families. Jay and Tessa arrive home at 7:14, and Tessa immediately goes upstairs to take a shower. At 7:38 Tessa joins her dad at the kitchen island. Jay has finished eating and is checking emails on his laptop as they sit together. The two banter and laugh as Tessa eats and Jay checks email. Neelam is upstairs doing homework. And Olivia is doing dishes. Another Tuesday is winding down.

Tessa and Neelam Shah have a dizzying array of after-school activities. These activities are a hallmark of the "concerted cultivation" style of parenting that has become the norm in middle- and upper-class families in the United States.[15] Parents are expected to orchestrate a series of enrichment opportunities that signal accomplishment and worthiness of both parent and child. Few parents would articulate this as the rationale; it is simply what one does.

When she was younger, Neelam played multiple instruments (along with her other activities). Now she dedicates herself to cello, swimming, and acting. She narrowed her focus to the cello when she reached middle school and plays in the school orchestra. Her cello teacher comes to the house for lessons on the weekend. The swim team requires eight hours of practice during the week and additional practices on Saturday morning. Neelam performs with an advanced acting group at the local repertory theater one evening a week and Saturday afternoons (even though acting is ten miles away and can be a trek with traffic). These activities require upward of fifteen hours a week.

Tessa also takes a two-hour weekly acting class at the same location (but on a different day). Tessa's activities are more varied: she is younger and has not found her passion. Tessa does look forward to yoga once a week and would like to take an art class. She is currently swimming and has tried and abandoned soccer, basketball, tennis, dance, and gymnastics. The opportunity for children to participate in an array of enrichment activities is part and parcel of the Perfect Parent myth.

But what does this array of opportunities mean for the parents? The details that Olivia juggles for the various enrichment activities for her girls become all too visible when she needs to leave town for a week. As part of her travel agency, Olivia occasionally visits a property or attends a conference. But a longer trip is unusual. For this five-day trip, Olivia makes a spreadsheet with a section for each helper (Jay, her dad, and her neighbor)(Table 3.1). She makes notes about who will do what to keep the girls' schedules going. Olivia's father has retired and regularly helps out. He has five entries for Monday alone. Included in the spreadsheets are the various cell phone numbers of the helpers she has enlisted for the week. She walks everyone through the details before she leaves. The spreadsheet documents and displays all of the coordination and orchestration that Olivia carries in her head at any one time. It is nothing short of extraordinary.

Rebecca Stewart also keeps the family schedule in her head. Invested in the relentless expectations of intensive parenting, she tracks an impressive amount of activities as well: three kids play soccer; two are in chess; two in swimming; two in gymnastics; and one each in Lego class, piano, and Cub Scouts. A stay-at-home parent with four young kids, Rebecca lacks Olivia's extended family. Rebecca is the organizer, orchestrator, and chauffeur for all of these various activities. And it is actually impossible to make it to a practice on time when gymnastics ends at the same time as soccer begins. Even on the weekends when two parents can be deployed, the Stewarts occasionally miss the game of their youngest soccer player, five-year-old Eric, because of conflicts with two of the other kids' games.

All in all, the Perfect Parent needs to be a facilitator and a cheerleader, keeping tabs on everything. While these numerous enrichment activities are technically for the children, they end up requiring serious investment from adults: someone has to sign up for activities, drive to practices, pay the fees, buy the equipment and clothes, keep said equipment and clothes clean, and be there to cheer for games or performances.[16] "Enriching" children is a serious drain on adults.

Nancy Huron, a single mom with one income, no support from her ex-husband, and a rigid schedule, allows her kids to each participate in one (and only one) activity: Dylan does karate and Melody gymnastics. And when the instructor suggests that Melody has a talent and could move up to the competitive gymnastics team, Nancy sticks with the existing class because she isn't prepared to upend the precarious schedule.

But there's more. Devoted parents don't just sign their child up for enrichment opportunities, make sure they have all the gear and materials, and get them to practices. Each activity *also* involves culminating events: soccer games, swim meets, dance competitions, play performances, music recitals, karate demonstrations. Despite these events being on an entirely

	Monday (School Holiday)	Tuesday	Wednesday	Thursday
Father AM		Drop Tessa off at school 8:15 am.	Drop Tessa off at school & then Neelam & Nora before 8:45 am for late start, or coordinate with Neighbor for her to drop older girls.	Drop Tessa off at school 8:15 am.
Father PM	Maybe pick up Tessa from swim at 7 pm.	Pick up Tessa from swim at 7 pm.	Pick up Tessa from swim at 7 pm.	
Grandfather AM	Come to our house and sit with Neelam. She will be doing homework but will be home alone.			
Grandfather MIDDAY	Friend will pick up Tessa around 10 am and drop off before swim if she is going.		Pick up Nora & Neelam from school at 1:55 pm and drop them both off at our house.	Pick up Tessa from school at 2:50 pm at the corner & drop straight off at Mathnasium.
Grandfather PM	Take Neelam to swimming at 4 pm. (Take Tessa to Mathnasium at same time).	Drop Neelam at swimming at 3:40 pm so you can pick up Tessa from school at 3:50 pm inside circle at school (she has after-school activity).	Take Neelam to swimming at 4 pm & come back to our house.	
Grandfather PM	Drop off Tessa at Mathnasium at 4:15 pm. Make sure Tessa takes all swimming stuff with her in the car including tennis shoes for dry land.	Drop off Tessa at Mathnasium at 4:45 pm. Make sure Tessa takes all swimming stuff with her in the car.	Drop off Tessa at Mathnasium at 4:45 pm. Make sure Tessa takes all swimming stuff with her in the car.	Pick up Tessa from Mathnasium at 4:15 pm and take to yoga from 4:30 pm–5:30 pm.
Grandfather PM	Pick up Tessa from Mathnasium at 5:15 pm & drop off at swimming before 5:30 pm. Wait for Neelam and pick her up from swimming at 6 pm.	Pick up Tessa from Mathnasium at 5:45 pm & drop off at swimming by 6:00 pm. Wait for Neelam and pick her up from swimming at 6 pm.	Pick up Tessa from Mathnasium at 5:45 pm & drop off at swimming by 6:00 pm. Wait for Neelam and pick her up from swimming at 6 pm.	
Neighbor MIDDAY		Pick up Neelam & Nora from school near swimming pool at 1:40 pm & drop Neelam at home.	Pick up Janice and Tessa from school at 1:15 pm & 1:30 pm and take them to Art Class from 2–4pm.	Pick up Neelam & Nora from school near swimming pool at 1:40 pm & drop Neelam at home.

TABLE 3.1 Spreadsheet for Olivia Shah's Helpers When She Leaves Town

different schedule from the original activities, faithful parents are supposed to show up to watch.

And, of course, these events are set without reference to parents' own schedules. Often they occur during the workday. And they are not negotiable. Melody Huron's summer gymnastics camp hosted a final "showcase" on Friday midday. Nancy simply couldn't get away. Her "lifesaver" neighbor, Kelly (a stay-at-home mom), took it upon herself to go in Nancy's place. The Thanksgiving school play in which Dylan was Abe Lincoln posed a similar challenge: 2:00 p.m. on a Tuesday. There is no way Nancy can be there; she consoles herself with the fact that he only has two lines.

THE PERFECT PARENT: MONITORING CHILDREN

It is a Wednesday afternoon in late October. The Stewart house is decorated with a large stuffed witch, ceramic jack-o-lantern figurines, and a cloth banner over the entryway that says "Happy Halloween." With her blond hair gathered in a low bun, wisps coming out at her temples, Rebecca Stewart sits at the dining room table and flips through six-year-old Peter's three-inch homework binder. She taps her dark pink nail on the page when she gets to the right worksheet (the binder has all of his worksheets for the year). A neon yellow paper at the front spells out the homework goals for first grade: "As a parent, you can help your child set up good study habits that will last a lifetime. . . . Your signature indicates that you have checked for completeness, accuracy and neatness."

Because of parent conferences, school ended early today, at 12:30 p.m. So after eating a quick lunch, Rebecca and Peter are getting an early start on homework. A bowl of celery sticks and a blue pencil case filled with markers, pencils, and glue are ready on the table. But Peter is having a hard time focusing. He asks for water. Just as Rebecca sets down the glass of water and gets Peter focused, five-year-old Eric gallops down the stairs naked, shouting "I'm a jumping frog."

Rebecca successfully puts shorts on Eric and diverts him toward a "math-manipulative activity" (a color-matching game) in the living room. Eric doesn't have homework, but the game makes him feel like his big brother. Screams of "Mommy! Mommy!" are heard from three-year-old Frankie upstairs. She has locked herself in the bathroom and eight-year-old Brittany can't talk her through how to unlock the door. Brittany fetches Rebecca, and Rebecca goes upstairs to unlock the door with a coat hanger. Successful, Rebecca soothes a hysterical Frankie.

While Rebecca is upstairs, Peter leaps up from the table to bother Eric in the living room. Back downstairs at 1:15 p.m., Rebecca corrals Peter back to the dining room table. Rebecca goes to help Eric with a pattern game. Less than five minutes later, Peter yells, "Done mommy!" She walks back into the dining room and after a quiet moment exclaims, "Peter! Peter! She's going to send your homework back." Peter's homework is not done. Rebecca returns to Eric in the living room, and Peter screeches, "EEEHHHH." Rebecca goes back into the dining room only to have Eric immediately call out with a question from the living room. This repeats four times over the next minute, Rebecca responding in sequence to Peter's and Eric's bleating questions.

By 2:11 both Rebecca and Peter are frazzled. Rebecca takes a deep breath and says, "You're losing focus. Let's take a break." But Peter keeps trying, randomly blurting out numbers. Kindly, she says, "You're guessing. Use your counters." Rebecca begins to lose her patience, telling him that they no longer have time to get a pumpkin for Halloween. Then, "Peter, this is your last day of homework for the week. This shouldn't be that hard!"

She changes tactics and suggests he just tell the teacher it was too hard. Peter protests, "I'm gonna finish it!" Mom says, "Okay, let's do it. I'm going to walk out of the room. You do it. And I'll grade it." Peter starts to cry. At 2:21 Rebecca insists, "Let's take a break." They start back up again fifteen minutes later. Rebecca gives Peter a spelling test and, finally, just as Rebecca needs to take Brittany to gymnastics at 3:15, they finish.

FIGURE 3.1 Rebecca Stewart Helping Peter with His Homework

AS ANY PARENT KNOWS, getting a young child to focus on home-work can be an exercise in futility. Rebecca Stewart's afternoon was typical: with frustration and exhaustion for all. She signs Peter's folder each night to acknowledge that he has done his homework, and the weekly packet documenting his work must be turned in every Friday morning. This is her responsibility as a parent (remember the instructions in the front of the binder). She also ensures Brittany gets her homework done each night. Rebecca carries these duties of the Perfect Parent close to her heart. Next year Eric will be in first grade and have his own binder. Before too long she will be monitoring homework for four kids.[17]

Rebecca implicitly understands that Peter's performance reflects on her as a parent. The teachers know which students are completing their work. Asking parents to sign worksheets makes them accountable to the school, and it intensifies the angst and frustration when homework doesn't go smoothly. The school functions as the voice of authority. They are not-so-subtly encouraging Rebecca to be persistent with her parental duties as homework manager—even when other demands (and children) eat away at her time and patience. The homework demands (not to mention the early dismissal time) presume a full-time parent at home.[18] Rebecca is a dedicated parent, but she also has four children under nine. And such school demands are nothing short of impossible for working parents, who rely on grandparents or paid help to help monitor homework (and take kids to activities).

In addition to conveying strong expectations about parental involve-ment and presence, schools also promote explicit ideas about how to use (or not use) technology. Rebecca shares how Peter's teacher has "got this whole thing [about screen time] . . . all the research shows how electronics takes away, like, this certain part of the brain." Their elementary school encourages a "no media on weeknights" policy.

But school is only one source of these expectations. The 2016 American Pediatrics Association recommendations highlight the expected role of parents to manage, monitor, and create "media-free" times and zones.[19] Contemporary media has overwhelmingly villainized the role of screens in children's lives: "Giving your child a smartphone is like giving them a gram of cocaine."[20] Headlines suggest in no uncertain terms that phones, social media, television, and digital games are a direct route to addiction, insomnia, and poor behavior.[21]

This messaging is particularly problematic, because devices are pervasive in contemporary American families—and they are not going away.[22] However, rather than provide parents a nuanced analysis of when and under what circumstances screens are problematic for children (which is what is really needed), Americans are fed a narrative of fear.[23]

This aspect of the Perfect Parent myth is confusing for parents. Schools integrate computer time into the classroom, they expect children to do homework online, and some schools even provide devices. So Nancy Huron lets Melody do "ST Math" (an online math game that the school has a subscription for) because Melody contributes points to her class total, but Nancy closely monitors one of Dylan's favorite games, "Bad Piggies," because she doesn't see it as educational (and once Dylan starts playing, it is difficult to get him to stop). For older children, technology is so intertwined with academic endeavors that restricting usage is close to impossible. Take Jay and Olivia Shah's daughter Neelam. She needs her laptop to write school papers (she also relies on Khan Academy videos to help her with math, sometimes finding the instruction more useful than what she receives at school).

Further complicating reality, entertaining children with videos and games provides practical value. Many children become engaged the minute a device lights up.[24] Parents use this to their advantage. Rebecca has "experimented this year" to figure out what "drives" Peter. If he finishes his homework without too much of a fuss, he gets thirty minutes to play on his mom's phone. And Nancy struggled for months to figure out how to help Dylan with his standardized testing anxiety. The promise of ten minutes of the game "Angry Birds" did the trick. Thrilled, she shares, "I swear it got us through ten days of testing."

For most families, rules about screen time are not strictly enforced. Rather, we see in-the-moment restrictions such as "No more TV after this episode," "Give me back my iPhone when we get to soccer," or "When the clock on the microwave hits 5:00 you're done." These restrictions are based on a series of contingencies. Have the kids been on a device for "too long"? Are they acting out? Are they tired and need downtime? Am I tired and need downtime? Do I have some work I need to get done? Does another child need me right now?[25]

Another obstacle to limiting technology is how technology can be used in creating "quality time." Jay and his daughter Neelam look forward to watching the Lakers basketball team and trash talking before, during, and after the game. Brenda and Cory's kids eagerly anticipate family movie night on Saturdays, when they eat pizza while watching an animated movie together. The high chair gets dragged into the living room for Tabitha, and the boys put their plates on the ottoman.

Employing screen time as quality time can begin spontaneously. One evening, for example, Olive shares how fast she ran at school over dinner, and claims she could keep up with Usain Bolt. This leads to the family animatingly discussing an imagined new reality TV show on which amateurs compete against professionals. Somehow the conversation moves to eating competitions, and Tim tells the girls about the hot-dog-eating champion who can "eat like twenty hot dogs in a minute." Tim chuckles and says, "You know, after dinner I think we are going to have to have some technology." So they watch YouTube videos: of Usain Bolt racing at the Olympics and a hot-dog-eating contest. Despite generalized prescriptions and a narrative of fear, screens can facilitate moments of togetherness and family bonding.

THE PERFECT PARENT: PRIORITIZING FAMILY

Rebecca Stewart glances at her phone and makes a small gasp. She immediately puts down the book she has been reading to the little ones on the couch. Standing up she declares, "Okay, kids, time to go." It is 4:42 p.m., and Peter's soccer practice starts at 5:00. Carrying Peter's shin guards and shoes to the bottom of the stairs, Rebecca calls up to Peter, "Okay. It's time to go!" After three calls, he yells downstairs that he can't find his socks. Rebecca sighs and goes to help him. At 5:04, Rebecca walks downstairs with a mostly dressed Peter and helps him put on his socks and cleats. As Rebecca tries to put on the shin guards, Eric jumps up and down in front of them and Peter squirms. Rebecca motions for Brittany and Frankie. Brittany has been practicing piano while Frankie has continued to "read" to herself on the couch. Ushering all of the kids out the door, Rebecca loads them into her minivan and heads to soccer.

Arriving at 5:20 Rebecca escorts Peter out of the car and onto the soccer field. As Peter practices, the three other kids kick a ball around on the sidelines. They all pile into the car again at 6:17. On the way home they drive by the library and, seeing the building, Rebecca smacks her head realizing she forgot to grab the books that need to be returned. Glancing at the floor by the passenger seat, where the library books should be (but are not), she notices the audio study guide for the California social worker exam. It lies amongst school announcements and a printout of houses for sale in the area. Rebecca laughs out loud at the sight of the study guide: "Like I'm ever going to get to that."

Rebecca contemplates getting take-out for dinner but decides against because, as she explains, "I'm big on them eating healthy." She hasn't gone to the store and needs to, but she decides they can make do with "breakfast for dinner" night. Upon returning home (and successfully mediating as the two boys fight over who gets to turn the doorknob on the front door), Rebecca checks the refrigerator and realizes they are out of eggs. The idea of breakfast for dinner is abandoned. She roots around in the fridge and offers frozen waffles, grilled cheese, or hot dogs to the kids. The kids decide on hot dogs (with a grilled cheese for Frankie). Everyone disperses as Rebecca prepares dinner for her and the kids; her husband, Nick, hasn't returned her calls so she assumes he is coming home late.

By 7:13 the kids have eaten and the dishes are in the dishwasher. Rebecca sends them upstairs in shifts for showers and bed. At 7:38 Nick's car pulls into the driveway. Rebecca is trying to get the boys calmed down and into bed. Frankie gets out of bed twice and Brittany finally gets in the shower. Suddenly, all is quiet. At 8:00 Rebecca walks down the stairs with an exaggerated tiptoe. Success! Three kids are in bed and Brittany is doing her math homework. At 8:10 Nick walks through the door. He stayed late to play ping-pong with the CEO, who likes to challenge Nick (as the reigning champion), then sat in his parked car for thirty minutes finishing up a work call.

As the two open a bottle of wine and munch on some prepared salads, Rebecca tells Nick about helping out in Brittany's classroom that morning while the little kids were in preschool. They asked her to give a talk about violence and bullying at school. It's a chance to use her social work expertise, and she is excited. But she has to find time to prepare.

Nick pulls out his laptop to take a look at his fantasy football team. Rebecca gets up and starts emptying, cleaning, and repacking the kids' lunchboxes. With mock exasperation, Rebecca tells Nick about how one of the kids complained that another kid had a make-your-own-cupcake surprise in their lunch that day. "I can't compete with the other moms!" she laughs.

REBECCA AND NICK STEWART moved to California in service of Nick's career.[26] While Nick has found professional challenge and satisfaction at SLH, Rebecca left her life as a licensed social worker. California doesn't allow her social work exam score to transfer. She has to retake a difficult exam that is only offered once a year. She is torn between her sense of herself as a professional and her desire to be a full-time parent to her four young children. Being the kind of mother that Rebecca wants to be leaves absolutely no time to study for the exam.

The Perfect Parent prioritizes children above other roles, passions, and opportunities. Even above his or herself. And for those in the economic position to be able to make the decision to work or not, the perceived trade-offs—between Perfect Parenting and Ideal Working—can be vexing.

According to Rebecca, "I don't get paid enough money to even make it worth it [going back to work]. But I miss it. I mean, I love what I do. That's the thing. I love social work. And when I start looking at these jobs I'm like, 'Oh, I want to be back out and working with these people.' But at the same time I'm like, 'Oh, but then my kids would suffer.' So, it's hard." The audio guide remains on the floor of her car and a large printed study guide on her bedside table. The yearning for work is real.

Rebecca faces a conundrum. As an educated professional woman, she found her work gratifying. But her identity as a mom—and her commitment to the myth of the Perfect Parent—trumps the angst that comes with losing her professional status and identity. Instead, Nick's salary enables her to invest in this "perfect" vision of parenting.[27] She devotes her time to monitoring homework, facilitating an impressive number of enrichment activities, volunteering at school, and feeding and clothing the kids. Proud of her children, Rebecca is glad she can prioritize this role. But we can't help but be struck by how often she talks about her "lost" career. Rebecca makes sense of this sacrifice by reminding herself that she *wants* to put her children first.[28] As Rebecca reflects,

> I'm pretty honest that my kids come first. . . . I recognize that my career doesn't pay that much. You know, it's not worth it to me to have somebody else raise them. Plus, like I said, I want to be the primary one [parent]. It's gonna be hard to find a job, because I don't want to miss their school performances. I want to be the one who picks them up if they are sick from school. So it would have to be pretty darn flexible.

Rebecca relishes her role at home, but she also isn't comfortable fully letting go of her professional self. When filling out our survey, Rebecca struggles with a question. "What is your occupation? I mean, I am technically a social worker. Do I get to put that?" Another time Rebecca recounts, "Somebody introduced me when I was doing this anti-bullying thing at the school and said I was a 'former social worker.' I was like, 'I'm not a former social worker. I have my license [in another state].' I was kind of like, 'No!

I went to school for a long time to do this.'" But this is the trade-off she feels she has to make.

Rebecca wants to prioritize her family and is proud that she is able to enact a version of the Perfect Parent that aligns closely with the myth. Yet her experience reveals how difficult it is to do. Even with parenting as her full-time focus—after giving up her professional self to pursue the ideal of the Perfect Parent—Rebecca simply cannot give each of her four children the attention she would like. Nor can she get them to their many activities on time, make sure every piece of homework is done, and host the mythical "family dinner." Wanting to be a good parent is, of course, worthy. But having sacrificed so much to the parenting ideal, it seems that the ideal is still out of reach.

WHAT GENDER IS THE PERFECT PARENT?

> WAKEY WAKEY BUSY DADS! Now is a good time to hand wash the kids' sports kits, make your wife's packed lunch and text your in-laws about plans for the weekend #husbandwork—@manwhohasitall

The "Man Who Has It All" tweets in the persona of a busy working dad, while sharing tidbits about getting through the day.[29] The British tweets are a parody of gender equity: snarky, funny, and revelatory. The words of advice frequently given to women sound ridiculous when gender roles are reversed. Following the tweet above, one woman replies, "If your wife's parents are coming you'd better add full deep clean of the house and carpets to your list as well as trip to the salon to do your roots, remove all body hair and have an exfoliating facial. It will reflect badly on your wife if you

Perfect Parent	Examples
"Quality Time"	Cory providing family dinner
Providing Enrichment	Olivia taking kids to multiple after-school activities
Monitoring Children	Rebecca monitoring and helping with Peter's homework
Prioritizing Family	Rebecca staying home to raise her children

TABLE 3.2 Elements of the Perfect Parent Myth

don't." The satirical tweets (and replies) highlight the gendered expectations and experiences of many women juggling the impossible myths of
Ideal Worker and Perfect Parent.

"The Man Who Has It All" highlights the ludicrous—but taken for
granted—expectations of women embodying gendered roles as wives and
mothers. Nevertheless, men face their own gendered set of expectations as
husbands and fathers. While stereotypical gender roles do not always align
with who actually plays the part of lead parent and primary worker, the
stereotypes affect the *experience* of inhabiting these roles. In the previous
chapter we discussed the experience of Brenda Finchley: since the Ideal
Worker is, ideally, a man, Brenda faces an extra challenge in her career: she
is, simply, not a man. Her husband, Cory, also faces gendered assumptions
as a stay-at-home parent. The Perfect Parent myth is the mommy myth;
and Cory is simply not a mom.[30]

This unexpected twist provides Cory with some freedom. He can more
easily reject some of the parenting demands. While Brenda cannot live
up to the Perfect Parent expectations (because she is a mom at work),
paradoxically, Cory is able to stand out as an extraordinary parent, even
though he does not zealously adhere to the Perfect Parent myth. Cory
does not, for example, actively monitor Bobby's homework, nor does he
put his children in multiple enrichment activities. Yet he "neglects" these
duties without worrying over them, as we saw others (mostly women)
do. Cory's days with three young kids may be long and draining, but he
doesn't carry the guilt of not being a Perfect Parent when the kids watch
TV in the afternoon. By not subscribing wholeheartedly to the myth, Cory
needs less help to cart the children to multiple activities (they have fewer).
His days are rarely frenetic, and he has been able to redefine parenting to
incorporate his own model of caregiving.[31]

It is not just that Cory does not fully subscribe to the Perfect Parent
myth. It is that, in many ways, he *cannot*. As a dad rather than a mom, the
expectations of perfection are not reinforced in his everyday experience,
whether through social interactions, media depictions, or cultural tropes.
Mothers, for their part, fortify these myths among themselves.[32]

Like many stay-at-home fathers, Cory isn't invited into mothering
groups or the clutch of moms at the park.[33] Cory does not see himself
reflected in media images, and he doesn't have other mothers who, together, craft stories about what parenthood should entail.[34] Instead, Cory

generally remains alone with his children, from the time they wake until Brenda returns an hour or two before bedtime. The downside of being atypical is the isolation; the upside is being less constrained by the tenets of the Perfect Parent myth.

EXHAUSTED AND EXHILARATED

Parenting is a tiring and never-ending task for everyone.[35] But as single working parents, Nancy Huron and Tim Andrews must figure out how to be a version of the Perfect Parent within the bounds of competing demands. Nancy never has enough energy to enact this ideal. Not only does the myth of the Perfect Parent expect total time and attention, but it is filled with injunctions about *how* that time should be filled (prepare family dinner, shepherd children to the right activities, monitor homework, restrict technology). After a long day at work, Nancy feels guilty that "my mind is not always 100 percent there" while playing with her kids. Tim jokes about the nature of his days one evening at the dinner table when "highs and lows" has turned into charades. When he leans back in his chair to think, his hands behind his head, the girls yell, "Relaxing!" Tim wryly responds, "No. I have not relaxed yet today. If I do that it might be a high, but it hasn't happened yet."

Stay-at-home parents can be tired too. Cory's kids call for him, as the default parent, in the middle of the night. Kyle has night terrors and is going through a hard phase, waking up two to three times a night. When Brenda tries to help, she faces a distraught Kyle insisting, "I asked for Daddy." So by Thursday, when the kids start fighting early in the day, Cory's patience is worn: "Every day is a hard day." Work might actually be a reprieve from long days at home with his three children. Cory explains,

> Yeah. I never really understood how peaceful a bathroom is. It's one of those things. It's like, 'It's so quiet in here.' Or you buckle everybody up in the car and you close the door and you walk around and it's like, 'They are so quiet when they are in their seats in the car and the doors are shut.' You know? So I think what is missed, especially with parents that work, they want to plan everything and do everything with their family because they are not around [during the week].
>
> Being a stay-at-home parent is great. But you have to realize, I'm never off. When the spouse or the other parent that is away wants to do

something special on the weekend, it's not any different for me. You want to go to Disneyland, that's great. We're just taking my day to Disneyland. It's exactly the same. They are just as dependent on me as they are at home. For everything. So I'm not getting away from my job. You are getting away from what you do, disassociating yourself from your job. . . . Well, I'll just get in the car and we'll go to Anaheim now. You know, that's hard. That's really hard. But their dependence [the kids] on me is nice too. They are not relying on someone else.

Alongside the many moments of discipline, shepherding, monitoring, and waking up in the middle of the night, Cory appreciates being a full-time parent. Having a close relationship with his kids is important, and he values being able to be there for them. "So if someone is sick, Daddy is taking care of them. If someone is sick at school, I can go right down the street and immediately get them."

Regardless of the exhaustion and frustration, the rewards of parenting are powerful. One evening when relating his dinner table "high," Tim talks enthusiastically about Olive coming to his office for the day and how they played ping-pong together. Another day we watch him laugh, grin, and bob his head as Olive and Hannah put on a performance in the living room, lip syncing to Adele. Remember that Tim *chose* to audition for a part in *Annie* with his kids, not just take his girls to rehearsal. Tim wants to be around his girls because they are fun.

The joys of parenting are often unexpected and appear in the little moments. Recall Nancy and her children having an impromptu dance party before bed. The light in Nancy's face as she "got down" with her kids was infectious. Or imagine Cory with Tabitha snuggled on his shoulder in a soft pink coat, smiling warmly down at Bobby, who is bouncing around him excitedly with the game ball in his hand—after his first baseball game of playing catcher. These moments of joy are seared vividly into our memories. Intense flashes of adoration and laughter. Interactions with children are not just exhausting, they are also memorable and fulfilling.

REMEMBERING THE END GOAL

Parents also feel pride in their children. Parents describe the numerous activities as "fun" for the kids, or something that is "good for them." But the frequency and intensity of such engagement suggests that they are also accomplishments—for both the parents and the children.[36] Seeing

children win a game or perform on stage is the ultimate in positive rein-
forcement for the time, money, and effort spent on parenting. Cory Finchley texts his brother proudly when Bobby makes a play in his first baseball
game wearing the catcher gear Bobby received from his uncle. Rebecca
Stewart calls Nick in excitement when they get a letter from school that
Brittany has placed into the gifted and talented program. Even though
Nancy Huron decides not to put Melody on the competitive gymnastics
team, she is obviously delighted by the invitation.

Despite the expectation and hope, however, dedication to the Perfect
Parent myth does not guarantee that children become successful grown-
ups. How do parents produce young adults who make "good" choices
(completing schoolwork, limiting their own technology use, undertaking
academic and then career hurdles)? Cello lessons do not ensure a musical
prodigy; monitoring homework does not ensure long-term success.

While unnerving, this lack of clear cause and effect can lead to greater
dedication to the myth itself. The elements of the myth cannot guarantee
that children will become happy and prosperous, but its guidelines are
nonetheless seductive, because they promise to do just that. Living within a
myth might be easier than admitting that raising children is an act of faith:
no one really knows how they will turn out, or how their lives will unfold.

Let's take monitoring technology as an example. We can see instances
when enacting this element of the Perfect Parent is, in fact, helping children learn regulation and self-reliance. Tim's girls are in a school with a
strict philosophy: zero technology in elementary school (no screens, digital
games, or even recorded music, and that includes no educational games or
homework that requires screens). Tim incorporates this directive into his
parenting in a modified form. He doesn't allow any screens or digital games
during the week (generally speaking: don't forget the YouTube videos of
Usain Bolt and the hot-dog-eating contest). He turns off the radio as they
get off the freeway exit to school. On the weekends, he bucks school policy
by allowing ten minutes of technology for each girl, for each day. Is Tim's
monitoring helping his children become people who can regulate their
technology use? Perhaps.

One Saturday afternoon, Olive's sisters decide to use their technology
time to watch an episode of an animated show. Olive is concerned that
she will get sucked into the show and lose her own technology time. She
explains to her dad, "Then I won't have any iPad time at rehearsal and I

really want to save it for rehearsal. . . . So I'm going to go outside and I'm going to rollerblade." She asks her dad to set the timer for the length of the show. Tim does. Olive has enlisted her father's help to avoid temptation. Self-regulation in the face of temptation is the gold standard in child development, and this looks like a clear win for Tim's parenting (although, truth be told, Olive does covertly go to a neighbor's house to watch TV every once in a while).[37]

However, before we assume that Tim's strict monitoring is the answer (and credit it to the Perfect Parent ideal), let's look at families who do not uphold such restrictions.[38] Take the Shah family. Daughters Tessa and Neelam each have their own top-of-the-line devices and few explicit rules governing use. One night, well after bedtime, Neelam catches Tessa watching Disney videos in bed on her new laptop when she gets up to go to the bathroom. The laptop lives in Tessa's room with no clearly specified criteria about when and how Tessa should use the machine. Her parents react with disappointment to the late-night binge watching, and they sit down with Tessa to establish that videos in the middle of the night are not okay. But they don't take away her laptop or begin to monitor her. Tessa, on her own, decides to move the machine across her room at night so that it isn't in arms' reach when she is in bed. Tessa is trying out a strategy for self-regulation, much like Olive does by rollerblading outside.

We see a similar story for each element of the Perfect Parent myth: those who fulfill the myth can seem to have good results, but so too can those who live in violation of its norms. Yes, Brenda and Cory's children are experiencing family togetherness and focused attention during family dinner. But the Shah family members, who often eat dinner in shifts during the week, still spend quality time playing board games on the weekend. Which is really superior?

And yes, enrichment activities allow children to develop new skills. But does anyone really think that seven-year-old Bobby Finchley will be less likely to get into college than eight-year-old Brittany Stewart because Bobby only pursues one activity? In fact, the presence of such activities actually limits time for unstructured and unsupervised play, the kind of time when children learn to overcome boredom and develop different forms of creativity and problem solving.[39] While fully prioritizing family might feel like the only way to enact the Perfect Parent myth, what are children missing by not having other caregivers—including relatives and even paid helpers—and not seeing their parents thrive outside the home?

There is, in fact, no one right way to parent. Yet the Perfect Parent myth directs actions and attention to only narrow conceptions of parenting. The myth does provide clear lines of action. But it does not direct people to think about the end goals—what *kinds* of humans do parents want to raise—nor does it highlight the multitude of alternative ways in which parents can provide the emotional support, structure, opportunity, and values to help children thrive.

Instead, the myth leads people to believe that they need a full-time parent at home. Because how else can they accomplish all of these injunctions? The narrative of the Perfect Parent demands it. Just like the Ideal Worker supports serving organizational interests with complete dedication, the Perfect Parent supports a division of labor that puts pressure on one person to stay home. And that sacrifice, the time required, is never enough. The Perfect Parent has no time for other endeavors. They don't get "me time" (particularly when the kids are young). It's difficult to find time to take care of oneself, much less work, when all of one's "physical, psychological, emotional and intellectual being, 24/7" must be devoted to parenting.[40]

And the final project, of being healthy—eating right, getting exercise—requires time away from working *and* parenting.

CHAPTER 4

WORKING TOWARD THE ULTIMATE BODY

Roger Waldo trains for an Ironman triathlon, despite his busy work schedule as a director at a large SLH property. He squeezes training workouts in during the early morning, occasional lunch break, and evenings after work. Roger looks forward to getting in a "real" workout over the weekend.

This Saturday Roger wants to swim—it is the event he's least comfortable with. But first he meets a friend for a 5:00 a.m. karate class. Getting up at 4:15 isn't hard for Roger; he wakes at 3:00 a.m. several days a week to exercise before driving to work. Tiptoeing out of the house in the dark with his family sound asleep feels normal. After the karate class he goes for a run. Next weekend he's running a local marathon with a friend ("no big deal" for Roger) so he takes a short, five-mile run this morning. He takes off from the karate studio, circling back to the studio in time for the 7:00 a.m. karate class.

After the second karate class, Roger hops in the car for a short drive to the gym. His energetic stride and broad smile belie the fact that he's already done three workouts today. Roger checks in on Facebook when he arrives at the gym. Workout bag in hand, he heads to the pool only to realize that he has forgotten to pack his swim trunks. Angry with himself, he immediately switches gears and heads to the spinning room. Checking Facebook again, he sees that his wife, Linda, has given a "thumbs up" to his location. The room is empty so he hops on a bike. He trains without any music since that's the Ironman triathlon rule and he wants to be fully prepared. The silence makes him notice his body—where he's sore, whether he needs a calorie boost for energy, how he's breathing. After an hour on the bike, Roger heads home.

Roger arrives home at 9:45 and makes himself a morning smoothie—protein pow-der, strawberries, mango, yogurt, and a number of supplements. Refrigerator open, he asks Linda whether she found the new high-protein yogurt that he had texted her about earlier in the week. She gestures at the appropriate shelf from her chair at the kitchen island. Declining his offer to share his smoothie, Linda nurses her coffee. Wearing yoga pants and a patterned exercise top, she is trying to motivate herself to hop on the tread-mill in the garage. But she has already been to the grocery store and the pet store this morning to stock up on household necessities and wants to sit for a minute. Roger drinks his smoothie standing at the island and grumbles to Linda that he forgot to bring his swim gear. Deciding to postpone the treadmill, Linda makes herself a parfait with fresh strawberries, blueberries, plain yogurt, and granola while they chat.

Finishing his smoothie, Roger goes upstairs to shower. It is 10:15 and the house is quiet. Their twelve-year-old son, Ryan, is still sleeping upstairs, and seventeen-year-old Sadie is out for a morning run. Too full now to do the treadmill, Linda moves to folding laundry in the living room. She puts the country station on the cable radio and hums to herself while folding. Roger comes back downstairs wearing sweats and a black base-ball cap. He props his white athletic-sock-clad feet on the coffee table and pulls out his laptop. The two chat as he browses through bicycle blogs, looking for reviews on the new bicycle he's been eyeing. He finds one for sale on eBay and excitedly calls Linda over to take a look. She feigns enthusiasm, reminding him that they need a new microwave after Ryan put foil in and the whole thing caught on fire.

At 10:45 Sadie wanders into the kitchen in a t-shirt and running shorts, and Roger quizzes her on the length of her run. Thirty minutes, she says, offering that she also did some sit-ups and pushups. Roger nods approvingly and queries, "How many sit-ups?" Sadie responds in mock exasperation, "I don't know. Just for, like, the length of the song." Roger shares the number of reps he did that morning. He did his sit-ups after the bike. Sadie rolls her eyes and laughs good naturedly at her dad. Shuffling down the stairs in his pajamas, Ryan overhears his dad telling Sadie that he likes to count his reps because he's not listening to music while he works out. Ryan asks his dad if it's boring to work out without music. Roger looks puzzled, contemplates the question for a moment, and responds, "I don't know what you mean. Well, kind of. I guess. Sometimes I get bored of my own thoughts, but I've become really attuned to my body in a different way. And you know there is going to be a trophy at the other end." Ryan muses, "Okay, I guess I can see that," as he opens the refrigerator to get some milk for his cereal.

WHILE THE ENTIRE WALDO FAMILY tries to eat well and stay in shape, Roger goes to the extreme. Training to be a literal Ironman,

Roger maintains a herculean exercise regime. Six days a week. Multiple hours a day. Often several times a day. Roger organizes his day around exercise and watches the food he puts into his body (trying, and mostly succeeding, to resist the miniature candies on the desk of an associate). The race is over nine months away, but preparation serves as an organizing principle for his daily life.

The Waldo family embraces the myth of the Ultimate Body. They each have internalized the importance of exercising and eating right. Ryan and his dad take karate together; Sadie is a dedicated dancer, and running and sit-ups keep her in shape for the dance team. Linda runs on the treadmill in the garage and takes regular exercise walks with her best friend. She also picks up the newest health drink or supplement that Roger has texted her about (on the advice of his trainer or buddies). She tracks them down and keeps the kitchen stocked. Aware of the latest health trends, they try to eat accordingly. Calories, supplements, and debates about the benefits of fasting serve as topics of conversation in the Waldo household. Each family member looks fit and takes care in their appearance.

WHAT IS THE MYTH OF THE ULTIMATE BODY?

The big-picture goal of the Ultimate Body myth is achieving health, energy, and longevity. However, in living within the myth, appearance can become a substitute for health. Roger Waldo worries about the fat he sees around his belly and strategizes about what calories he can cut to lose more weight.

It's never enough. Airbrushed billboards, advertisements, and the covers of health magazines displayed at supermarket checkout lines glorify beautiful and toned bodies. Headlines offer six-pack abs, protein powders that bulk muscles, and foods that shred fat. At some level people understand that the models themselves do not look as fit in reality as they do in technicolor. Photoshop sharpens the chisel and hides the imperfections. But it is hard to ignore the images from advertisements, social media influencers, and favorite entertainers: a man's sculpted chest in an Equinox advertisement or a woman's bikini body in a beer or car commercial. The gendered myth of the Ultimate Body flaunted in the media presents powerful, muscular men and beautiful, thin women.[1]

With the exception of Roger, the thirty and forty-something adults in these families do not actively strive for six-pack abs. They are just trying to stay healthy—get some exercise and eat right. But the pressures of working and parenting regularly sideline efforts to do so. When Linda Waldo can't fit in a morning workout (and attends to the laundry instead), she feels guilty. When Nancy Huron stops waking up at 4:00 a.m. to walk on the treadmill, she worries about the consequences. Rather than simply managing their health, all are living within the Ultimate Body myth. Consequently, they all feel shame, frustration, or a sense of failure when they don't measure up. The images in the media make clear that people can (and should) always do more to cultivate their bodies. And like each of the myths, one never actually "achieves" success. People can always do more (even Roger), and it's never clear what's really enough.

The myth is a sheer impossibility. Even professional athletes, whose days are filled with bodywork, can only sustain such visible health and ability for a short time. For those simply trying to remain active while working and parenting, there is little chance of being perfectly, ultimately in shape. Moreover, the means for accomplishing this impossible dream are constantly shifting. Competing headlines scream for attention, and the weary consumer does not know what to believe.

Although a general scientific consensus concludes that inactivity is a public health problem, ideas about what to do have changed substantially over time.[2] Over the past forty years, recommendations have ranged between fifteen and sixty minutes of exercise a day. Should someone get thirty minutes of sustained exercise or perhaps just an efficient seven-minute burst?[3] Food guidelines are even more confusing. Are eggs among the healthiest foods on the planet?[4] Or does their cholesterol make them too dangerous for people to eat?[5] As new data come in, advice changes. In 2000, the American Heart Association reversed their earlier recommendation to suggest an egg a day was perhaps okay.[6] "Superfoods" such as acai and goji berries, kale, spirulina, wheatgrass, and flaxseeds seem to rise and fall with the seasons.[7] Marketers design catchy slogans to bring new foods to the mainstream, while offering minimal scientific evidence of their benefit.[8] Cookbooks and health gurus promote trends in detox and elimination diets, from the low-fat diets of the 1990s to the Paleo and Whole30 of the 2000s. Each diet touts the benefits of avoiding certain foods and eating others. And each promises to be "the solution."

These changing guidelines and marketing strategies create problems for those striving to be an Ultimate Body. Even if someone were to find the time and energy to fully dedicate efforts to the project of the body, expert opinions evolve.[9] It's hard to keep up. And, of course, bodies change over time: what might be healthy exercise at one phase of life would be debilitating at another. People can never fully control their bodies, despite their efforts. In the end, all bodies age, get sick, and break down. Even an Ultimate Body would, of course, expire.

Despite the challenges, Roger regularly reads health blogs, tries new shakes and protein bars, cuts out carbs, and knows the latest superfood. He subscribes to health and fitness magazines and spends hours online researching fitness equipment. Roger's regimen helped him lose a substantial amount of weight in the five years before our study began, and he is dedicated to keeping off the weight and pushing his body to new achievements.

For Roger and the employees of SLH, fitness and health are not only valorized by society, they are expected in the workplace. Unlike many organizations, SLH takes an active interest in the health and wellness of employees.

It is the first Friday of the month, and employees filter in to the monthly "health and wellness" meeting at the corporate headquarters. Teresa Davies walks in with a friend from IT, chatting softly, and takes a seat in one of the black padded chairs toward the back. The room buzzes with anticipation. At 9:00 a.m. a jubilant man strides into the room belting a bright, "Good morning!" to the assembled group. The charismatic man is David, CEO of SLH's parent company.[10] David starts the meeting with his standard question: "Who exercised this morning?" Four people raise their hands (not Teresa, who makes a joking grimace). David quizzes each on what they did and makes a show of handing out a dollar to each exerciser. A new employee says she worked out to a kickboxing video. David has her come to the front of the room and asks her to demonstrate a move. Too embarrassed to climb on the desk in the front of the room, as David jokingly suggests, she makes a few halfhearted punches and sits down. David continues, "Who exercised last night?" Another two or three hands (again, not Teresa). He questions them for details and hands each a dollar.

The meeting moves on to nutrition, and David asks if anyone has a "nutrition update" to share. One woman talks about how her husband brought his blood pressure down significantly with the "Forks Over Knives diet and some Dean Ornish."[11] David enthusiastically probes, asking several questions: "Does he look different? What does he eat?" Eventually David turns to the group. "It's funny she mentioned this because I had

wanted to talk about blood pressure today. It's the best indicator of health. High blood pressure often leads to inflammation, which is why I wanted to know how he looked."
After a brief lecture on HDL and LDL cholesterol, the correlation between cholesterol and blood pressure, and the pharmaceutical companies' motivation to sell us drugs, David asks for other nutrition stories. One man says that he and his family have been eating vegan for a month. Another man says that he has stopped eating sugar and gone gluten-free: consequently, it has been "effortless" to lose twenty-five pounds over the last four to five months. David picks up on this theme and talks about sugar and toxins—"it's all about inflammation." He reminds people not to go "overboard with the sweet stuff."

Employees share stories and look to David for answers. One person laughingly recalls her grandfather eating eggs and bacon and living to ninety-three; someone else describes the issues his mom had taking Lipitor. Teresa nods in agreement; her mom recently suffered a heart scare and ended up in the ER. One man talks about problematic interactions among drugs for older patients. David highlights a new study out this week that says statins cause cancer. "Has anyone heard this?" A shaking of heads, no. As the health conversation winds down, David turns to SLH updates.

After acknowledging work anniversaries, David calls Teresa and two others to the front of the room with much fanfare. He tells a short story about each, handing Teresa a gift certificate to the Cheesecake Factory for going "above and beyond." Then several executives stand up to give updates on recent hotel acquisitions and the status of major properties.

At this point, David changes gears again, asking everyone to break into small groups for this month's activity. He asks each small group to talk about what it means to be "in the moment." After a few minutes of group discussion, David has groups report back. Teresa talks about making a sandcastle with her son at the beach. Someone else mentions mobile phones ruining the moment. The meeting closes with David's standard line: "What do we say?" Everyone chants one of the firm's core values, "Make it better!"

ALONG WITH MONTHLY wellness meetings hosted by David, the SLH CEO, Noah, sends out regular emails sharing health tidbits. Nick Stewart summarizes the general sentiment: "Sugars are bad, leafy greens are good." A clear message comes from the top ranks of SLH: we expect you to be good workers and healthy people (in the largest sense of the word). This focus on the Ultimate Body at SLH is explicitly tied to a theory of productivity. Jay Shah explains,

> David's deal always is, "Healthy people, happy people are going to produce results." So, results are almost a given. If you love being here, and

you pop up like toast every morning, and you treat everyone with respect, as humans, the results just happen. That's basically the philosophy.

SLH puts their money where their mouth is: they will pay for gym memberships at one of three high-end gym chains in Southern California for corporate employees. Tony, a single director in his late twenties, takes full advantage of this perk.

> They pay my gym membership. Equinox, you know. That's a badass gym, right? Why do they pay you for your gym? Because if you work out, you feel happy. You feel energized. When you come into work sloppy, you don't want to work. You just want to be drinking buckets of coffee and trying to make it to the end of the day. When you work out, you feel energized. You're happy. You're ready to go. So, I think the small things like that make a difference.

This attitude filters throughout the firm. While they may not pay for his gym membership (he's not at the corporate office), the focus on exercise and wellness at SLH allows Roger Waldo some flexibility. His colleagues respect his "crazy exercise schedule." If Roger has to start his morning team check-in meeting from the car and sit in the parking lot until the end of the meeting (because traffic was bad and cell reception is terrible between the parking lot and meeting room), his staff cuts him some slack because he has been exercising (and commuting) all morning. However, like each of the myths at SLH, this attitude of acceptance is also one of expectation. When the boss asks them to raise their hand if they exercised this morning, in front of their colleagues, the correct answer is clear.[12]

Men and women alike are expected to eat well and take care of their bodies, but they face somewhat different challenges as the myth competes for priority with working and parenting. The people that raised their hands at the 9:00 a.m. monthly "health and wellness" meeting to say they exercised either don't have children, have someone else to care for their children in the mornings, or are trying to fit in exercise when the kids are sleeping. The participants in the meeting were silent on the logistics of preparing whole foods, or doing the "Forks Over Knives" diet. The complexities of following these injunctions to care and feed the body, given all the other demands on SLH employees, are not part of the advice provided in the health and wellness meeting. That is because someone *other* than the SLH employee is generally doing that work (like Roger's wife, Linda).

THE ULTIMATE BODY: STAYING FIT

On a Thursday in the early evening, Lisa Phillips walks across the room at a knock on the door. A petite brunette with an infectious smile, Lisa gives the girl standing on the stoop a hug. Natalie, a former student, has brought Lisa some new running shoes—her favorite brand (Nike) and colors (purple and grey). Natalie smiles at Lisa's excitement and says, "They went on sale, I couldn't resist. With my employee discount it was such a good deal." Natalie works at a large running footwear chain and knows Lisa's size and style by heart. Although they have been friends for over ten years (Lisa was Natalie's middle school teacher and they have been close ever since), the two started regularly running together on the week-ends about a year ago. Natalie had texted Lisa earlier that night about the shoes, asking if she wanted her to get them and bring them over after work. The two get out their phones to plan a running date for the upcoming weekend. Lisa's weekend plans are filled with sporting events for her three children, but they settle on Sunday, early evening. Lisa is happy to have running in her life: "I fit it in whenever I can. Generally, three to four times a week. But the kids are older now, so I don't have to worry....They are okay here by themselves for an hour while I go exercise, which is awesome."

REGULAR EXERCISE is a key element of the Ultimate Body. People proudly and happily advertise physical activity on social media. Lisa Phillips will post an image from her running app (mileage and current pace) on Instagram, commenting, "Quick summer run equals super fun!" or "First run of the new year! So very, very cold this morning!" These posts receive numerous likes and positive comments. Roger Waldo too marks and measures his fitness achievements. It may be a photo on Facebook after a long bike ride, a post tagging the friends accompanying him on a ten-mile run, or a quick check-in noting when and where he is exercising (often at an hour others are sleeping or having a morning coffee). When Roger writes "morning run with the boys" or "70 miles with this great group! Nice way to start the weekend!" (along with a picture of smiling people on road bikes), he collects numerous "likes" and encouraging comments from his close to a thousand Facebook friends. While Roger plans his life around exercise, most people are trying to "fit it in" around other priorities and commitments. So they feel pride when they succeed—and advertise their accomplishments on social media.[13]

When it comes to busy professional parents, exercise is the elusive goal of many and the realized goal of few. For many of the consistent exercisers (and this may be their secret), it is also a fun and social endeavor. Lisa runs with Natalie and sometimes her daughters. They chat and gossip along the way. Roger has his karate and running buddies who "keep him honest." For those with young kids, exercise is harder to fit in. It happens less regularly and often at home when the children are asleep. Jumping on the treadmill in the garage doesn't seem to warrant a Facebook post, so these people have fewer accolades and no friends encouraging them on when, arguably, their actions may be more impressive.

Nancy Huron's alarm blares. It is dark outside and she takes a moment to focus on the clock at her bedside. 4:30 a.m. The house is silent and both her kids are asleep. It's now or never. For the past few weeks Nancy has been getting up each morning to walk for forty-five minutes on the treadmill in the garage. She recently had a serious health scare and is now on a medication that makes her feel horrible—lethargic and moody. Starting the day on the treadmill helps get her energy up. It makes her feel like she is doing something proactive about her health. But she has been up late the past two nights working. And last night six-year-old Melody had a night terror at 11:00 p.m.: "The first time that has happened in years." Nancy is utterly drained. She pauses, takes a deep breath, and forces herself to push off the covers. She makes her way downstairs to the cold, dark garage and wonders how long she can keep this up.

NANCY HURON'S morning exercise peters out after a month. She physically can't do it. She needs sleep to function as a worker, as a mother, and as a person. There are simply not enough hours in the day for Nancy to attend to all of the other demands in her life, sleep an adequate amount, and fit in attention to her body. She is left with lingering guilt about not getting exercise and fears about her health. She continues to walk on the treadmill on most weekends and keeps her fingers crossed that it is enough to keep health issues at bay.

THE ULTIMATE BODY: EATING RIGHT

Linda Waldo stands at the island in her kitchen telling Roger about the Dr. Oz detox cleanse that her best friend, Edith, just finished. Edith brought her up to date during their weekly "catch up" walk (while the kids were in lacrosse practice). Edith lost six pounds in three days and "she feels a lot better"; Linda has decided to give it a try. She shares with Roger that you are supposed to take a "cleansing" bath every night with lavender and Epsom salts. Roger laughs and says, "That doesn't do anything." Linda chimes back, "Yeah. But maybe it smells really good!"

Reading up on the ingredients she needs to add to the shopping list, Linda says, "I need to buy almond butter. And they say we shouldn't have peanut butter anymore." Roger muses, "Who is they?" Linda chuckles, "I don't know! But they do say that, whoever they are." She reflects, "Mostly it's because the kind of peanut butter we buy is Skippy. You're definitely not supposed to eat Skippy." Linda continues peering at her iPhone. She needs a multivitamin and an omega supplement: "We have that. We have fish oil. And flaxseed. But I need to get some probiotics. . . . It's $17 for this little bottle of probiotics!" While chatting she has searched the probiotics online and turns the phone to show Roger. He exclaims, "$17! Skip those!" And she says, "No!" He responds, "Well, what are they for?" She chortles, "It's to push things through the digestive system." He jokes, "Kale is going to do that all on its own."

A week later Linda is on her second day of the Dr. Oz detox diet. "Today has been pretty rough. I've basically just felt horrible and nauseous. I've had a headache all day. They say you will feel better on the third day, but I'm not sure." Earlier she told Roger she would make him a grilled chicken salad for dinner. "But I just can't grill it. I can't. Otherwise I will break." She muses, "I guess I could just put it in the oven and bake it." After she puts some chicken breasts in the oven, she ruefully makes her evening shake: blueberries, kale, cayenne, mango, avocado, and coconut water. She sighs, "I am just really hungry. And I have no idea the point of all of these ingredients. I don't feel any better. Honestly, I'm feeling pretty dumb today."

Linda lasts the full three days of the detox diet. She even does the "silly" cleansing baths. She loses four pounds but gains back two almost immediately. Once it is all over she tries to make sense of the experience: "So, I like this concept that maybe it was good for me. But I don't know why [it was good for me], even if it was. I am SO never doing it again." Linda resolves to just get on the treadmill in the garage more often.

LINDA WALDO IS WILLING to consume elaborate shakes that "taste disgusting, are pretty thick, and take awhile to get down." She trusts Dr. Oz that somehow, in some way, this experience is "good for me." The myth of the Ultimate Body promises that following the latest cleanse or diet, or eating the latest "superfood," will produce the healthier, slimmer body that Linda wants. Aside from the energy expended keeping up with the latest trends in eating, following these trends takes time and money. Linda finds and purchases the ingredients and makes the shakes, while also feeding Roger and her kids. The specifics are different but the commitment is the same in the Shah family.

Olivia Shah stands at her large kitchen island cutting a pineapple at 7:30 a.m. She chunks the fruit and saves the core to the side. Then she pulls open the vegetable drawer where she stores the juicing ingredients. She brings out kale, celery, apple, ginger, and a large bunch of Swiss chard, adding it all to the juicer set up next to the sink. Her daughter reminds her not to forget the pineapple core, and it goes into the juicer as well. The machine starts spitting out green liquid into a waiting pitcher. Olivia pours four large glasses of juice. Both girls take a sip, providing commentary on the taste—one suggests adding oranges while the other thinks it needs more ginger. Green juice at the Shah house is a family activity, and one that happens daily. Jay has just returned from the gym and takes a long drink, adding his two cents about the taste. Olivia tells him about the new protein powder that she picked up, following the tip that David, CEO of SLH's parent company, recently shared with Jay.

While the girls sit at the table drinking their green juice and eating yogurt, fresh berries, and cereal, Olivia moves to making a fruit snack for each of them to take to school (and one for Jay to take to work). She puts the cut pineapple into three matching Tupperware containers and starts peeling a papaya to add to the mix. After the fruit snacks are stacked at the edge of the counter, Olivia turns to making three lunches, in three separate Tupperware containers. Today, everyone gets a pita wrap with hummus.

THE RATIONALE FOR THE GREEN JUICE is clearer to the Shah family than the health shakes to Linda Waldo. As Olivia describes, "We are eating all this good food, fresh fruits and fresh vegetables, and this is purity for the body." The Ultimate Body is mindful of what goes into it. The Shah family's commitment to green juice is just one part of their diet. Olivia and Jay will occasionally do a cleanse together: they recently finished a twenty-one-day fast. "No gluten, dairy, or sugar. Lots of fresh spices. Ginger. Garlic. Protein shakes." Jay has the newest tips from the monthly health and wellness meetings; Olivia has her favorite podcasts. They stay up on the latest health news and are always game to try something new that will make them feel "cleaner," like the feeling they get from green juice.

Olivia dedicates several hours of her day to cooking and preparing healthy food and demonstrates her allegiance to the Ultimate Body. The Shah family's everyday diet is organic and vegetarian, and consists of meals prepared from scratch. Just getting the family fed and out the door in time for work and school takes an enormous amount of effort. Olivia also cooks almost every night (usually with help from her mom). In addition to Indian, they do Mexican or some other genre one night a week. (When we spent time with the Shah family, we eagerly looked forward to joining whatever scrumptious dinner was served in their house). In order to have the right ingredients and enough food on hand, Olivia shops several times a week and generally goes to two or three different grocery stores. In addition, she makes a weekly Costco run for organic produce (very helpful for the juice drawer). Her newly remodeled kitchen also has an industrial-sized refrigerator and freezer. The floor-to-ceiling cupboards house various flours, grains, and bulk ingredients.

Finding enough time for this degree of food preparation requires daily juggling. While Olivia does have a considerable amount of help, her ability to continually put healthy, homemade, and quality food in her family's mouths is a serious achievement. The collective time and energy that goes into food preparation at the Shah household is a lesson in how difficult it is to enact the myth of the Ultimate Body.

THE ULTIMATE BODY: PRIORITIZING THE BODY

Jay Shah leaves for work at 8:30 a.m. while Olivia Shah drops Tessa off at the elementary school, then Neelam at the middle school. Arriving back home around 9:00, Olivia goes into the kitchen to clean, dry, and put away each element of the juicer. Then she pulls out the blender to prep her post-workout protein shake. While working in the kitchen, she watches a webinar on her iPad about how to use social media to better market small businesses. She is trying to move into a new market niche—planning trips with a social overlay—in which tourists engage with the local community in a productive way. Clients might volunteer their time to paint a school or bring supplies for a local orphanage. Olivia feels passionately about using her expertise to do good in the world. After she wipes down the kitchen, she finishes the webinar over a cup of green tea. At 10:30 the doorbell rings.

Thursday is one of the two days a week that a personal trainer comes to Olivia's house. On other days she will drive twenty minutes to swim at the gym pool or go for a long walk. Exercise "me time" is precious. Sandwiched between cooking, working, and parenting, she considers this her only real "downtime." Olivia and the trainer spend the next hour and fifteen minutes in the garage gym doing cardio, lifting weights, and performing resistance moves (which help her manage the pain from a serious injury many years ago). The garage is well-equipped: a treadmill, stationary bike, weight bench, free weights, resistance bands. At 11:45 she is done. After the trainer leaves, Olivia realizes she doesn't have time to shower before a noon call. After the work call, she cleans up and gets dressed, finishes her protein shake, rinses the blender, and spends a couple of *hours working at one of two mahogany-colored wraparound desks that line the large upstairs alcove near the girls' bedrooms. At 2:45 p.m. she heads out to pick up the girls from school. The rest of the afternoon cycles between pickups and drop-offs for various kids' activities and cooking dinner. She will finish up work tonight after everyone is in bed. There just aren't enough hours to get it all done while the girls are at school.*

OLIVIA SHAH WORKS HARD to fit in exercise, even though it often means getting less than six hours sleep. Her workouts are her personal time; her time to recharge and reduce stress. For Olivia, exercise serves as a natural extension of the time she spends feeding herself and her family the right foods. Yet it is also the single activity that isn't colored by her role as a wife, mother, and worker. Olivia doesn't waste a moment of this precious time. She would rather sacrifice sleep than time with her personal trainer. By framing exercise as "me time" (in fact, exercise as her only "me time") Olivia highlights her allegiance to the Ultimate Body myth. The sanctity of using "me time" to improve the body demonstrates it as a moral good to herself and those around her. For Olivia, it makes sense: this is how people should be spending those precious few moments away from work and children.[14]

In reality most people don't spend all of their "me time" prioritizing their bodies. "Me time" can be spent socializing with friends, watching TV, or enjoying a few moments alone.[15] "Me time" includes all of the activities focused on the self (and not working or doing things for others). But people feel compelled to justify their nonvirtuous "me time" when it does not serve the myth of the Ultimate Body. They have precious little time to themselves.[16] People rationalize nonvirtuous "me time" through multitasking. Roger Waldo and Nancy Huron often use their commutes to call friends and family (and make the occasional work call). Nancy reflects, "It's my only quiet time when I can actually have a conversation and not be interrupted." Layering a necessary activity (driving to and from work) with the nonvirtuous "me time" of calling a friend feels like an acceptable way to enjoy a personal moment. It provides a rationale for not prioritizing the body in the nonwork, nonparenting moments.

People describe their secret pleasures with an embarrassed laugh—the decidedly not virtuous forms of "me time." Facebook, Pinterest, the tabloid website TMZ, and reality TV shows like *The Bachelor* serve as welcome antidotes to busy lives. One afternoon Linda Waldo declares,

"I should be doing laundry, or getting on the treadmill, but I'm just not in the mood. I am taking one hour to watch *The Bachelor*. God forbid!" Linda rebels against the expectations of the Ultimate Body in which all "me time" is dedicated to self-improvement. Not even multitasking with the laundry, Linda relaxes on the couch and simply enjoys the show. For Nancy Huron, having a glass of wine in the evening while watching TV or flipping through a *People* magazine similarly feels decadent. In these moments people are willing to deal with the residual guilt that accompanies decisions to not prioritize a myth but instead just relax.

We applauded Linda and Nancy for accepting that these moments are what they need to get through their busy days. These types of downtime are normal and perfectly acceptable ways to relax. Linda and Nancy are not claiming that watching TV is useful or enriching. They are not parroting the SLH line that focusing on health and wellness will make them more productive at work. Even though claiming a productive positive relationship between "downtime" and "worktime" is common.[17] But these two are unabashedly taking the time for themselves, not for anyone else. And in these moments they are rejecting all the myths.

The myth of the Ultimate Body has three components (staying fit, eating right, and prioritizing the body). Everyone in these families is aware of the myth but few are fully able to enact it.[18] It just takes too much time. Each of the other orienting myths requires intensive effort and dedication. Everyone needs just a few more hours in the day. In order to fit it all in, many make similar choices to those of Nancy Huron and Olivia Shah—giving up on a few hours of sleep.

THE ULTIMATE BODY: (NEGLECTING) SLEEP

Work has been crazy and Katrina Garcia feels tapped out. Yesterday required a not entirely unusual fourteen-hour day at work. And four-year-old Charlotte had a hard night. Katrina laments, "She woke up in the middle of the night screaming, and all she wanted ... She just wanted to be with us."

Today is Katrina's day off and her day alone with the kids. Charlotte and her two-year-old brother, Matt, are anxious to go outside. After breakfast they spend a half-hour in the backyard having a tea party, and Katrina tries to keep Matt from throwing things. By 9:17 a.m. Katrina has had enough. They return inside and she puts Mickey Mouse Clubhouse on the TV. Katrina and Charlotte settle on the sofa while Matt stands a couple feet from the screen. Katrina's eyes start to close. At 9:33 Katrina receives a phone call from work about the pricing for an item they want to sell for Black Friday. She stands up and moves out of the family room. Charlotte wanders into the kitchen and starts looking in the cabinets for snacks. After the call ends, Katrina gives each kid a donut.

Katrina returns to the couch. With notepad in hand, and Matt on her lap, she begins making a grocery list, getting up periodically to check the cabinets. Charlotte, perched next to her mom, takes the shopping list and starts to draw on it while watching their favorite 10:00 a.m. show, Doc McStuffins. Doc has diagnosed a new disease that involves too much time indoors. Katrina mumbles, "I think I have that disease, I'm falling asleep." Charlotte's request, "Look at my drawing!" evokes a "mmmmmhhh" from Katrina. As the show ends, Katrina revives herself and tickles the kids from the couch. When asked, Matt says he'd like to "do something!" But the next show is another of Charlotte's favorites, and Katrina stretches out with a blanket on the couch to rest a bit longer.

KATRINA GARCIA SPENDS HER DAY OFF, and her one day a week alone with her kids, trying desperately to stay awake. She regularly leaves the house at 5:00 a.m. to work a twelve- to fourteen-hour day, then comes home to two high-energy toddlers, a dinner that needs making, and a house that always seems (to Katrina) to be in disarray. She is thoroughly tapped out. And yet she still feels bad about not getting to the gym. Every once in while she goes in the morning on her day off—when she manages to get up at 4:00 a.m., leave, exercise, and return before her husband, Franco, goes to work. But most often that feels like a fantasy: "It's impossible. Literally I don't have an hour to go to the gym. Like there's no hour."

While clearly and justifiably exhausted, Katrina doesn't talk about lack of sleep as something she feels guilty about. She feels guilty about not working out. Exhaustion is the norm. Similarly, while Olivia Shah makes a point of prioritizing exercising in the morning, the cost of this virtuous "me time" is not trivial. She regularly stays up past midnight—occasionally to 2:30 or 3:00 a.m.—figuring out client itineraries and responding to emails. In her words, "Making sure I get in my 'me time' in the mornings just makes work even harder."

Nowhere in the Ultimate Body myth do people focus on sleep. In fact, in Western professional culture, the people operating on minimal sleep are valorized as the "sleepless elite."[19] The very fact that these people are labeled "elite" suggests that they are to be envied and emulated. Even though caring for the body promises health and wellness, people generally

FIGURE 4.1 Katrina Garcia on Her Day Home with the Kids

ignore the damaging health effects of exhaustion. From the short-term dangers of driving with too little sleep (it's like driving under the influence of alcohol), to the long-term association between sleep deprivation and negative health outcomes (such as cancer, depression, diabetes, and weight gain), there is a new and welcome recognition of the importance of sleep.[20] But sleep hasn't yet taken hold as an element of the myth. And even if it did, perhaps it would simply feel like one more failure to tally when work and parenting take precedence.

One challenge of integrating sleep into the Ultimate Body myth turns on the fact that sleep appears to be a passive, unproductive time (although the amazing, necessary things that happen to bodies while people are sleeping are well documented).[21] It doesn't fit the notion of virtuous "me time." The myths of perfection highlight productivity, mastery, and achievement. Sleep doesn't fit with agentic, individualistic notions of accomplishment. Unless sleep is reframed as *doing* something (for example, as the time when brains are encoding knowledge and solving problems), we suspect it will endure outside the aspirations for an Ultimate Body.

Although these individuals viscerally experience the effects of exhaustion, it is rarely enough to motivate changes in sleep patterns. Given the choice between sleep and exercise, exercise often wins. The choice between sleep and work doesn't feel like a choice; there is too much work to be done. Jay Shah tries to go to bed before 10:00 p.m. Getting more sleep was his New Year's resolution after he read somewhere that "every hour you sleep before midnight is worth four hours of sleep." It rarely happens. Jay still finds himself closer to 11:00 p.m. and often midnight. But he continues to leave the house every morning by 5:00 a.m. to get to the gym before work. Sleep may be important, but people treat it like a luxury. And, of course, Jay receives public recognition for his commitment to exercise when he raises his hand at the SLH wellness meeting—signaling that he prioritizes his body. What would valorizing sleep look like? Proudly counting out the number of hours of sleep in a night, much like the number of miles on a run?

THE GUILT OF NOT HAVING THE ULTIMATE BODY

Exercise feels good physiologically and psychologically, bringing endorphins, accolades from friends, and peace of mind. Lisa Phillips exercises as a "sanity thing," for reasons beyond looking good. Struggling with severe early onset arthritis, Lisa has discovered that running is the best way to manage the pain. Nothing else works as well. Lisa's fit frame belies the fact that her body is not under her control.

As Lisa knows, the body is fallible. It is not an airbrushed vision of perfection. The body is an unpredictable and often uncooperative vessel. Weight

Ultimate Body	Examples
Staying Fit	Roger's daily and weekend fitness regime
Eating Right	The Shah family's green juice
Prioritizing the Body	Olivia squeezing in exercise between work and parenting
(Neglecting) Sleep	Katrina's exhaustion on her day off

TABLE 4.1 Elements of the Ultimate Body Myth

loss, health concerns, stress—these chronic issues motivate lifestyle adjustments and turn exercise into something that feels both good and necessary. Indeed, the primary concerns for these thirty- and forty-something-year-old parents revolved around health, stress reduction, and dealing with chronic pain. They suffer from debilitating migraines, stomach problems, back injuries, severe arthritis, and multiple forms of cancer. Their focused efforts to diet and exercise offer the hope of keeping health issues at bay. Exercise promises energy, longevity, and health. For some, it does help manage chronic pain and increase daily well-being. Yet the idea that diet and exercise *is the solution* can become a source of shame and worry. And making the time to exercise and care for oneself can be a daunting challenge.

This guilt ignores the fact that working out and eating healthy foods require substantial resources that not everyone has. Personal trainers, gym memberships, home exercise equipment, fancy juicers, probiotics, and organic greens are all expensive. And leaving the house to exercise means that someone else needs to be watching small children. Lisa Phillips and Olivia Shah are able to manage this, in part because they have older children. Cooking a healthy meal requires planning, shopping, and coordination. These activities take significant chunks of time. When people are trying to be Ideal Workers and Perfect Parents, there simply isn't time to be or do more.

THE BURDEN OF THE ULTIMATE BODY

The Ultimate Body, while a valued myth in its own right, often takes backstage to Ideal Worker and Perfect Parent. Unlike parenting (children expect attention) or working (colleagues expect availability), failing to eat a healthy meal or exercise doesn't leave anyone in the lurch (except for those friends one has arranged to exercise with). So people push it aside: "There is just not enough time to do the work I want to do and work out." They fit it in around the other myths (running while waiting for a child's practice to finish) or shove it to the very beginning or end of the day when other responsibilities wane (before colleagues look for an email response or children awaken, or after the family goes to bed). When "squeezing in" exercise leads to 4:30 a.m. treadmill attempts and 5:00 a.m. gym workouts, cultivating the body often becomes a solitary endeavor. The phrase "me time" highlights why attending to the body is often thrust aside. We resonate with their struggle.

An expectation of individual responsibility baked into the myth implies that those that fail simply don't have the necessary willpower to make it happen. If the Ultimate Body is an individual's responsibility—and all that an individual needs is self-control—then failure is a *personal* failure.[22] But even dedication, good intentions, and financial resources can only take people so far. When Franco goes to work, for example, Katrina simply can't leave the house alone: she has small children to watch. Yet rather than push back on any of these myths, people take on responsibility for failing: accepting individual responsibility for their appearance, physical performance, and even their genetics.[23] The project of the body—which is another way of saying, perfecting one's physical body—has become an exercise of self-discipline rather than an understanding, and acceptance, of biological fact.[24]

This mandate for individual accountability is fueled by consumerism and marketing of athletic products. Advertising such as Nike's famous "Just Do It" campaign suggests people simply need determination, with no excuses.[25] Consequently, the body becomes something other than a physical identity or source of well-being. Recall Lisa Phillips and Roger Waldo posting on social media about their runs. Not only do they highlight their commitment to the Ultimate Body in their posts, the collective response reinforces that belief. The body is a personal project, a place in which success and mastery can be displayed. The pleasures that come from exercise and listening to the body can become subsumed by counting calories and counting steps. Appearance serves as evidence of success (the proxy for being fit, eating right, and being "healthy"). People want results they can see, because the physical form signals individual success and control over the body.[26] The benefits of being good-looking radiate out into the workplace and beyond.[27]

People take on this belief in individual responsibility wholeheartedly. They *want* to adhere to the myth: attending to their bodies in the "right" way is experienced as emotionally satisfying, morally worthy, and scientifically justified.[28] The focus is not on the doing of exercise (and diet) per se, but on the doing of activities that are good, moral, and virtuous.[29] Moreover, rather than paying attention to how the environment, genetics, or access to health care either impairs or enables health, individuals take on the entire burden of "fixing" their bodies. Framing the project of the body as a site of freedom, choice, and responsibility cannot help but lead to angst when efforts fall short.

This is not to say that exercise is bad or not pleasurable. Individual efforts to shape the body can, and often do, result in positive outcomes. Such outcomes are more expansive than physical heath—the myth also perversely connects the external markers of health with attractiveness and likeability.[30]

Yet no amount of exercise or green juice will preserve youth.[31] And the pressure on the individual to achieve these goals undermines differences in underlying health conditions. Although the Ultimate Body promises the body is malleable, the body ages and can never be fully controlled. Thinking of the body as a project under individual control is misguided. The body begins "fighting back" when people push it too hard and ignore their physical limitations.[32] And when tasked with the individual responsibility for "health," attention is diverted from other actors—society, the state, or even the health care system—that are also responsible.[33] These families in Southern California have access to abundant fresh fruits and vegetables, and to adequate health care, and they live in neighborhoods relatively free of environmental toxins and full of green space. Perhaps this makes it easier to be healthy? Perhaps it makes it easier to believe that their health is something that they, alone, control?

All of the myths of perfection keep the gaze squarely on individuals, and on individual responsibility for thriving at work, raising good kids, and being in good health. With a phone in hand, people can check in with a colleague, coordinate a child's after-school activity, and track their daily progress of steps. Technology enables (and exacerbates) these myths and encourages using them as a yardstick for people's accomplishments.

PART II

WHY IT IS GETTING HARDER

CHAPTER 5

THE PROMISE OF TECHNOLOGY

Roger Waldo spends Tuesday nights at the hotel. This saves him four hours in the car (he has a two-hour commute) and makes it possible for him to take a ten-mile evening beach run with his trainer. This Tuesday he works until 5:30 p.m. then goes running. Appreciating the sun over the ocean, he pulls out his phone to snap a photo of the view. Posting the picture on Facebook, he captions, "Sunset run on the beach, what a privilege!"

Making his way back to the hotel, Roger grabs a protein bar and returns to his room to shower and dress for an evening reception. At 8:45 he heads to the Convention Center and Visitors Bureau. Chatting with a local restaurateur, Roger doesn't flinch and maintains eye contact when the phone buzzes in his pocket. Guessing that it's the hotel pinging him, he artfully offers to get them both a drink and checks the phone on the way to the bar. Nothing pressing, but it's always good to be sure. He doesn't stay long at the party, an hour or so, before returning to his hotel room. He goes to sleep almost immediately.

At 6:30 a.m. Wednesday morning Roger sends each family member a good morning text before heading to the hotel gym to lift some weights. First a simple good morning to his wife, Linda. Then Roger sends a quick reminder to his twelve-year-old son, Ryan, to save their favorite show, The Walking Dead, to watch together when he gets home. Finally, he texts seventeen-year-old Sadie—the first of generally a half-a-dozen texts to his kids during the day. Roger is a proud father. Pictures of Sadie in her dance uniform and Ryan with his bass guitar sit prominently on his desk. He talks about his kids often, and his colleagues are up-to-date on their latest achievements.

When Roger returns to his hotel room to shower and get ready for work, he plugs in the phone and turns the volume up high, checking whenever anything comes in: "I hear it go bing, I check it. I just do." By 8:00 he is munching on a piece of fruit and drinking a Powerade from the hotel café. After a quiet half-hour in his office, Roger runs the daily morning meeting with his team. As they go around the room giving status reports, Roger approves the "no-brainer" deals and offers rapid-fire guidance on what prices to negoti-ate. Then it's off to the property-wide leadership team meeting that starts at 9:00. On his way he stops to pick up a cup of strong room service coffee, joking with the kitchen staff as he makes his way through the kitchen.

At the leadership meeting Roger waits for his turn to report out. He googles a new Odwalla protein bar he saw recently and sends a picture of it to Linda, asking her to pick some up when she's at the store. When Roger is in a meeting that he describes as "off his radar," he'll take the opportunity to either send a text to Linda or check in with one of the kids.

During the subsequent executive committee meeting, Roger knocks out a response to a work email on his phone while someone is talking about the breakfast buffet problems. Boom. Dealt with. Then his head is back in the meeting. According to Roger, "Shifting from one gear to the next is something that you have to do. Because if you can't multitask, then you're going to die. You're going to be overwhelmed. There just isn't enough time in the day." He can get a hundred emails an hour and often spends chunks of each week-end at his dining room table cleaning out his inbox.

He heads home Wednesday after a forty-five-minute swim at the hotel pool. Home by 7:30 p.m., Roger relaxes with the family before going to bed at 9:00. He lays out his workout clothes and packs his overnight bag before bed so he doesn't wake Linda in the morning. Thursday starts at 2:50 a.m. with a swim and karate class before driving back to the property. Waking from the alarm on his phone, he quickly checks for texts from his morning workout buddies. All clear. Using his phone as a flashlight in the predawn darkness, he slips out of bed and gets dressed. After exercising, he grabs coffee at the Circle K before starting his 6:15 drive back to the hotel. He's back in the office for the 8:30 team meeting. Roger is not exaggerating when he says, "I do more before ten than most people do all day."

ROGER WALDO'S MOBILE DEVICES help him manage a hectic schedule. He stays on top of endless meetings and emails by multitask-ing. He cracks open his laptop in the evenings, and stays close to his fam-ily through regular texts throughout the day. He diligently maintains his workouts, tracking his times and posting his accomplishments on social media. We are exhausted just watching Roger. The weeks are busy, but Roger manages. Over the weekend he maintains the intensity, leaving at

6:00 a.m. for a weekend bike ride, returning home by 11:00 with plenty of opportunity in the afternoon and evening to spend "quality time" with the family and catch up on work email.

Roger engages the myths of Ideal Worker, Perfect Parent, and Ultimate Body more than many. Roger is always available to everyone. He is constantly coordinating, talking, and texting with Linda, his co-workers, his exercise buddies, and his children. He regularly sends Linda items to add to the family shopping list or to let her know when he's running late. Roger's phone is his savior, "I'm able to head things off, help my overall career progression . . . it's also a great tool for me to communicate with my family and friends." His smartphone allows him to feel in control of his life, and he lives in fear the battery will die.

Technological advances historically have come with the assurance that they will make lives easier to manage,[1] and advertising capitalizes on this promise.[2] The rhetoric around phones amplifies a sense of individual accomplishment. People control their devices and so they control their lives: the rectangular block in the hand, the personalized screen, and the rapid back and forth of texts and emails. The feel, look, and weight of these devices create a visceral experience that provides a sense of power over various roles and demands. Unlike the newest wearable technologies, people *know* they can put the phone down. It is under their control. Yet it is also intimate. Slipped in a pocket, it is both close to the body and separate from it. This gives people a feeling of control over their devices while allowing technology to become embedded in their aspirations, accomplishments, and sense of self.

WHAT IS THE PROMISE OF TECHNOLOGY?

The story goes like this: smartphones allow individuals to be accessible and prepared. They enable people to be available for the unexpected work call or to finish a project on the couch at home in the evenings. They help people coordinate parenting activities—getting children to after-school activities and being up on the latest homework assignment. They aid in the quest to be fit and healthy. Fitbits or the spectrometer in phones (and smartwatches) make it easy to calculate "steps," and any number of apps will track food intake, sleep rhythms, and pain levels. With dexterous fingers, one can easily sign up for a spinning class or post a photo of a morning run on Facebook or Instagram. And it's true. These technologies enable people to do more. But that isn't the full story. Despite the moments of multitasking when people revel in feeling that they can do it all, technology is subtly encouraging them to change, shift, and amplify what it means to "be" any one of the three myths.

This shifting explains what Roger calls his "love-hate relationship" with his phone. The fact is, no matter how close he comes to enacting the myths, Roger is *not* always in control. And his reliance on communication technologies can undermine his attempts to "do it all" as much as it facilitates them. One night Roger checks his phone just before falling asleep and finds a 9:00 p.m. email from his boss asking for an updated spreadsheet ASAP. His heart sinks and temper flares. But he begrudgingly gets out of bed, opens his laptop, fixes the spreadsheet, and sends it off. Such tools have ushered in a new culture of availability. And now, in order to be the Ideal Worker, Roger has to be available at 9:00 p.m. (or later). As he describes,

> I've got this leash that's attached to me. I'm at a wedding . . . I'm at my daughter's dance competition, . . . and I feel it go (buzzing sound). I know it's there. So, now, all of a sudden, I've got this in the back of my mind. It's now triggered that, the first available break, I need to go check that out. . . . I'll be working in the yard. I've got a project that I want to do. I'm going to paint this fence. Well, I've got my phone in my pocket. I'm painting the fence [spraying sound]. And then the phone goes off. Stop. Now, my intention was to finish this fence during the day. But now I'm dealing with an issue at work, which needs to be dealt with, but I'm not finished, and I'm in a fifty-minute conversation—or I'm dealing with something, and the whole family's waiting to go, but work is more important than us being at the carnival. But I've got people waiting for me.

Roger's experience suggests that a focus on such technologies as tools for individuals is misplaced. In truth the phone is a link to other people and other demands. It creates the expectation that everyone with a smartphone is on the hook to be available and responsive. The image of Roger, with his phone in hand, striding through the hallway of a hotel, sitting through a meeting, or advertising his ten-mile sunset run on the beach, masks the inherent *connectivity* of technologically mediated lives.

As Roger so succinctly puts it, "I've got people waiting for me." The specific functions of these technologies (near ubiquitous connectivity, asynchronous text and email) literally put *other* people at his fingertips and allow him to reach them. But technologies also allow them to reach him. With a phone in hand, humans become people-with-information, people-at-the-ready, and people-on-call.³ Individuals can do anything on demand—request (or run) a financial report; coordinate a pickup from swimming; confirm that a running partner is on their way; and manage the inevitable collisions of work, family, and body. Phones encourage the micro-coordination of logistics on the fly.⁴ Yet it is those on the other end of the device that enable people to do and be more, not the technology itself. Those people on the other end also have ideas, expectations, and needs that give them power.

CREATING THE ON-DEMAND WORKER

Franco Garcia holds his two-year-old son, Matt, on his hip as his wife, Katrina, reminds him to grab the Gatorade on the kitchen counter. It is Saturday afternoon, and the family is getting ready for a visit to a local amusement park. As he walks into the kitchen, Franco pulls his phone out of his cargo shorts pocket. He pauses at the entry to the kitchen, as Matt reaches up to grab the brim of his baseball cap. Franco laughingly chides, "Hold on Buddy." Ducking his head to avoid Matt's grasping hand, Franco taps a short response to an email with his right thumb. Less than a minute later he pockets the device, picks up the Gatorade, and is back in the hallway grabbing jackets and his wallet (Matt still on his hip). Ten minutes later, Katrina puts Matt and his four-year-old sister, Charlotte, in their car seats. Franco stops for a moment outside the driver's door and checks email on the phone again. He reads an incoming message and taps out a quick reply, sighing before getting behind the wheel and taking off.

Parking the car forty-five minutes later, Katrina Garcia tries to rouse Charlotte, who fell asleep the minute they got on the road. Franco walks to the back of the car to pull out the double stroller. He stops before opening the trunk and checks his email again, pausing to answer another message. Franco grumbles under his breath, "This client's going to be the death of me." An important client is due to arrive at the hotel on Tuesday and is just now, on Saturday afternoon, finally replying to a series of messages that Franco sent last Monday. Franco feels pressure to reply and forward the information to the necessary colleagues so they can prepare for the client's event. Franco sends one more message, shakes his head, deposits the phone in his pocket, and proceeds to enjoy the park with his family—not checking the device again for the rest of the afternoon.

FRANCO GARCIA DOESN'T regularly engage with email when he is with his family. He turns his phone on silent mode and keeps it on the kitchen counter, glancing at it every couple of hours in the evenings. He rarely responds to incoming messages—at least until after Katrina and the kids have fallen asleep.

Today was unusual. The urgency of the impending event and the client's lack of responsiveness led to a scenario in which Franco felt he had to check repeatedly and answer immediately. And while this might be frustrating, it doesn't upend his life. He feels good about the result. The phone actually acted as "a lifesaver." He was not forced to go into work, call into work, or even stay home and respond to emails on a desktop computer. His phone converted what could have become a major last-minute scramble into a minor inconvenience. Franco can simultaneously be an Ideal Worker in the moment (responsive and available) and a Perfect Parent, enjoying an afternoon of quality time with his family at an amusement park.

Professionals frequently engage in this type of technology-enabled work, and many employers provide phones, laptops, or other means of accessing work outside the office.[5] These technological "perks" allow people like Franco to be there for the unexpected emergencies while providing a degree of flexibility. They also change the expectations for what does and does not need to be accomplished. Franco doesn't have to tie everything up before leaving the office. If a particular project takes longer than anticipated, he knows he has the option to finish later that night and can make it home for dinner.

The ability to keep up with work while maintaining temporal autonomy and independence is highly desirable.[6] Until it becomes too much.

Like many, Franco describes his technology as incredibly useful, all-consuming, and occasionally problematic. On the one hand, he asserts that the *best* thing about his company-provided phone is "[a] sense of security. An understanding that even though I'm not on property I'm still fully connected and understanding what's happening with the operation." On the other hand, his description of the *worst* part of technology is eerily similar to the best: "My mind is always on work. There are far fewer times that I'm afforded the ability to just really disconnect from work and recharge."

Like Roger Waldo, Franco feels constantly tethered to work. He's able to go to the amusement park and have quality time with his family. But he's never truly off. Franco knows others expect him to be available, and not only does he return the expectation, he has begun to expect it of himself. In using technology to be constantly available—and therefore allowing himself to be available to others—Franco participates in amplifying what it is to be an Ideal Worker. The same phenomenon—a ratcheting up of expectations of what it means to enact the myth—is true for all the myths of perfection.

ENABLING THE OMNIPRESENT PARENT

As a junior high school English teacher, Lisa Phillips has a particular expertise in social media. She knows all the social media apps and how kids are using them. When she drops thirteen-year-old Danielle off for a sleepover, the mom of the house (Lisa's friend) asks for help. She wants to figure out if her daughter is dating a certain boy. The teenager won't let her mom follow her on Instagram, and the mom is dying to know what's happening. Lisa promises to investigate. Luckily, Danielle follows both the girl and boy in question. The next day, and after being sworn to secrecy, Danielle shows Lisa that both kids have called out their new relationship on their Instagram bios with emoji hearts. Mission completed, Lisa sends a text to the other mom giving her the scoop (Figure 5.1). The two process the news with shared mom humor.

FIGURE 5.1   Lisa Phillips's First Text Messages to Her Girlfriend

A few days later, on the way home from soccer practice, Lisa and her daughters stop for a donut. Lisa notices a boy in the store—the same one who, according to Instagram, is dating her friend's daughter. Lisa jokingly texts about this to her friend (Figure 5.2).

FIGURE 5.2   Lisa Phillips's Second Set of Text Messages to Her Girlfriend

After laughing at the other mom's reaction to her daughter beginning to date, Lisa smiles and says, "It takes a village these days."

FIGURE 5.3 Lisa Phillips and the Girls at the Donut Shop After School

Many teenagers live much of their social lives online (on social media or multiplayer games). Between her kids at home and her kids at school, Lisa Phillips follows her daughters, many of her daughter's friends, and ex-students that have graduated from her class at school on Instagram and Snapchat (she doesn't allow Twitter and they don't use Facebook). Her frequent use of social media makes her a valuable commodity among other moms. She helps them interpret what is going on in their children's lives online: a murky and often confusing space for parents.[7]

Lisa and her husband Dave track their children's online activities and friendships in a manner more akin to mentorship than surveillance. After a day at an amusement park or beach, Dave will nonchalantly pick up one of the girls' phones from the table and start scrolling through her photo feed, asking questions and showing interest. Lisa will make a lighthearted challenge, scrolling through Instagram posts together and "testing" her daughters to see if they actually know each of their followers by name. She asked Lauren to delete a post that didn't quite feel appropriate—"too morbid"—and they talked about never putting your phone number on Instagram, even privately to a friend.[8] Lisa wants her daughters to understand how social media plays a role in their esteem and sense of self.[9] She also encourages positive social media use, one week suggesting that Danielle post an Instagram picture for the birthday of a friend's younger sibling.

Lisa is trying to meet the demands of being a "good mom" in the context of busy and technologically saturated lives; she jokes that this is "why I am getting an ulcer." Knowing what kids are up to in digital spaces is difficult when children have their own phones, tablets, and laptops. Teens will leave a social media site that has become overrun with adults, create multiple social media accounts in order to trick parents, delete texts they don't want their parents to see, and leave their phones in approved places or carry multiple devices to get around GPS tracking.[10] Whether making a technology contract with a child, installing a tracking app on a phone, or thinking about their family's "digital culture," parents feel the pressure to help their children navigate a complicated online world.[11] But they often don't have the expertise and resources to know what to do.[12] There is always more parenting to be done, as the task of monitoring children shifts daily. Beyond changing the capacity for how much parents can monitor their children, these technologies usher in more existential concerns about whether monitoring protects children or undermines their psychological development and ability to become self-reliant adults.[13]

Ironically, technology also puts parents at the beck and call of their children. When everyone carries a phone, parents can be enlisted to pick up a child with a simple text or call. This is both a blessing and a curse. Such just-in-time parenting allows flexibility, but it often means more time spent waiting and an inability to plan ahead. One night, Lisa finds herself waiting for a call from Danielle to be picked up from the big eighth-grade dance. Lisa had encouraged her to go—emphasizing that Danielle only had to text and she would pick her up *any* time. Danielle texted at 8:30 p.m., asking to be picked up early. Lisa immediately dropped what she was doing and hopped in the car. But by the time she arrived at the dance, Danielle had changed her mind and wanted to stay longer. So Lisa sat in the car outside the dance waiting (watching a Netflix show on her phone). Technology is allowing her to be "there" for her child, while increasing the demands of parenting.

PROMISING THE TAMED BODY

Katrina Garcia just went through a stretch of long days and exhausting nights. Working ten to fourteen hours a day and raising two small children has started to get the best of her physically. She has gained a little weight and is unhappy with how she looks and feels. Katrina turns to technology to help her lose a few pounds. She tries a few diet apps to help her track food, and a fitness app to track her activity. None of them are quite what she wants. She gets a sense of her activity and learns a bit about calories, but the effort to log in and track is just too much in her busy life: "I felt like it was too complicated, like too much information. I just need simple. Like just to pay attention. . . . I just need it to be like, 'Hey, stop putting food in your mouth. That would be a good idea.'"

Katrina glances down at her new Fitbit. Her brother-in-law and sister-in-law both have one and gave her the device for Christmas (at her request). She loves it. Katrina started wearing the device after the holidays (after all that eating at her parents' house) and appreciates that it doesn't actually require her to do anything—it just logs what she is already doing and helps her feel better about it. After walking the kids to the park today in the wagon and going up and down the stairs in the house, she has gotten her steps in.

Four-year-old Charlotte wanders over and notices Katrina looking at her wrist. Charlotte pipes up, "Mom, did you get to a five yet?" (Five lights mean that Katrina has met her daily target of ten thousand steps). Katrina points the band toward her daughter and happily replies, "I'm there today!" Charlotte gives her mom a hug before going back to coloring on the floor. Tracking mom's steps has become a family project. Katrina recently saw her in-laws at a birthday party and was surprised when they noticed she had lost a few pounds. She can't help but grin a little when relating the story. Now she is trying to convince Franco to get one too.

KATRINA GARCIA TURNED TO technology when she wanted to lose some weight. Using her Fitbit, Katrina lost five to ten pounds and got back to her "comfortable weight." The device helps her stay attentive to her daily activities and encourages her to do more. Katrina loves that the Fitbit made visible what she was already doing and gave her a sense of accomplishment and control over her body. Such activity-tracking tools measure the bodily inputs (such as food and steps) that determine specific outputs (such as physical or mental performance). The ability to track and measure the body is a form of technological accountability that is often talked about as the "quantified self."[14] However, becoming a quantified self comes with benefits and costs.[15]

As with the Ideal Worker and Perfect Parent, technology can heighten the expectations of what is possible for the Ultimate Body. Counting calories and tracking exercise are not new. Roger Waldo has maintained a journal for years in which he writes down his daily exercise. However, technology allows for new forms of monitoring, and people can track what is happening to the body with a range of technologies and indicators.[16] It is easy to transform the possibility of tracking one's health into an expectation and even a responsibility to do so. If someone chooses not to track calories and steps, are they rejecting the possibility of being an Ultimate Body? Tracking promises greater control over the body. But seeing the numbers doesn't make them changeable. The promised control—especially in the context of a myth that places total responsibility for health and wellness on the individual—means that when technologies report numbers that don't match the desired ones, people are left with frustration, are distraught, and become alienated from the project of the self.[17]

Tracking numbers for oneself is just the first step. Eventually Katrina might share her personal data with others in real time: making comparisons, getting sent updates on her progress compared to an algorithmically decided norm, and being accountable to global ideals of what it means to be "healthy" and "normal." Roger Waldo could post more than a picture of the sunset after his run; he could post his distance, pace, and time using an app like Strava. He'd have more detail than he keeps in his journal, and he would get accolades and perhaps some new challenges from his friends' responses. The Ultimate Body, as with the other myths, is an escalating expectation.

MAKING ALL THE MYTHS ALL THE MORE IMPOSSIBLE

Ideal Worker, Perfect Parent, and Ultimate Body: these myths have been part of American society for far longer than smartphones or social media platforms. They promote unreachable aspirations. Although there is a reasonable, and not entirely unwarranted, temptation to blame the fundamentally unattainable dreams on technology, this is too simple a diagnosis.[18] Technology didn't create the impossible dreams, it simply reframed them, adding new promises and new opportunities for failure. Technology amplifies the expectations associated with each myth, as well as exacerbates the myths by putting them in greater contact with one another. But the myths themselves were never compatible with one another.

With the help of these tools, people manage to pull multiple myths off in certain moments. Tim Andrews can put in quality time with family (Perfect Parent!) and work from home in the evening and on weekends (Ideal Worker!). Even when he doesn't squeeze in time on the treadmill, Tim can go to bed feeling like the dynamic, fully engaged person that the technological age demands him to be. When people feel they are living the myths of perfection, technological tools often seem to be helping. However, technology does not actually reduce demands on time or attention. Tim has to choose between folding laundry, getting on the treadmill in the bedroom, or clearing email. Email often wins. Usually, laundry "kind of falls by the wayside" and the treadmill gathers dust.

Even with all of technology's promises and capabilities, the myths compete for people's attention. What's more, they frequently collide. And technology isn't a panacea.

After a busy weekend, Tim Andrews's Tuesday morning has gotten out of hand. He has taken the day off to get his three girls ready for a long 4th of July trip with his ex-wife, Tonya. The plan is to take the girls to Tonya's house after meeting the painter he hired to paint their living room. Tim moves with efficiency, packing lunches for the girls to take with them on the road trip. The painter was scheduled to come at 8:00 a.m., but it's almost 8:20 and he hasn't arrived.

As the clock approaches 8:30, things start to get hectic. Late last night Noah, Tim's boss, sent a meeting request for an 8:30 a.m. conference call. Tim accepted the call without thinking (despite the lack of warning, inconvenient time, and fact that he had officially taken the day off work). Of course, the painter shows up just before the call is slated to begin. Now Tim finds himself distracted as he tries to prepare for the call, show the painter around, and get the girls ready to head out the door.

Tonya wants the girls at a certain time and even with his careful planning, the morning is starting to fall apart. The conference call begins. The painter needs input. And suddenly Tim's daughter Olive begins to pepper him with questions about their lunches. Tim waves her away as he tries to concentrate. Olive frantically calls her mom to say that they don't have lunches. Still on the conference call, attempting to focus on what his colleagues are saying, Tim starts getting texts from his ex-wife about whether or not he has prepared lunches. Once the call ends, Tim mollifies Tonya (via text) and the girls, assuring them that, indeed, they do have lunches and everything is ready to go.

Later, Tim wryly admits, "All three of those things collided at the same exact time and so I didn't really do any of them well. . . . It was just a horrible clash of all this stuff. . . .

I made some assumptions. . . . I wasn't my best. I wasn't my best dad, I wasn't my best employee, and I wasn't my best customer."

IN HIS EFFORTS TO BE an Ideal Worker and Perfect Parent while managing his household, Tim Andrews experiences a clear moment of collision. Everyone—the painter, his boss, his girls—needs him at exactly the same time. Greeting the painter and getting the girls ready and out the door was challenging but manageable. The conference call (and back-channel texting with his ex) pushed him over the top. Hannah pipes up to suggest, "Maybe next time schedule all this stuff on different days." Tim nods. "I should have realized that the morning was going to collide between the painter and the timing with the kids. And I should have said no way can I call in at 8:30 a.m."

So why did Tim accept the call? He had taken the day off and the request came in at 10:00 p.m. the night before. His inclination to take the call was habitual. He lives with the mantle of the Ideal Worker. This is the myth Tim doesn't question, even on his day off. And the smartphone allows both Tim and his boss to assume he is available.

Technology subtly shifts, often without anyone noticing, what people think is possible—both for themselves and those around them. Tim thought he could be available; his boss expects him to be. Olive knew she could reach her mom on the phone; Tonya knew she could reach Tim by text. What had been a small morning snafu exploded into a larger one, with multiple stakeholders, agendas, and schedules.

Such incidents reveal that technology doesn't only introduce top-down power dynamics: it's not just the CEO who expects availability. On a different morning, Tim responds to an email from his colleague Frank about a forecast that Frank is waiting on. Tim promises to get it done by noon. Such exchanges are not just about expectations or authority, they are about interdependencies. By automatically saying, "Sure, I'll have those spreadsheets to you," Tim is being a good friend and colleague. He *wants* to be a good friend and colleague. Tim emphasizes how much he appreciates the collegial relationships he has at work:

> These people are really more like my friends than co-workers. So, I think there's a huge feeling of none of us wanting to let each other down. And so, one of the ways we show that to each other is being responsive

through the use of technology. . . . I mean, none of us walk around saying, "Oh, I worked four hours this weekend." That's not the kind of culture.

But in upholding these relationships, and being the kind of person and professional he wants to be, Tim uses technology (perhaps without even realizing it) to tighten the interdependencies that are part of working with others—inside and outside of the workplace. The more he responds, even out of friendship, the more work there is to do outside the office. Ignoring a text from either his ex-wife or girlfriend also carries serious consequences: a missed pickup, a potential argument with his ex-wife, or an inadvertent insult to his girlfriend. Technology changes the ways that people display commitment to each other. And while such intensification is not caused by technology in and of itself, the tools force a reevaluation of what responsiveness looks like and what nonresponsiveness means.

CHAPTER 6

CREATING A SPIRAL OF EXPECTATIONS

IMAGINE YOURSELF amidst a mass of people—work colleagues, work friends, old friends, other parents, family members, babysitters, your kid's teacher. And to each of these people, you are connected by a string.

Once upon a time (before the possibility of constant availability), these strings were slack. Expectations for each other were not constantly activated. To ask something of someone (or tug at the string), people made a phone call, wrote a letter, maybe even sent a fax, and the communication act traveled, with some degree of swiftness, over the string, tugging slightly at the other person.

Sometimes the recipient didn't feel the tug (they didn't check voicemail or the mail carrier was delayed). The sender understood this possibility and didn't take immediate offense if the person didn't respond right away. But more often than not, you would feel a little tug yourself. Maybe in an hour, a few days, or even a month, as the person communicated back. Occasionally the message traveled instantaneously: perhaps someone picked up the phone when it rang. Occasionally the message got dropped entirely: perhaps the answering machine was full or no one was home to take a message. It was impossible to gauge what would happen when you picked up the phone to make a call. This may not have been the most efficient way to communicate. Missed connections were inevitable, and it could be difficult to coordinate and keep track of people. But all the slack involved certain freedoms.

Now, everyone's strings are pulled taut. People seem to be standing at attention, with any number of strings vibrating between them and those they need, love, and rely on. When someone wants someone else's attention they just have to give the string the tiniest of tugs (send a text, leave a Snapchat video, drop an email) and the tug is felt instantly, with force. The person on the other end can't help but jerk toward the invisible string. And whoever started the tug assumes the recipient got the message. They know that if a response isn't forthcoming it is because someone else made a *choice* not to respond. They may be more or less forgiving of that choice. But people no longer assume that someone missed the call. Instead, it is assumed that they *avoided* the call.

The ability to give a tiny tug and to get an immediate response can be intoxicating, emotionally satisfying, and stress relieving.[1] At least until someone realizes that the string pulls both ways. I am just as much at your beck and call as you are at mine. Everyone feels the need to be everything to everyone else, without natural barriers or separations.[2] As strings tighten, expectations of what people want from one another intensify. This changes what it means to strive for an ideal.

That doesn't mean people don't love technology. Franco Garcia experiences a sense of accomplishment when helping solve a client's problem, even though it is on his day off. Tim Andrews feels competent when he successfully coordinates the complicated schedule for his girls and manages an out-of-town trip. Roger Waldo displays real pride when he posts on social media about his fitness routine. Moments like these are motivating. They perpetuate the sense that professional parents can use technology to live the dream.

However, and this is the tricky part, as people do more through technology—send work emails from home, coordinate with babysitters at the last minute, keep kids on a digital leash, track and share the latest fitness feat—expectations of what is possible shift. Information and communication technologies have blown open the shared capacity for connection, coordination, and surveillance. And in so doing they have changed how Ideal Workers, Perfect Parents, and Ultimate Bodies behave.

Although technology allows people to do more, it also makes it more difficult for them to keep up. It creates a spiral of expectations. It is not simply a matter of trying harder, engaging with technology more fully, or somehow being better at time management.[3] In promising to help people achieve their aspirations—making things more flexible, controllable, and efficient—technology masks its role in amplifying the demands and increasing the scope of these myths.

WHAT IS THE SPIRAL OF EXPECTATIONS?

People are not, in fact, "living up" to an ideal at all. What they are actually doing is *changing* the ideal: specifically, changing the ideal to make it all the more impossible to achieve. The spiral explains both the promise and the frustration of technology (Figure 6.1). It clarifies how technology can provide both short-term feelings of accomplishment and a pressing feeling of being out of control or always behind.

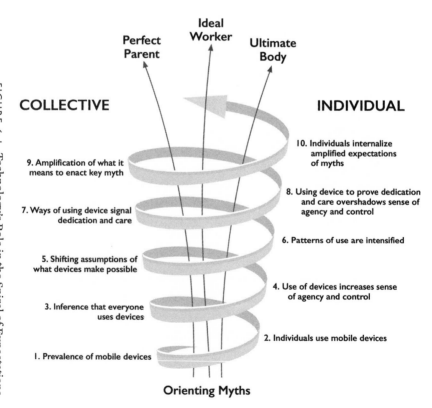

FIGURE 6.1 Technology's Role in the Spiral of Expectations

Ideal Worker

Perfect Parent

Ultimate Body

COLLECTIVE

INDIVIDUAL

10. Individuals internalize amplified expectations of myths

9. Amplification of what it means to enact key myth

8. Using device to prove dedication and care overshadows sense of agency and control

7. Ways of using device signal dedication and care

6. Patterns of use are intensified

5. Shifting assumptions of what devices make possible

4. Use of devices increases sense of agency and control

3. Inference that everyone uses devices

2. Individuals use mobile devices

1. Prevalence of mobile devices

Orienting Myths

The spiral of expectations represents the interplay between individual experience and collective norms.[4] The right-hand side of the spiral visualizes the changing ways in which individuals experience their devices and understand the myths. The left-hand side of the spiral lays out the collective norms and assumptions that emerge from, and shape, the individual experience of use. In the center of the spiral are the myths, which simultaneously influence how people use their devices and change in conjunction with use.

Taken as a whole, this spiral provides an overview of the relationship between emerging communication technologies and the orienting myths. The same myths that motivate people to use technologies in certain ways are amplified in collective processes of use. It's a dangerous, mutually reinforcing process: as individuals adapt to the collective, and the collective adapts to individuals, the myths grow and become more extreme, and it becomes more difficult to uphold any one of them, no less all three.

Let's explain.

First *mobile devices become available* and more affordable (1). They promise to help people do more. As a result, individuals start using them and *taking advantage of what they enable* (2). And as *people see those around them using these devices* they naturally infer that others have the same new capacities that they do (3). They begin connecting with each other through their devices. They feel like everyone is at their fingertips, and it is intoxicating. *People feel more in control* and are convinced that technology will help them be the kind of person (worker, parent, body) they want to be (4). Of course, *these dreams and desires are informed by prevailing myths* about the Ideal Worker, Perfect Parent, and Ultimate Body.

As these devices become prevalent and people become increasingly attached to the capacities they provide, *everyone (individuals, families, organizations, societies) collectively begins to shift their assumptions* of what technology makes possible (5). If everyone is using their phone to be available—and, at the same time, uphold a version of the myths—it becomes normal for people to coordinate on the fly, answer texts immediately, and be at-the-ready for each other.

Colleagues, friends, and family take for granted that messages are received and replied to with something approximating immediacy. Further, knowing that others are running a six-minute mile increases the pressure to reach a goal, log it, and compare it to others.[5] The same social pressures surface when Tim Andrews receives the Sunday morning email from his colleague Frank or Lisa Phillips is asked to track Instagram for a friend. With these shifting assumptions of what devices make possible, *individuals intensify their own patterns of use* (6). People are more available to work, to monitor their children, and track and share health data. These *acts of availability and responsiveness signal dedication and care*—dedication to the project of work, parenting, and the body (7). And dedication to each other. Responsiveness becomes a sign of respect and love. Availability becomes a signal of competency and reliability.

In making sure to signal dedication and care to the people that matter, *individuals find themselves more and more available, not wanting to offend.* People don't simply respond to a message because they can. They respond because not responding is interpreted as disrespectful. They respond because they *care.* Even if they don't love and respect that person, they care that others think of them as a responsible and dedicated colleague or friend. Tracking exercise becomes a proxy for care of the body and a dedication to health and wellness. Eventually, this need to signal care and dedication overwhelms the thrill initially experienced when using these devices. The experience of individual agency begins to shift. *Individuals feel more at-the-ready for others than in control of their lives* (8).

The *collective expectations of what it means to be a good colleague, good parent, or healthy body expand* (9). And this shift is subtle. As a whole, we may not even notice it happening: people focus more on trying to accomplish their dreams than on interrogating the dreams themselves. No longer can an Ideal Worker miss a client message on their day off. No longer can a Perfect Parent be unaware of a child's location and actions. No longer can an Ultimate Body fail to track (and share) the details of their food and exercise. The core elements of the myths of perfection are the same (be available, monitor children, exercise regularly), but what it takes to enact the element has ratcheted up (be more available, do more monitoring, track more metrics).

Collectively, *people internalize amplified expectations* of what it means to be an Ideal Worker, Perfect Parent, or Ultimate Body (10). Even as they might be able to laugh at the impossibility of it all, they still hold themselves up to the ideal. We know we do. And now everyone expects more of themselves. For these have become technologically enhanced dreams: the ideal person is always at the ready, always there, always in the know, always watching. This person can't help but notice how he or she measures up and, consciously or otherwise, judge him or herself in terms of shifting ideals. *Along with increased capacity comes increased impossibility.* There is more to be done than anyone has time for.[6] *Technologies enable people to better enact the orienting myths—and ensure that nobody can live up to them.*

Magazine covers and popular books regularly discuss the impact of technology on everyday life. But rarely do people take a step back to think about how technology shifts collective and cultural expectations. Like many, we love our devices for helping us manage the day to day. And we hate them for escalating our sense of what's possible and expected.

A SPIRAL POWERED BY SHARED EXPECTATIONS

The spiral of expectations explains the love-hate relationship with technology—in part by rejecting the widespread language of individual addiction to devices. Despite a real attachment to devices, and reasonable concerns about this attachment, the language of addiction often used to describe people's relationships with these tools suggests that technology use is purely an individual issue. Such a narrow focus on individuals, and individual responsibility, is problematic: in fact, technology addiction as a pathology is supported by only weak clinical evidence. Moreover, the addiction narrative prevalent in popular discourse promotes fear, uncertainty, and self-blaming.[7] The focus on addiction directs attention to individual solutions for the overuse of technologies rather than to understanding *social* expectations and *collective* pressures that have led to the intensification of expectations.

Similarly, calls for individuals to disconnect and disengage from their technology perpetuate the idea that individuals can, in fact, make a unilateral choice to walk away from their devices.[8] Certainly it is important to point out that individuals do have agency and are not passive in how they choose to engage with technology.[9] But advice to disconnect ignores the fact that much of what people are doing on their devices is living up to the expectations of others: their organizations, those they depend on, and those who depend on them. Taking a "technology detox" may be a liberating experience.[10] But such injunctions ignore interdependencies and the many ways in which people express dedication and care through technologically mediated communication.

These interdependencies cannot be easily ignored. Being aware of expectations and mutual dependencies is essential to being culturally competent. As a result, people feel they are constantly connected whether or not they actually are—simply because they have internalized shared expectations of connectivity.[11] People may be able to disconnect from devices for a day or a weekend, but how can any one person reject technology and manage their day-to-day life as a working professional (when colleagues expect availability) or as an engaged parent (when schools operate through email and automated progress reports)?

Any effort to truly disconnect from digital devices requires collective effort and a shift in shared expectations. In order to increase productivity, some companies have mandated quiet time when workers are not to email or interrupt each other. Other companies have experimented with a rotating night off when co-workers explicitly cover any work demands that come up on someone's night off.[12] These shared efforts are a first step toward enabling individuals to break the cycle of expectations emanating from the workplace.

The common fear that people are retreating into an isolated world of screens and flying fingers, ignoring the "real" world, feels overblown to us. Not only did these professional parents regularly put down their devices, they also engaged with those around them. Most focused intently on maintaining face-to-face relationships and were very cognizant of when and how they checked their phones and emails.

Recall Franco Garcia. He described his phone as a tether to work, but he actually left it on the kitchen counter for most of the evening. Similarly, when Tim Andrews found himself drawn to the phone while playing with the girls, he was so disturbed by his own actions he became adamant about declining calls and leaving his phone in his pocket (this happened before we spent time with Tim and his family—our presence did not provoke this awareness). Rarely did we see mobile devices interfering with interpersonal relationships. It was harder for the kids to regulate their use without parental intervention, of course, and there was variation among families, but on the whole we did not observe technology dampening interactions.[13]

We generally observed clear technology etiquette. Glancing at a phone in the middle of a conversation was unusual. People would excuse themselves from a conversation first. We didn't see family members checking their phones while at the dinner table or ignoring each other in favor of screens. Parents take seriously that it is their job to teach teenagers to maintain eye contact and engage with the world around them.

That said, smartphones allow people to inhabit multiple roles at once (such as work colleague, friend, family member, and fellow parent from the soccer team). Even though people might be good at masking the intrusion of one world into another (think about a babysitter's text arriving in the middle of a business meeting or an inquiry from a colleague coming in on a Friday during family movie night), the intrusion is still there. An individual might artfully answer the babysitter by texting under the conference table, but the string pulling one into another sphere is not without a cost.

Tim Andrews is aware of the calls even when he leaves the phone in his pocket. Every time he feels a buzz he can't help but wonder who called and what they want from him. This is its own unique form of stress—and one that isn't apparent to those watching him interact with his girls or joke about the laundry. Franco Garcia knows his client might be emailing while he's enjoying his day off with his family. Even though it doesn't influence his family in any observable way, it's in the back of his mind. He can't just let it go. This is the source of internal stress. Technology tightens the strings whether people respond or not.

A SPIRAL POWERED BY THE MYTH OF THE INDIVIDUAL

Technology is also a bit of a red herring. It is the instrument, rather than the agent. Roger Waldo doesn't "do it all" with his phone. He does it with the help of others. Roger's successes are not an individual accomplishment. Looming over technology use, then, is the myth of the individual.

The myth of the individual is at the heart of each of the myths of perfection. Although not everyone dreams of completing a triathlon, or their child winning a dance championship, these myths promote and idealize individual accomplishments. They feature a heroic worker (who is valued for his or her commitment), a devoted parent (who is rewarded with a successful child), and a fit body (who is recognized for looking good and sharing accomplishments). The individual is the focal point of each of these myths.

For workers, the executives gracing the covers of business magazines reinforce the image of the individual as the harbinger of corporate success.[14] With regard to parenting, the cultural narrative is one of the "mom" standing alone, solely responsible for her child's upbringing and credited with her accomplishments.[15] Athletes and movie stars provide visible evidence of an individual's ability to cultivate their image, and blogs, social media, magazines, and news reports offer pronouncements about how individuals can and should control and shape their bodies.[16]

In each of these images of perfection, success is attributed to individual effort and individuals are responsible for overcoming structural or environmental barriers that might stand in their way. Americans celebrate people who do it all, and call out individuals as the source and representation of triumph. Employees see their work-life problems as individual problems, rather than problems demanding an organizational, governmental, or societal response. This framing of individual "choices" makes them feel in control and empowered.[17]

Americans like to solve their own problems. In so doing, though, there is a deep resistance to seeing shared issues as collective responsibilities. The meta-myth underlying all three of the orienting myths (Ideal Worker, Perfect Parent, Ultimate Body) is the myth of the individual. Technology intensifies this myth, as well, masking the intricate network of human support that withstands tension, protects people from collision, and truly keeps it all together. The truth of how individuals strive to enact these myths is not about technology. It is not, in fact, an individual story at all.

PART III

HOW PEOPLE SURVIVE AND THRIVE

CHAPTER 7

INVISIBLE WORK IS REAL WORK

It is a lazy Saturday around the house for Jay Shah and his family. Generally an early riser, he sleeps in until just after 7:00 a.m. He quietly makes his way downstairs to their home gym. After his workout, before heading back upstairs, Jay grabs a bowl of fresh fruit salad sitting invitingly on the kitchen island (green juice only happens on weekdays). Jay's wife, Olivia, is diligent about buying organic fruit and having it cut and ready for Jay and their girls, thirteen-year-old Neelam and nine-year-old Tessa. She says that is the only way they will eat fruit—you have to put it in front of them.

The house is quiet; Olivia has gone to the gym to swim and the girls have yet to emerge. Jay pokes his head into each of the kid's bedrooms. Tessa is still sleeping and Neelam is propped up in bed reading a novel, The Life of Pi. *Jay showers and answers a string of emails from work while sitting on their freshly made bed—deep red throw pillows over a simple white blanket. By 9:20 Jay is clean and dressed in dark jeans and an artfully faded t-shirt. He spends the next four-ish hours going back and forth between personal finances and answering a stream of work-related emails at his desk in the upstairs alcove.*

Family life begins to buzz around him. Olivia returns from the gym and showers before heading to the other desk for an hour of work (some clients are waiting on travel itineraries). Neelam comes out of her bedroom and tells her mom that Jay's aunt called earlier and she was supposed to call her back. Olivia replies that the aunt called her cell and they compared schedules as she was driving home. It won't work to go visit them tomorrow. When Jay asks why, Olivia relates that his uncle is going to London tomorrow. "Ah well," he says. "We'll find a weekend."

Neelam heads downstairs to get a bowl of fruit then curls up on the sofa with her book. A bit later Olivia heads downstairs to start on lunch. At 1:15 p.m. Jay stretches and wanders downstairs. Neelam is still deep into her book. She looks up when Jay comes down the stairs and says, "Okay. I am SO close. I only have like ten more pages of this book. I am going to go in a bubble."

Olivia has laid out vegetarian BBQ for lunch—Tofurkey kielbasas and Haloumi grilling cheese that they had at a Greek restaurant recently and she wanted to try. She is peeling cucumbers and laying out condiments. Jay turns on the large gas grill in the back patio. Tessa prances into the open kitchen. She has cut the neck, arms, and bottom of a t-shirt in a Flashdance style as instructed by a YouTube video. She twirls in front of her mom, declaring, "This is the shirt I decorated." Olivia replies dryly, "You mean cut." They both smile.

At 1:30 everyone sits down to eat. They have a lively chat about last night's dinner with family friends. Tessa asks if they have any mangoes left, and Olivia rolls her eyes, knowing that her daughter is really asking for someone to cut her a mango. Between the fruit bowls for the morning and the lunch condiments, Olivia has no intention of jumping up to do more chopping. Eager to please, Jay volunteers to do it and ends up slicing himself—twice. But it's nothing a band-aid can't fix. Olivia laughs, with a slightly mocking tone and says, "Dad is not used to using kitchen knives."

Lunch complete, they all head back to their own activities. At 2:40, Jay comes back from running an errand and Neelam asks if people want to play "Clue." When everyone agrees she sets up the board game. The first game goes relatively fast, over by 3:00. Jay pulls out his phone. He glances at the screen, typing in small bursts as the girls hand out the player cards and get the board set up for the next game. The second game is a nail biter, lasting almost forty-five minutes.

At 4:00 there is a knock on the front door. Neelam jumps up to let in her grandparents. Her grandpa (Olivia's dad) is driving her to theater rehearsal while grandma is coming to help prepare dinner. Neelam and grandpa soon drive off. Olivia goes into the kitchen to start chopping and prepping vegetables with her mother. Tessa retreats to her room. Jay sits on the couch downstairs reading a magazine about golf. Eventually he makes his way upstairs to work on the forecast for one of the hotels that has been refinanced. All in all, a good Saturday.

JAY SHAH IS A WELL-RESPECTED executive at Silver Lake Hospitality—valued within the company for his work ethic and responsiveness, adored by his two accomplished daughters, and admired for his healthy lifestyle. His co-workers, friends, and family see Jay as the de-

FIGURE 7.1 Olivia Shah's Mom Helping in the Kitchen

finitive success story—a person admired for who he is and what he has accomplished. Jay is indeed terrific: personable, hard-working, loving, stylish. He deserves the accolades.

But Jay does not stand alone in his successes. Think back to Jay's Saturday. The bed made, the fruit cut, the food purchased and laid out for lunch, his daughter picked up and taken to her afternoon activity. Jay doesn't have to worry about what he will eat, whether the house is clean, how his children will keep up with their busy schedules, or how he will fit in a workout. Jay had time to exercise, put in several hours of work, and be a devoted family man who grilled lunch and played "Clue." We can't help but note that when Jay says, "We will find a date" to get together with his uncle, he means that Olivia will work it out. Olivia is in charge of organizing visits with his extended family and generally coordinating their calendars. She is the one who plans for dinner and does much of the preparation (often with grandma). So while Jay is a loyal nephew who visits his uncle an hour away, he is able to be this person because of the work being done behind the scenes. Olivia and those she relies on are the force making much of his life possible.

We marvel at all that Olivia manages in a day—with great calm but too little sleep. Olivia has her own forms of support. Her parents regularly help with picking up and dropping off the girls at various activities. In addition, ample financial resources from Jay's work allow them to engage significant paid help. Olivia has two women assist with the household work. Rosa does a "deep clean" every other week. Martina does light cleaning and laundry, and helps prep food for dinner several afternoons a week.[1] Jay and to an extent Olivia are able to engage as fully as possible with the myths because of the help they receive.

Not only do these myths of perfection suggest that everyone *should* be doing it all, they encourage everyone to believe that others *are* actually doing it all. By focusing attention on the individual, the myths mask the work that has been done by others that enables a person like Jay to project himself as a certain kind of worker, father, and body.[2] His co-workers don't see the 6:30 p.m. text Jay sends to Olivia that creates more space in his workday—he needs to stay late and can't pick up Tessa from swimming. Jay doesn't have to wonder if someone else can take care of it. He knows Tessa won't be abandoned. The work of others makes Jay's life not only manageable but gratifying.

The Shah family is but one example. Many parents who manage the domestic front do not have Olivia's additional layers of help. Many full-time working parents do more (or less) than Jay to participate in household work. But every parent who works full-time is supported by the work of someone else. At the most basic level, a full-time job expects a parent to be at work more hours a day than public schools are in session. Someone needs to watch the kids during the gap, and somehow all of the domestic duties that working parents barely have time for need to get done. Working parents need someone to do invisible work to simply get through the day.

WHAT IS INVISIBLE WORK?

It is burrito night for Tim Andrews. Returning from his neighbor's house, Tim laughs rue-fully at himself as he stacks the small "borrowed" chunk of cheddar next to the tortillas on the counter. With no cheese in the house, he was forced to ask a neighbor for this nec-essary ingredient. Tim opens the refrigerator to find two almost overripe avocados, a tub of sour cream, and half a jar of salsa. He searches a nearly empty cupboard for a can of refried beans and declares, to no one in particular, "Okay. It is time for a grocery list." His nine-year-old daughter, Hannah, who has perched herself on a stool in the kitchen, pipes up, "I can help!" She grabs a small pad of paper and announces, "I'll make the list." She immediately asserts that she wants "three thousand waffles" and writes this in large print across the entire pad. "I don't think there is room for that in the freezer," Tim jokes, but then notes, "Yes, we have gone through them all. We need waffles."

As he begins to grate the cheese, Tim hears animated talk filtering in from the other room. Eight-year-old Olive and five-year-old Chloe are arguing over a Barbie car, and it sounds like Chloe is trying to grab the car from her sister. Chloe's upset voice carries into the kitchen: "I DON'T want people to undo the car or take it apart." Tim patiently calls out, "Chloe, play nice with your sister and use your words." Hannah, intrigued, leaves her shopping list to wander into the family room. Tim takes the pad of paper and, on a new page, writes "waffles" in small print, as well as "milk, beans, bananas, carrots, cheese, bread, hamburger meat, buns, tater tots, and frozen taquitos." He places the list on the island in the middle of the kitchen, muttering that he's usually a better list-maker than this. He was out of town over the weekend, and the week has gotten out of hand. He goes back to making burritos.

Over dinner the girls chatter, laugh, and play charades as they tell Tim about their respective days. Olive informs Tim that her mom says she needs some new clothes. Tim protests, "I just got you some." With mock exasperation Olive replies, "Daaaad, that was like five months ago. We need to do it again." Tim laughs, "Okay, we'll try and find time next weekend." The talk of clothes reminds Tim that he forgot about the laundry. He slaps his head and pops up. "I forgot to turn on the dryer." Now he has a load of wet clothes backed up. "Darn," he mutters. "That could have been working for me this whole time." Tim hustles into the garage to start the dryer. He needs to have clothes done before school tomorrow.

When the girls go upstairs to shower, Tim heads to his upstairs office and calls his mom to coordinate the next day. He is going to Palm Springs to do a site visit at an SLH property, which means a two-hour drive in the morning. He will make the girls' lunches tonight after they go to bed, and his parents have agreed to come at 7:00 a.m. and take the older girls to school. They will watch Chloe all day (she hasn't started kindergarten *yet), then pick the girls up after school. Tim should be home after dinner. He confirms the plan with his mom.*

Hannah comes into his office, freshly showered, and wants to look at the evite for her birthday slumber party that they made over the weekend (sleepover, arts and crafts activity, dinner, movie—but not pizza, "everyone has pizza"). Tim logs onto the website so she can look at it again, and he texts his ex-wife, Tonya, reminding her that he has tomorrow covered. Until Tonya finds a full-time job, she watches Chloe and picks up the girls after school. Tim picks them up from her house after work on his nights to have the kids (two nights during the week and every other weekend).

After a pause, he sends Tonya another text: "Is there any issue with my parents having them all day?" Sometimes Tonya bristles when his parents step in to help—they are stricter than both she and Tim. Tonya writes back quickly, "Fine. No problem." He replies, "Great." Tim puts his phone on the desk and herds Hannah into the bedroom to read stories with her sisters, then he tucks them in. At 9:00 p.m. Tim comes back down to retrieve the laundry from the dryer and extract the girls' clothes for the next day. He's pleased he hasn't fallen asleep on their bed. Ignoring the rest of the laundry, he dumps it on his bed and grabs his phone from the office. He heads back downstairs and collapses heavily on the couch. He calls his girlfriend, Betsy, who lives an hour away. Then it's time to make lunches and go back upstairs to answer a few emails on his computer. Tim ends up making a call at 10:30 after receiving an email that his dad was having trouble figuring out the website of the local library. Finally, bed.

T I M   A N D R E W S is the primary worker in his family and default parent in his home. Tim makes a salary that puts him on the top end of middle class, but with alimony and three children he watches his budget closely. He hopes his car makes it a few more months before giving out. Tim does all the Physical Work required to run a home: shopping, cooking, cleaning, and laundry. Unlike Olivia, he doesn't have paid household help. But like Olivia, he also takes on much of the Mental Work that goes into planning these everyday activities: making shopping lists, planning birthday parties. He regularly does the Coordinating Work of lining up help (with his ex-wife, parents, and babysitters). Last, Tim engages in the Emotional Work of keeping track of the state of mind of those around him.

For example, when Tim checks his email before bed and discovers that his dad is aggravated because he can't find the children's activity page on the website of the local library, he doesn't just ignore the message and go to sleep. Tim calls his dad and the two get on their respective computers.

FIGURE 7.2   Tim and Hannah Andrews Looking at Her Birthday Invitation

Tim helps his dad navigate the website and pick some activities he thinks Chloe would like to do. Tim then prints out the schedule to bring to his parents. It may mean an extra thirty minutes before getting to bed, but Tim wants his parents to feel appreciated and good about the plan for the day.

The work that goes into running a household has been the focus of numerous books and articles. Arlene Kaplan Daniels coined the term "invisible work" in 1987 to describe the largely unpaid work done by women in households.[3] Many scholars delineate between different types of invisible work (using different terminology but capturing similar underlying ideas).[4] In practice, the person who does the work (physical) is not always the one who remembers that it needs to be done (mental), sets it up (coordinating), and is mindful of how it affects others (emotional).[5]

Despite forty years of conversation and progress, we see frequent laments that much of this work is still neither visible nor valued.[6] Even though men can do this work, as Tim Andrews ably demonstrates, household work is still understood through a gendered prism that influences both society's expectations and Tim's experience. The invisible work of running a household (the Physical, Mental, Coordinating, and Emotional

Work) is implicitly thought of as "women's work," with women often doing the lion's share, even in dual-income households.[7] Logically, everything would get done faster and more easily if everyone pitched in to get the invisible work done—but both genders generally assign these household tasks to women.[8]

The "second shift," a term coined by Arlie Hochschild, describes the additional time spent on childcare and housework that working mothers perform *after* they come home from their jobs outside the home. The extra hours are for what we call Physical Work, and they don't account for the time spent engaged in Mental, Coordinating, or Emotional Work. Today couples share more of the childcare and housework.[9] But the division of labor is nowhere near equal in most families, especially if we take into account all types of invisible work—Physical Work, Mental Work, Coordinating Work, and Emotional Work.[10]

A great deal of invisible work lies behind visible efforts to be an Ideal Worker, Perfect Parent, and Ultimate Body (Table 7.1). When Tim's parents take the girls to school in the morning so he can go to a work meeting in Palm Springs, they do the Physical Work that supports Tim as an Ideal Worker. When Olivia's father takes his granddaughter to play practice, he enables Olivia to cook family dinner in service of the "quality time" essential to the Perfect Parent—while simultaneously enabling her children to be in enrichment activities, also part of being the Perfect Parent. When Olivia leaves freshly cut fruit for Chad in the morning, she provides the healthy food necessary for an Ultimate Body. The more we live in terms of the myths, the more we need help.

CAN TECHNOLOGY DO INVISIBLE WORK?

New technologies promise that some of this invisible work can be offloaded to smartphones and smart appliances. It is indeed possible to bypass some of the Physical Work. The idea that devices do invisible work *for* households began with early domestic technologies such as dishwashers and washing machines and continues today.[11] However, the technologically enhanced capacity to do more often shifts expectations and increases the amount of work there is to do. It is well documented that the "time-saving" domestic technologies that households embraced after World War II did not translate into less time on unpaid housework. Instead devices such as vacuum cleaners and washing machines changed

	Physical Work	Mental Work	Coordinating Work	Emotional Work
Description	Childcare Shopping Cooking Cleaning Gardening Laundry Bill paying Transportation of children to and from activities and appointments	Planning childcare and activities Maintaining shopping and to-do lists Tracking doctor and other appointments Remembering to pay bills and make purchases (e.g., presents)	Arranging schedules of children, often enlisting others Providing logistic information to others (e.g., start and end times, addresses) Scheduling housecleaners, contractors, and other home services	Being sensitive to the needs of others Expressing appreciation and maintaining positive relationships with others
Role of Technology	Tech automates some Physical Work (e.g., auto bill pay, online shopping) and helps in finding others to do the work	Tech offers reminders and can distribute Mental Work (e.g., shared calendars and lists)	Tech serves as a tool for just-in-time Coordinating Work (e.g., texts) and connects users with those that can coordinate for them	Tech enables small gestures of appreciation in Emotional Work (e.g., emoticons and emojis)

TABLE 7.1   Invisible Work of Managing a Home

our ideas about how often we should clean our houses and wash our clothes. In fact, those with a washing machine spend substantially more time on laundry than those households without.[12]

Concerns aside, Roomba robots *do* vacuum. Touted as the "Family Hub," smart refrigerators not only keep food cold, they can digitally send a shopping list and automatically purchase food.[13] But machines that legitimately do invisible labor for people are still unusual. Typically, smartphone applications connect people with anonymous others who will do the work for them. This is the goal of much of the platform economy. Individuals can now open an app and have a fair amount of Physical Work done for them. Groceries and household supplies can be delivered via Amazon (although drones occasionally deliver them, it's still more often people). On-demand gig work is often about matching people who want invisible work done with those who will do it. Doordash or Postmates finds people to deliver take-out food at a moment's notice. HopSkipDrive promises to send someone to drive kids to where they need to go. Taskrabbit is the go-to for finding people to perform any number of tasks—from doing handy work to organizing a closet or waiting in line. There are tools to facilitate Coordinating Work as well. Zirtual is a matching service for finding virtual assistants who will reschedule a doctor appointment, book travel, empty an email inbox, research where to go to dinner in a new city, or sign kids up for summer camp.

These applications are a spin on the promise that technology enables us to do and be more. But the fact is, technology isn't *doing* the work—that is still reserved for people. However, in making these connections less personal and more anonymous, these services also reduce social cohesion and interdependencies between people.[14] In a pinch, or even worse an emergency, there are limits as to what the gig economy can provide.

Despite the promises of the platform economy, the families in our study were not intensive users of on-demand services, grocery delivery, or even Amazon Prime. Perhaps this is because we left the families in 2015 when the platform economy was in its infancy. Or perhaps this is because the platform economy doesn't truly solve these challenges. Instead, we saw these families use their smartphones to text, check in, and organize the day with others.

INVISIBLE WORK CANNOT BE SOLVED BY TECHNOLOGY

Individuals use their technology to connect with the people they know and rely on, and who know and rely on them. Tim Andrews's mobile device helps him communicate with those he works with, the various people who help with childcare, the person he hires to paint his house, and his long-distance girlfriend. And his device allows him to do the Coordinating and Emotional Work that such relationships require. He does all this by text. He started a Google calendar for his ex-wife and girlfriend to share the Mental Work of tracking the girls' activities and pickup times. But like everyone we studied, he doesn't find maintaining the calendar worth the effort. The daily schedule is too unpredictable, and just-in-time texting ends up working better in the moment. As a result, technology doesn't allow Tim to offload the Mental Work of knowing who has to be where and when.

The strings of connection and obligation between Tim and the people around him are only tightened by the rapid-fire back-and-forth texting in his day. Technology also participates in hiding some of the invisible work being done to scaffold lives and uphold the myths.

Tim and his network become more interdependent and at-the-ready. Tim is, in fact, *more* reliant on others at many moments throughout the day. When he recounts what makes his life overwhelming, Tim says, "All logistics. Just logistics. Everywhere you look there is something. Scheduling is crazy." Tim's experience is representative of every family we spent time with. This increase in logistics is fundamentally how technology intensifies feelings of being out of control. But every family does this differently. Everyone relies on a different structure of support to get invisible work done as they strive for the myths of perfection.

CHAPTER 8

SCAFFOLDING DREAMS

INVISIBLE WORK REQUIRES a language to make it visible. Demarcating Physical, Mental, Coordinating, and Emotional Work enables us to describe what people are doing. Patterns emerge in how families distribute and manage this work, which correspond to different structures of support. Each structure relies on various forms and combinations of invisible work to keep a household running. Like the scaffolding used to support the construction of a building, an exoskeleton of support scaffolds Jay Shah, and each family in this book, in their efforts to achieve perfection.[1] In fact, it makes the version of the life Jay lives fundamentally possible.

We examine these scaffolding structures to reveal the benefits and challenges of different models of support—and to underline the simple fact that there is a lot to do and no single or right way to get it done (see Figure 8.1 for a visual depiction and Table 8.1 for a description of the structures of scaffolding). Some forms of scaffolding alleviate stress on one parent while increasing it for another. Some are more egalitarian but create substantial stress for both parents. Some structures are more or less isolating, complicated, or fragile. The structures of scaffolding shape the possibilities and constraints of everyday life.

Single Scaffolding occurs when one person (usually not engaged in full-time work) takes on the bulk of the invisible work to manage the home; in so doing, this person devotes themselves to

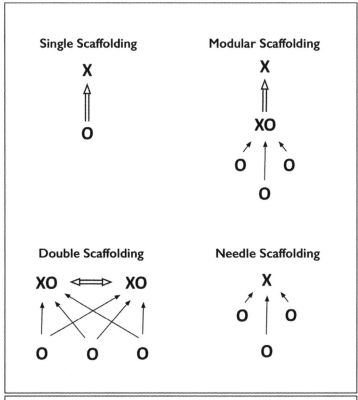

Single Scaffolding

Modular Scaffolding

Double Scaffolding

Needle Scaffolding

LEGEND
X   Person striving for one or more myths of perfection
O   Person or entity scaffolding Person X
    (doing some or all of the invisible work so X can pursue myths)
XO Person simultaneously striving for the myths of perfection and
    scaffolding someone else who is striving

FIGURE 8.1 Scaffolding Visualizations

supporting—scaffolding—their spouse's efforts to uphold the myths.[2] The structure supports one person in their efforts be an Ideal Worker, Perfect Parent, and/or Ultimate Body. For example, a parent (Person X) could start each day at the gym, put in a full day at work, and come home to spend quality time with the kids over dinner, but only if someone else (Person O) takes the kids to school and picks them up, prepares and serves food, and takes care of everything else in running a household and managing a family's relations to the community. The other person does all of the invisible work for the family, even if they too are attempting to enact one or more of the myths.

	Single Scaffolding	Modular Scaffolding	Double Scaffolding	Needle Scaffolding
Description	Principal person in charge of Mental, Emotional, Coordinating, and Physical Work Specialized role in which person doing invisible work supports the efforts of another Privileges one worker's career	Principal person as the central hub Hub manages Mental Work and does extensive Coordinating and Emotional Work with paid and unpaid help Offloads much of the Physical Work Having someone act as hub often privileges one worker's career	Two people jointly share Mental, Emotional, and Coordinating Work Physical Work done jointly or coordinated with outside help (paid or unpaid) Does not privilege one career	Principal person with sole responsibility for Mental, Emotional, and Coordinating Work Relies upon paid and unpaid help for assistance with Physical Work Maintaining career is crucial for financial stability
Benefits	Stable and flexible Bounds Coordinating and Emotional Work within family Little conflict because decision making concentrated in one person Flexible to changes in demand Uncomplicated	Agile and resilient Multiple people help with invisible work, especially Physical Work Able to redeploy help when demands change	Shared Greater equity in distribution of all aspects of invisible work Duplicated knowledge of details of invisible work provides stability and flexibility	Autonomous Little conflict because decision making concentrated in one person

	Single Scaffolding	Modular Scaffolding	Double Scaffolding	Needle Scaffolding
Challenges	Separated	Centralized	Stressful	Precarious
	Isolating for solo support; financial pressure on primary worker	Requires financial or familial resources	Ongoing negotiation of all invisible work between couple	Requires financial or familial resources
	Asymmetry can lead to tension and dissatisfaction for both persons	Pressure on hub to manage invisible work can lead to frustration	The more both prioritize career, the greater the stress	Changes in schedule or help require major adjustment
	Not compatible with two full-time jobs			
Examples	Nick & Rebecca Stewart	Dave & Lisa Phillips	Teresa & Chip Davies	Nancy Huron
	Roger & Linda Waldo	Jay & Olivia Shah	Franco & Katrina Garcia	Tim Andrews
	Brenda & Cory Finchley			

TABLE 8.1 Structures of Scaffolding

Modular Scaffolding is built on one person acting as the hub for invisible work (Person XO), engaging in a substantial amount of Mental, Coordinating, and Emotional work while relying on (or outsourcing) a network of paid and unpaid help (Persons O) to do some portion of the Physical Work. By relieving themselves of some of the burden of Physical Work, and cultivating sufficient scaffolding, the person who acts as the coordinating hub has the opportunity to live a version of the myths.[3]

To the primary worker (Person X), Single and Modular Scaffolding may be experienced as identical. For example, a parent could come home to a clean house, fed children, and an organized home without it being apparent (or relevant) who is doing the work to make it all happen—Physical Work could be performed by their spouse or people the spouse has hired, cajoled, or developed friendships with. To the hub, a Modular Scaffolding structure is a very different life: a life of less Physical Work but intensive amounts of Mental, Coordinating, and Emotional Work required to maintain a lattice of scaffolding.[4]

Double Scaffolding appears in families in which spouses do their best to share the invisible work, including the Physical and the Mental Work.[5] These couples engage in Coordinating and Emotional Work with each other (checking in, dividing responsibilities, and regular gestures of kindness and appreciation). They often engage outside help for support (Persons O), but share or divide the tasks of hiring and coordinating. In this structure each parent (Persons XO) is afforded time to enact some version of the myths around working, parenting, and exercising while keeping up with the invisible work. The day-to-day management of hectic lives can be stressful for both parents, especially when both partners strive to be Ideal Workers.

In the final structure, *Needle Scaffolding*, a sole person holds the weight of the invisible work while also working full-time.[6] In families with a single working parent, a sole worker (Person X) has no choice but to find scaffolding. Needle Scaffolding relies on a variety of supports: paid help and often an assortment of friends and family members who help manage logistics and the Physical Work (Persons O). The lone worker is, by default, in charge of all the Mental Work and regularly engages in Emotional and Coordinating Work to maintain a critical network of external help.

SINGLE SCAFFOLDING: BRENDA AND CORY FINCHLEY

Bobby is the slowest eater of the Finchley clan. Tonight, Brenda came home later from work than usual, and Cory had based the time of dinner on her arrival. Now, minutes before bedtime, their younger children finished and excused, Cory and Brenda are sitting at the table trying to get Bobby to finish his dinner. Cory sighs, checking the clock. When Bobby finally takes his last agreed-upon bite, Cory hops up to clear the plates and does the dishes—ready for some alone time in the kitchen. Brenda orchestrates the return of the toys strewn in the front room to their rightful places: dinosaurs, blocks, dolls, a giant foam alphabet mat. While she is hustling the kids toward bed, Cory enjoys a much needed moment of quiet. It is a long day managing three young children—only one of whom is in full-time school.

Finishing the dishes, Cory makes three sippy cups—two with water and one with milk—to bring to the kids before bed. Two-year-old Tabitha wants her zebra pajamas. They are dirty but Cory promises to wash them tomorrow. Narrowly avoiding a PJ-inspired tantrum, he sits with Tabitha in the rocking chair in her room while she drinks her milk, her bedtime routine.

Meanwhile, Brenda supervises the boys' toothbrushing and moves them toward bed. After a warning not to jump on the bed, she tucks four-year-old Kyle and seven-year-old Bobby into their beds to await dad's goodnight. After dad comes in for a kiss the boys fall quickly asleep. It's 7:46 p.m.

Cory and Brenda meet on the sofa and catch each other up on their day. At work Brenda found a performance review that had been missing; Cory has been planning Bobby's birthday party for next weekend. She asks who is coming. He got one face-to-face RSVP, one email RSVP, and one by text. He explains who the kids are—there's the "Good Jack" and the "Bad Jack." At 8:00 they turn on their Monday night television show. A few minutes in, Cory hears Kyle whimper and cocks his ear, listening to see if he will wake. He doesn't.

Cory is dragging the next morning. The kids go to bed promptly, but Kyle regularly wakes up with night terrors and wants his dad to soothe him. Cory likes that his kids automatically turn to him, but it can make for a long day when he's sleep deprived. After they walk Bobby to school in the morning, Cory takes Kyle and Tabitha to Costco. It's good to get out of the house. Brenda used the last of the creamer in her coffee this morning, and he wants to check the children's book section to see what he might find for Bobby's birthday. He finds a book with six different Dr. Seuss stories for only $10. A good deal. He also picks up food for Bobby's baseball team because he's on for snacks next week. He finds a plastic tub to store the dog food for only $4. The kids eat samples in the store, which makes lunch pretty simple. When they get home, Cory makes sure to wash Tabitha's zebra pajamas with the other laundry.

Fast forward two weeks. After a successful birthday party for Bobby last weekend, this Saturday Brenda has to meet some clients at the hotel at 4:00 p.m. Shortly after she leaves, Tabitha trips and hits her head up high on the temple. Lots of bleeding. Cory thinks it might need stitches. He doesn't hesitate to take everyone to the ER for a Saturday adventure. As he grabs shoes and steers the kids to the car, he texts Brenda asking about the location of the insurance cards. She texts the location with a query, "Why?" Cory intentionally delays responding. There is no point in telling her about Tabitha now—she would just turn around and come home and there's nothing she can do. No need to worry her. She might as well do the meeting. Emergency dealt with, he texts Brenda while she's on her way home an hour and a half later. Turned out to be just a little nick. All is fine.

Single Scaffolding privileges one career in a family. Brenda Finchley can act like an Ideal Worker because Cory is there to pick up the slack. He does most of the Physical Work and the Mental Work of the household. He plans birthday parties and knows the names of the kids at school. He remembers what needs to be purchased and purchases it. While stay-at-home fathers are still somewhat rare, Cory acts as the solo support in a Single Scaffolding structure.[7]

Not only does Cory scaffold Brenda as an Ideal Worker, he also scaffolds her parenting. Cory's invisible work allows Brenda to show up to baseball games just as they begin and come home in time to ask engaged questions at family dinner. He does the Coordinating Work of figuring out her timing, the Physical Work of preparing dinner and doing dishes, and the Mental Work of deciding what to cook. By engaging the kids when she gets home and orchestrating toy pickup after dinner, Brenda helps with some of the Physical Work. This facilitates Cory getting a bit of uninterrupted alone time in the kitchen after a day of childcare and household duties. But it also allows Brenda a few moments of quality time with her kids.

Single scaffolding is flexible because the solo support is available to take care of an issue—both the regular and the unexpected, like doctor's visits. Tabitha isn't the only one who has made a visit to the ER. Kyle recently knocked out one of his front teeth, and last year Bobby busted his lip at school. Each time Cory was there and able to drop everything to deal with the injury. This form of scaffolding is also stable because the invisible work is concentrated in one person. It involves minimal Coordinating and Emotional Work because there are fewer people to keep track of and appreciate. And Cory does the Physical and Mental Work in the way that he wants it to be done.

Brenda and Cory are responsive to each other throughout the day, and the ability to communicate by text keeps the string of connection between them drawn tight. Thus when Cory chooses to ignore Brenda's text asking why he needs the insurance cards when he is en route to the ER, he is challenging the expectations of constant availability fostered by mobile devices. Even this decision is a form of Emotional Work: Cory is purposefully shielding Brenda from worrying about Tabitha so she can focus on work.[8]

Brenda engages in more Emotional Work with her spouse than other primary workers we observed. She takes the pulse of the household when she walks in the door and inquires about the details of Cory's day when they relax on the couch in the evening. She supports his passion for photography even though her bosses tease her about leaving early every Tuesday at 4:00 p.m. so he can take a photography class. Brenda shares,

> I think he should always have *something*—he tries to take one class a semester, sometimes two, just to have an outside-of-little-kids interest. I mean, really, it's so important to do something other than just be here— it's nice for me to have something other than just work, and it's nice for him to have something other than just home.

Being the solo support and maintaining the home is, in essence, an isolating full-time job. Taking on a full-time job, or even most part-time jobs, while doing all the invisible work is nearly impossible (particularly while the children are young and not in school). We see solo supports struggle with this realization. Cory talks about the loss of his professional identity— the job he left because it didn't make financial sense. Even if only temporary, giving up a professional identity can cause personal stress and dissatisfaction, not to mention financial insecurity for the stay-at-home parent.[9]

Single Scaffolding focuses the full brunt of the household work on one person. Even though Brenda notices, appreciates, and attempts to shoulder some invisible work, she leaves Cory and the children for long periods each day to go to work. Occasionally irritation bubbles up. One evening Cory and the kids arrive home at 7:26 p.m. after baseball practice. The kids expect Brenda to be waiting for them only to discover that she is not home when they pull into the driveway. Although Cory and Brenda have been texting about her working late, the immediate chorus of, "Where is mommy!!" receives a curt and irritated reply, "She's still at work. She probably won't be home until NINE." And when Tabitha asks, "Why is

Mommy not home?" Cory cannot help but exclaim, "That's a good question!" When Brenda works late, he doesn't get a break.

People who act as solo supports can feel devalued while managing the invisible work.[10] Currently, Rebecca Stewart maintains the home and scaffolds Nick's efforts to be an Ideal Worker at SLH. They talked about this division of focus when the family decided to move to California for Nick to take the SLH position. But without any external help it is difficult for Rebecca to strive to be the Perfect Parent to four young children while doing all the invisible work: the kids are often late to their various activities; one child may end up playing video games while she helps another with homework; and dinner is rarely as healthy and complex as she would like.

Rebecca looks to Nick to scaffold some of her parenting efforts but repeatedly fails to enlist his help. As Rebecca recounts, "Sometimes he just gets caught up working and kind of loses track of time . . . when I don't call him he'll say, 'Why didn't you call me?' So he just kind of expects that I will." The ease of sending texts and making phone calls means that Rebecca trades Physical Work for Coordinating Work by allowing Nick to assume she is his source of just-in-time information and reminders. The frustration increases when she follows his request and calls him in the evening to ask if he is coming home in time for dinner—and the call goes to voicemail. Rebecca feels resentful of the silence.[11]

Rebecca's experience is not unique. Invisible work is generally devalued: by Nick, by Rebecca, by most of these families, and by society as a whole. It is not clear that Nick understands the exhausting challenge of wrangling four small children, and his lack of responsiveness to her texts and calls means that Rebecca is always the parent of last resort. When Rebecca gets frustrated, Nick quietly retreats—staying in the driveway on a work call until after the youngest kids are safely tucked into bed.

Nick, as the primary worker supported by a Single Scaffolding structure, feels a different set of stresses. Nick struggles with migraine headaches and reports the highest level of work-family conflict among these SLH workers, even with Rebecca as his full-time support. The financial pressure to provide, combined with Ideal Worker expectations and a desire to be successful, make it difficult for him to push back on work demands.[12] He says, "I've been so busy, sometimes our family life is better if I just don't come home if I'm going to be stressed out and need to work." He is confident that Rebecca has the household covered. Nick knows that

Rebecca will lead the family, set the agenda, and, as he lovingly describes, "Just [be] kind of the glue to the whole place." With Rebecca focused on the home, Nick focuses on being an Ideal Worker: "Someone's gotta make some money in this world."

Why can Brenda grasp what Cory needs at the end of the day while Nick fails to understand that Rebecca needs a break? Perhaps the switching of gender roles makes a difference for Brenda and Cory.[13] With each in an atypical role for their sex, Brenda cannot help but notice what she, as the wife, is "supposed" to be doing around the house. Cory similarly understands the demands of being an Ideal Worker and how his work helps her and the family: "I've made the concession to that [her career]. It's like, if that is my part, to allow her to give it her all, I can't have any animosity or resentment. That's not fair." Like same-sex couples who make deliberate decisions about who does what, Cory and Brenda understand and appreciate what each is doing for the other and how this contributes to the well-being of the family in a way that we do not observe when men and women hold more gender-typical roles.[14]

For many, the Single Scaffolding structure is not a permanent model. Rather, families who can afford it choose this structure when kids are young and need constant care. Rebecca and Cory both talk about going back to work eventually. Linda Waldo and her family also have a Single Scaffolding structure. She didn't work when the kids were little. Now her children are teenagers and she is underemployed: working a family-friendly job as a lunch lady in her son's junior high. As her kids get older she is actively planning her "next move" (either returning to her occupation as an accountant or figuring out something new such as being a real estate agent). Stay-at-home parents often go in and out of the workforce.[15] But when a family tries to organize around two careers, Single Scaffolding is insufficient, and families begin to cultivate outside help.

MODULAR SCAFFOLDING: DAVE AND LISA PHILLIPS

Lisa Phillips leaves at 7:00 a.m. to make it on time to her middle-school classroom in a low-income district thirty minutes away. To make the morning manageable, she packs school bags and sports clothes for each of her three kids the night before. There is always something to pack for, and keeping up with laundry is near impossible—she is embarrassed but resigned to the large piles of clean laundry that litter the upstairs alcove. Each child is in at least two sports at any point in time. Today is one of the three days a week that Lisa drops the kids off at her mom's house in the morning, often hungry and in their pajamas (but with packed bags!). Grandma Edith makes the kids' lunches, feeds them breakfast, and gets them to school on time. The other two days a week Grandma comes at 8:00 a.m. when Dave leaves for work and takes the kids to school.

When her school day ends, Lisa's day as a mom begins. Today her school had a half day, and she is on a mission to buy the baseball pants that Harry's baseball coach requested—the ones with the stripe running down the side. Two sporting goods stores later, she scores the pants and makes it to the local elementary school in time to pick up thirteen-year-old Danielle and seven-year-old Harry. A mom friend with similar-aged kids has dropped Danielle at the elementary school while picking up her own child. By getting her kids in one place this friend is a mini lifesaver. Lisa has a close relationship with many of the parents, and she appreciates that "mom friends are always there if I need help with my kids." Today it shaved a few minutes off of the frenzied afternoon schedule. The three of them make a quick stop at home (Harry forgot his cleats) before heading to the baseball game. They arrive a few minutes after 4:00 p.m. Danielle settles onto the bleachers while Lisa visits with the other moms. Eventually Lisa sits down with her daughter and texts the swimming coach, giving him a heads up that Danielle will be late tomorrow afternoon because she has soccer tryouts. Lisa jokingly texts, "I hope you can forgive us," with a smiley face and prayer hands emoticons. Lisa thinks the coach is a bit of a jerk, but she is willing to make nice because she doesn't want her daughter to be punished for being late to practice.

Dave bounds onto the field. He came directly from work, changing at the office. Last year Lisa carted Harry to all his games and watched from the bleachers. This year Dave stepped up and volunteered to be an assistant coach. Athletic by nature, he enjoys being involved and it is a good justification for urging Harry to show more spunk on the field.

At 5:45 Lisa answers a call from Grandma Edith. Edith bought twelve-year-old Lauren dinner after picking her up from soccer, and the two of them are at home. Lisa and Danielle leave the baseball game a bit early, picking up pizza for a very hungry Danielle on the way. While Danielle gobbles some pizza, Lisa and Edith confer briefly about the day. Then Edith heads home to eat dinner with her husband.

At 7:25, Dave and Harry arrive home. As they walk in the door Lisa gestures to the pizza box on the dining room table. Phone to her ear, Lisa chats with Dave's mom to arrange a get-together for Saturday evening. Dave heads upstairs to change. Lisa hangs up the phone and Harry pleads with Lisa for plain noodles instead of pizza. She obliges with a grumble, filling a saucepan with water as she fires off requests to the girls: "Danielle turn off the TV and start on your homework; Lauren, have you studied for your math test?" Both girls trudge slowly upstairs. She says to no one in particular, "Why isn't anyone doing what I say?"

After eating his noodles, Harry sits at the dining room table to work on his English homework. Dave returns with his laptop and sits beside Harry while checking email. Fifteen emails came in during the game, making Dave a bit nervous. It's now 8:08, and Lisa sits on the other side of Harry, helping him with a reading passage on Sammy Sosa. Lauren bounds downstairs excitedly to share a good grade on an English test—earning a high five from Dad and a smile from Mom. At 8:28 Danielle yells down for Dave to help format her science study guide. Dave heads upstairs to help, and Lauren follows to work on a paragraph for English.

Danielle has finished the study guide, and she heads downstairs in a panic when she realizes she can't find the teacher's email to check her answers. Lisa reminds her that she gets those emails too and pulls up the study guide answers on her phone. Lauren comes down to read Lisa her English paragraph. Lisa suggests one word change and declares it "beautiful." Approaching 9:30, Lisa helps the girls finish their homework, Dave directs Harry to put on his pajamas and brush his teeth.

After the girls go to sleep around 10:00, Lisa texts her mom to confirm the next morning's schedule. She ends the exchange with a smiley face text and the words "you're the best!!!!!" Lisa climbs into bed to watch an episode of Nashville *(her favorite). She generally tries to go to sleep by 11:00. Dave sets his alarm for 5:50 a.m. so Lisa can run before work. Dave acts as her backup because Lisa doesn't trust herself to wake up to the alarm.*

DAVE AND LISA PHILLIPS each have full-time jobs, three activity-packed children's schedules, and both exercise regularly. Managing it all is only possible because of the web of support that Lisa has cultivated. This Modular Scaffolding allows Dave and Lisa to both enact versions of each of the myths while keeping their lives generally afloat. Life feels sustainable to Dave and Lisa. Unlike in a Single Scaffolding structure, however, Lisa does not do it alone. Yes, she engages in invisible work. And Dave helps. But their resilience comes from a web of support: Lisa's mom, neighbors, and other parents.

In Modular Scaffolding, one person acts as the central hub, offloading as much of the Physical Work as possible with a large network of potential helpers. Lisa shoulders the Coordinating Work. The texting starts first thing in the morning and ends right before bed. As Lisa explains, "As soon as I get to school I text my mom the schedule for the afternoon so she knows what her little part in it is. And then if it involves Dave, then I'll let him know. If it doesn't involve him, then I just let him be." By picking up Henry (with the right pants) and getting him to baseball (with his cleats), Lisa is scaffolding Dave's ability to fulfill his work responsibilities and be the Perfect Parent. He can show up directly from work and coach his son's baseball team.

Lisa keeps a number of other moms on speed dial for both repeated engagements (regular car pools) and just-in-time help taking kids to and from activities. Along with Grandma Edith, these friends support Lisa and Dave as Perfect Parents whose children are fully engaged in after-school sports. Lisa is also close with her neighbor Susie. An animal lover who works from home, Susie walks the family's elderly dog three to four times a day. Susie confides, "I don't have kids; the animals in the neighborhood are like my kids." Susie scaffolds Lisa and Dave by taking dog walking off the to-do list: Lisa and Dave's deep and long-term commitment to their neighborhood and community fosters their Modular Scaffolding.[16]

With this network of support, Lisa stands in the middle, orchestrating it all. In addition to a large amount of Coordinating Work, Lisa does most of the Mental Work: knowing who needs to be where when, who is overdue for a check-up, or who needs new pants. But it is hard to overstate how much Lisa's mom, Edith, does to make their life manageable. When the oldest girls were three and one, Edith quit her full-time job to help out because she didn't want "a nanny raising her grandkids." Edith's husband is able to financially support the two of them. So for the past eleven years, the kids have had their Grandma on hand.

Edith takes on a lion's share of the Physical Work of transporting kids; making lunches; grocery shopping; and making dinner: putting spaghetti and meatballs in the crockpot, leaving a homemade cake on the counter, or sliding a rotisserie chicken into the fridge and texting Dave and Lisa to let them know what they can count on for dinner. In this way, Edith does some of the Mental Work as well. She generally knows what is (or most likely isn't) in the fridge and what to get at the store. And while Lisa does all the laundry and Dave is in charge of keeping the house tidy, Grandma occasionally takes it upon herself to run a vacuum or scrub a floor—to do the "deep clean that they never get to."

Modular Scaffolding with its lattice of supports requires extensive Emotional Work. This falls on Lisa. She maintains close ties with the many mom friends who regularly help her, and she is always attuned to Grandma Edith's state of mind. Regular texts of appreciation and joking emoticons accompany the daily volley of coordinating messages between Lisa and her mom.

Over Lisa's spring break, the two had a leisurely breakfast, chatting and catching up (and they went to get their taxes done). Lisa enjoys breakfast with her mom. But it is also part of the Emotional Work she does to make sure her mom knows how much she is valued. Dave and Lisa agree that she has a right to pipe in, given her role in their lives, even if they do not always implement the suggestions. They support Edith's rules when she is alone with the kids: no devices in the car, unload the dishwasher, eat everything on your plate.

With Lisa's supports in place, Modular Scaffolding can be an agile and resilient structure. Agile because Lisa acts as a central hub for coordinating and can find help if an issue arises. Resilient because there are, ideally, a number of people on the bench who can be called upon to pick a kid up from school, grab something at the store, or step in at the last minute.

Cultivating and maintaining Modular Scaffolding, however, is an ongoing effort. People come and go as kids change sports teams, babysitters quit, and neighbors move—and someone may get sick or be out of town. Relying solely on unpaid support from friends and family, Lisa's scaffolding blurs the lines between friendship and support.[17] Lisa values these people for more than their instrumental benefits. Such informal ties and personal relationships give the family a sense of rootedness, connection, and community.[18]

That said, Modular Scaffolding is not without its challenges. Dave and Lisa's shared attachment to the Perfect Parent myth intensifies their exhaustion: their three kids participate in a total of nine enrichment activities. With their busy schedules, Lisa remarks that they "are never all in the same house at the same time anymore!" Dave and Lisa "divide and conquer" all week long, calling on various forms of scaffolding (including each other) to get through.

And as the hub, Lisa runs herself ragged. Lisa's workday typically ends at 4:00 and she doesn't work summers—lending to the assumption that she can take on the bulk of the Mental, Coordinating, and Emotional Work for the family. As a teacher, her work schedule is well-aligned with the children's school day, and she has cultivated a great deal of support for the Physical Work. Yet the invisible work of the household happens alongside maintaining her career.

The time and stress associated with being the hub make it a challenge for her or him to delve fully into professional life (particularly given the prevalence of Ideal Worker norms in many workplaces). We see this compromise in Jay and Olivia Shah's family. The Shah family is fortunate that Jay makes enough money to support the family. And Olivia explains that she maintains her travel business "more to keep my sanity" than because they need the income. But this reality also means that she feels unable to fully engage in her professional career. According to Olivia, "Jay is definitely the breadwinner in our family, so I think that I need to prioritize supporting him more than I need to focus on my work. And that's really just where I am right now."

This can be hard for a hub that believes strongly in the Ideal Worker myth. According to Olivia, "As a stay-at-home mom there is definitely that, 'Oh, yeah. I cook for the family. I take care of the kids.' But there is also the feeling of, you are not good enough. Or you are not quite productive enough. Or you are not smart enough. Because I had worked before, and then you don't, and you feel like, I am going brain dead." In American society, the career that takes the back seat is often the woman's.[19]

GENDERED DIVISION OF LABOR

When asked about the details of the daily schedule, Dave Phillips nods sheepishly to Lisa for the answer. They both know—and don't question—that she has it all in her head. Lisa knows that Harry needs striped baseball pants and texts Danielle's swim coach about the scheduling conflict—doing a bit of Emotional Work. Lisa keeps track of homework (asking about Lauren's math test and having the teacher's emails on hand) and coordinates with Grandma Edith to make sure everyone is fed and transported. That's not to diminish Dave's help with the Physical Work. He regularly does the dishes and picks up around the house. He makes everyone's bed before going to work. He is in charge of all house cleaning (except when Edith takes it upon herself to run the vacuum). Dave is always there to help—but he isn't doing the Mental Work and keeping it all in his head. He isn't doing the Coordinating Work; he is *being* coordinated. And he doesn't feel the same responsibility for everyone's feelings and take on the Emotional Work.

To say that Dave and Lisa have a set of gendered assumptions about their roles does not negate the many ways that they reject the sexist assumptions built into the Ideal Worker, Perfect Parent, and Ultimate Body myths. They *both* spend evenings and weekends watching (or coaching) the endless number of kids' sporting events. Both help with homework. Both cook and clean. They have remained in their community despite a better job opportunity for Dave out of state. But the privilege of coaching falls to those who are being scaffolded themselves: people who enable someone like Dave to engage more fully in the Perfect Parent myth.

In Single and Modular Scaffolding, the extensive Mental, Coordinating, and Emotional Work remains largely invisible and often performed by women.[20] Many women who do get help from a spouse still often find it easier to deploy their spouse to do Physical Work (for example, take a child to a birthday party, go to the dentist, or drop something off at the post office) than have that person share in the Mental Work (such as RSVP-ing to the party, buying and wrapping a gift, scheduling the dentist appointment, or calling the internet company when service goes out). Men helping with Physical Work still leaves women with the Coordinating Work and the Emotional Work of appreciating their spouse's efforts.

The Finchley family has resolved these gendered norms by simply switching roles: Brenda works and Cory does the "women's work" of being the default parent and doing the invisible work as the solo support. For the Phillips family, Lisa and her mother do this work. It's a lot for Lisa: having a career, being a mom, coordinating and keeping everything afloat. But neither of them thinks that Dave should be doing more of it. Their Modular Scaffolding solution has been to find others to help. The popular press and blogs suggest that this is not unique, and the prevailing assumption is that mothers bear the brunt of the invisible work.[21]

Invisible work as women's work extends beyond wives and mothers. We see gendered roles among the *others* who help Lisa and Dave. Because even when Lisa is not doing the Physical Work herself, other women are. Other moms help with carpool. Susie, their single female neighbor, walks the dog. And of course, Dave and Lisa rely on Lisa's mom, Grandma Edith. This multigenerational support from her mother is a gift to Lisa, and it liberates her from the full responsibility of the household. But it also perpetuates the fact that this *is* women's work. The Phillips family is not unusual in this way; two-thirds of our families rely (or have relied) on a mostly female network of extended family for caregiving.

In other families, household help are paid. Rebecca and Nick Stewart pay for a house-cleaning service that employs women. Nancy Huron hires a pair of sisters for babysitting services and pays for school day care, staffed mostly by women. Olivia Shah pays Rosa and Martina to help with house cleaning and daily chores. When this work is hired out, poor and immigrant women are often the backbone of support—helping privileged women accomplish more rather than raising the value of the work itself.[22] The gendered expectation is unquestioned and itself invisible.

In both Single Scaffolding and Modular Scaffolding, the person in the center of the scaffolding structure is spending substantial time and energy supporting the person with the primary career (though Modular Scaffolding can enable the hub to focus on a career as well).[23] In families in which both parents are advancing their careers and living in terms of the myth of the Ideal Worker, we occasionally see structures emerge in which parents attempt to share all forms of invisible work more equally.

DOUBLE SCAFFOLDING: TERESA AND CHIP DAVIES

Chip Davies walks in the door with seven-year-old Max trailing a few steps behind. Wearing t-shirts and jeans, Chip and Max have just returned from Chip's office. Max has his Nintendo 3DS open in his hands and hums along with the Mario music coming from the handheld game device. Chip drops his keys by the front door and tells Max he's going to take a quick shower. Max turns on the television, leaving the 3DS game open on the couch, and circles the coffee table as he watches the TV.

This is a new routine. Max attended the after-school care program at their local elementary school until about two months ago. Chip and Teresa had traded off picking Max up at 6:00 p.m. Teresa would often stay a few minutes to check in about the day and make friendly chatter with the care providers. But Max started having run-ins with the staff. They called Chip at work when Max walked to the after-school portable from the front parking lot rather than from the playground. Another day at pickup the staff outlined to Teresa how Max hadn't wanted to be in the room where the other students were playing. Chip and Teresa didn't feel like the staff was giving Max a chance, but there was little they could do. The final straw was one afternoon when Max wasn't feeling well and didn't want to play outside. The ratio of kids inside to outside meant that the staff needed Max to stay outside. Max lost it. Later that week Max came down with a cold and was home sick all week. Chip and Teresa simply gave up and pulled Max out of after-school care.

Now Chip picks Max up after school at 3:30 p.m. and brings him to work for several hours. Chip is an engineer at a company doing contract work. He can make up the hour he misses each day picking up Max by working every other Friday (a day he usually has "off" to keep his hours at a stable forty). Max is quiet, and Chip's colleagues don't seem to be too bothered with Max hanging out in Chip's cubicle. Teresa is happy with the new arrangement. "Kids just need to be kids and sit and play."

Today Chip and Max picked up a Chipotle quesadilla on the way back to his office, making it a late lunch. His curly head bent over his 3DS, Max moves between his camp chair and the inflatable mat from REI in the corner of Chip's cubicle. At the end of the day, Chip realizes they forgot their tae kwon do outfits this morning, so they skip the 7:00 p.m. class and head straight home. Teresa arrives home at 7:20, and Teresa and Chip chat about their days. At 8:15 Chip sets up Max's laptop with a math puzzle game for him to play. Chip and Teresa both have their laptops out. They check Facebook, track packages, and peruse bike gadgets on Amazon. Teresa also does some work. Teresa asks Chip if he's hungry at 8:38. But he's not. After Chipotle, Chip ate the granola bar from the work vending machine that Max hadn't wanted. Teresa happily agrees when Chip offers to make her some sourdough toast. She's eight weeks pregnant and has been having a hard time keeping food down. Teresa tells Chip that she texted her mom and asked her to come spend the night. She realized they had an early ultrasound with the doctor in the morning, and she asked her mom to take Max to school.

At 9:15 Chip asks Teresa if she's heard anything about a science project due this week. Teresa queries, "No, I haven't. Have you looked on the classroom web page?" Chip replies, "Yes. I looked on the web page. I didn't really see anything. But the sheet that came home with homework said that there is no spelling this week. They should be working on their science project due Thursday." But Teresa and Chip have not heard about this. Chip asks Max, "Do you know anything about the science project? What is it?" Max continues playing his game. Chip continues, "I am not going to ask you to do it tonight. I just want to know the truth. You need to be honest with me. Nothing is going to be different tonight, but I need to know what your science project is." Max says, "Well, it has something to do with the lifecycle of a butterfly." Teresa and Chip laugh, pleased to be making some progress. Teresa googles "lifecycle of a butterfly." Chip doesn't get a response about when it's due. But it's better than last week when Max mentioned in the morning that he needed to dress up like Martin Luther King Jr. for wax museum day. They decide to leave the butterfly project alone tonight and return to their laptops. This is where Teresa's mom finds them when she arrives at 9:53.

TERESA AND CHIP DAVIES maintain two full-time careers. Teresa is a director at SLH; Chip an engineer. Double Scaffolding has two parents and two primary workers involved with the Physical, Mental, Coordinating, and Emotional Work. Despite the recent hiccup to their daily routine, Teresa and Chip are used to sharing the full range of invisible work.

They share the Physical Work. Chip regularly does laundry; Teresa cleans as she goes, grabbing a wipe when she walks in the door to wash a spot off the wall. Grocery shopping is either a joint activity on the weekend or done by whoever remembers on the way home. Each parent generally cooks for him or herself, asking the other if they want something. But they often just graze after eating a big lunch at work. They share taking Max to his regular doctor appointments and managing school drop-offs and pickups. Both were engaged in Emotional Work with the after-school childcare provider during conversations about Max's "transgressions." Teresa was more likely to stay and chat at the end of the day, but the school called Chip when there was a problem. They even share the Coordinating Work. Chip works out the summer camp schedule; Teresa will call her mom for backup. They share (and sometimes neglect) the Mental Work—they don't maintain a shopping list, and Max's school deadlines are hard to track. Chip is better at remembering dates. And Teresa often coordinates social events through Facebook.

Double Scaffolding means shared responsibility. Such distributed ownership requires a great deal of communication and negotiation between partners because decisions about who will do what are always in flux. In some families, the amount of negotiation is reduced by an agreed-upon specialization of certain types of invisible work.[24]

For Teresa and Chip, the daily figuring out of Max's school drop-offs and pickups is based on work demands. There is regular discussion about who will take Max to the doctor and who will schedule or cancel a visit. Teresa sometimes has a hard time getting out of the office, so Chip is used to updates by text. They deal with the occasional surprise of an empty refrigerator when no one went to the store. It helps that their parenting style does not reflect the Perfect Parent myth. They enroll Max in few activities (tae kwon do doesn't last long), family dinner is not part of their daily routine, and they are less attentive to homework and media restrictions than parents such as Rebecca Stewart. In fact, Teresa resists those social pressures and posts complaints on Facebook when someone makes a judgment about someone else's (or her) parenting. And while they both love to do long bike rides for good causes such as a yearly charity bike ride, neither is fully dedicated to the Ultimate Body.

Double Scaffolding allows and requires each adult to dedicate time and energy to work *and* home. Teresa and Chip each provide scaffolding for the other's efforts at working, parenting, and exercise. This provides them with flexibility to manage life's little glitches. It's working out for now, but Chip and Teresa miss the paid after-school childcare. It was predictable, easy, and always available. They paid to have the Physical Work of basic childcare covered for predictable hours. Chip's ability to step in when things reached a breaking point with Max's after-school care was a lifesaver. When a child doesn't fit in easily, much less has special needs, the formal nature of childcare programs (and schools) often fails the needs of families.[25]

In the long run, however, Chip and Teresa need more help. They turn to Teresa's mother. They move from their studio to a two-bedroom apartment, and Grandma lives with them during the week. On the weekend grandma helps with Teresa's nieces and nephews. Chip remembers how Teresa's mom showed up like "magic" to help when Max was born. They need that magic again, especially with another baby on the way. Teresa is fortunate she will get six weeks paid leave with the new baby. She can take up to six months unpaid leave according to California law (she decides on three months). She plans to come back for a few weeks during that three-month period, to get people through the year-end craziness.

It helps that Chip does not have the pressure to work extended hours and be fully available like Teresa and other SLH workers.[26] While he is a salaried engineer, as a contract worker he is actively discouraged from working over forty hours a week. Indeed, Double Scaffolding works better when only one parent has Ideal Worker demands.

DOUBLE SCAFFOLDING AND THE FALSE "CHOICE": FRANCO AND KATRINA GARCIA

Franco and Katrina Garcia also rely on Double Scaffolding. With two toddlers and both parents striving to be Ideal Workers, daily life can be stressful. While they often feel overwhelmed in the moment, they are proud of what they have accomplished in the aggregate. Katrina and Franco have staggered their days off to minimize outside childcare to four days a week—Katrina is home alone with the kids on Mondays and Franco is with them on Sundays. Saturday is their one day together as a family.

They have also negotiated complementary daily schedules. Katrina leaves early and Franco stays late. As the manager of a chain of bakeries, Katrina leaves between 4:15 and 5:15 a.m. and aims to be home at 4:00 p.m., but it's often closer to 5:00. Franco acts as "mom and dad in the morning," waking the kids and doing the morning routine. He leaves in the morning around 7:00 a.m., and he is usually back between 7:00 and 7:30 p.m. Katrina has the hours at the end of the day, and more often than not she makes dinner. Neither of their children are in school, and Katrina's half-sister, Carrie, lives with the family and serves as the primary caregiver four days a week. In order for this arrangement to work for everyone, they have clear start and end times for Carrie's workday. Carrie often spends the evenings in her room or goes out with friends. Her job is to provide childcare for Franco and Katrina—she doesn't do additional invisible work for the family.

Together, Franco and Katrina have established schedules that allow each parent to average over eleven hours away from home every day, with nearly fifty hours a week of face time in the office and forty- to sixty-minute commutes each. Franco and Katrina text during the day to keep each other updated on the schedule, check in when one has an important meeting, or request an item at the grocery store on the way home. Their Double Scaffolding becomes stressed when their work demands heighten simultaneously, but they communicate, negotiate, and generally juggle it all.

Although Franco and Katrina share the invisible work, it is not proportionate. Breakfast is simpler, the morning time shorter, and the children's needs fewer. The evenings (when Katrina is in charge) are longer and more demanding. Kids are cranky and Katrina is exhausted. She tries to get them outside for a bit, clean up the house, and make dinner. She carries more of the burden of the invisible work, even within their Double Scaffolding structure.

When women and their families take on the masculine Ideal Worker myth without rejecting the feminine Perfect Parent myth, working parents and mothers in particular feel the strain.[27] Although both Franco and Katrina are exhausted, it puts a particular strain on Katrina.

Katrina Garcia arrives home at 5:54 p.m. She is two hours late because of bad weather and traffic. The second she walks in the door, four-year-old Charlotte runs to the door, flinging herself on her mother declaring, "You're working too much!" Having been out of the house for over twelve hours, Katrina responds with a passionate affirmative, "I knoooooow!" and gives her daughter a hug. Katrina hands Charlotte some stickers to placate her, as two-year-old Matt starts grabbing at Katrina's phone. When Katrina gives him a flashlight instead he throws it to the ground and makes a fuss. She offers crayons, Legos, Elmo, bear. "No. No. No. No." Matt doesn't want any of those things and bursts into tears when Katrina turns to speak to Charlotte. Exasperated, Katrina says, "What do you want? I have been home ten minutes and you're making me crazy!" During this exchange, Carrie quietly disappears upstairs, officially "off" for the night.

And so it goes while Katrina tries to make pizza for the three of them. Franco is working late. At 6:45 when he texts to see how things are going, Katrina tells him that Matt is being a handful. Walking in the door at 7:40, Franco tries to do his part. He immediately takes both kids upstairs to put on their pajamas. Katrina picks up a few Legos and then sits on the couch to watch TV. Charlotte wanders down and sits next to her mom. When Franco brings Matt downstairs, Katrina reaches out to hold him. Franco replies kindly, "No, I'm giving you a break." Later when their son toddles over to Katrina, gesturing for a snack, Franco stops Katrina from getting up and says, "It's okay. Sit down. I can get it." At 8:10 Katrina starts doing the dishes. When Franco offers to do them, Katrina says she'd prefer to do them if he will keep Matt from crying. Franco nods. She is stretched to the limit.

Katrina Garcia is conflicted. She gets satisfaction from her work and her kids. Although the sheer amount of time that she's at work means that she misses things at home (as does Franco), she is equally committed to being an Ideal Worker and Perfect Parent. Despite her daily life being exhausting and stressful, Katrina gushes about the big picture.

> I'm just super happy. I feel very, very blessed for what I have. And to be given the opportunities at work that I have been given. . . . I know I work hard, and I show myself, and I prove myself, and my boss is very happy. . . . Home, too, I have two kids, I have a boy and girl; I have a house; I have a yard; I have a husband; we're all healthy. You know, all that stuff. . . . There's not really more that I'm wanting.

Katrina and Franco contribute almost equally to the household income, identify strongly with their careers, and share parental duties more than most. But the gendered assumptions of the (masculine) Ideal Worker, (feminine) Perfect Parent, and (women's) invisible work creep into every scaffolding structure—even those in which the parents attempt to share this work equally.

Franco feels pressure to be able to support the family financially. He describes the lessons he learned from his parents: "[T]he male role in my family was . . . well . . . I have to take care of my family, regardless of what happens." He says, "I would love to get myself to a position where Katrina doesn't have to work. Even if we had to change our lifestyle a little bit." His mom helped for a while when they lived closer to her, now it's Katrina's sister, but best of all, in Franco's mind, would be Katrina as primary caregiver. It's implicit that caregiving is a family responsibility, a woman's responsibility, and ideally the mother's responsibility. Franco acknowledges that these ideas are "just in my head, what I've always expected."

At the same time Franco supports Katrina's passion for her job. They work in the same industry and regularly compare notes about customers and problematic subordinates. Franco and Katrina feel the strain of contradicting ideals. Both love their jobs and support each other in striving to be Ideal Workers. They are both stretched thin. Both also love their children and carry gendered ideas about what is best for them. When circumstances change, Katrina makes a "choice" that she wouldn't have made if life had been easier and if gendered assumptions didn't prevail.

Several months after Katrina talked about how her boss appreciated her hard work, the owners of the bakery where Katrina works decide to sell. The new owners reorganize the staffing—putting her out of a job. Simultaneously, her sister, Carrie, moves away to get married, and Franco takes a new job with a higher salary and more responsibility. When it all happens at the same time, Katrina thinks she will "never regret the time with my kids" and stays home as the default parent. It was less of an active decision than a constellation of forces propelling her into the home full-time. Having Katrina at home fits Franco's image of a mother raising the children. Katrina misses the purpose and satisfaction she received from her job. But having a clean house, getting a full night's sleep, and running regularly is marvelous.[28] Her errands get done, she loses a few pounds, and she does more with the kids. Reducing the complexity of daily life brings real benefits and helps Katrina accept the gendered role for now.

Katrina and Franco's situation is not uncommon, but this opting out of the workforce has unanticipated costs.[29] Mothers return to the labor force with fewer opportunities and are penalized for violating a key element of the Ideal Worker: the prioritization of work over other domains of life.[30]

When it comes down to it, although Katrina "chooses" to prioritize family over work, it is a false choice. It's hard to maintain two full-time careers. If the demands of work and family were more compatible, the invisible work more visible and shared, and the daily struggle to enact incompatible myths not so overwhelming, Katrina certainly wouldn't have made this "choice." Katrina would rather both work and parent.[31] Reflecting on her work after being home for just a few months, Katrina is clearly nostalgic for the excitement and challenge of her professional job.

> Yes, I was doing fifteen people's jobs. . . . But I was fine, and we were moving forward, and I was having positive sales growth and we were good. . . . I really liked my job, and that's why I did it, you know. I liked the challenge of training new people and trying to hire and build a team . . . coming up with new ideas and trying to see if they are going to work. So as far as that stuff goes, I really liked it. . . . I would totally do it again. . . . I'm not even opposed to going back right now.

Katrina contemplates returning to the workplace. But she becomes momentarily deflated when she learns that Charlotte's kindergarten will be half-day. And grade school will be less than six-and-a-half hours a day (with one day a week getting out early!). How are they supposed to make that work? Katrina complains, "I'm like, where is the other hour and a half [of an eight-hour work day]? Like what is going on?"

Unsupportive school schedules are just one example of the incompatibility of the Ideal Worker and Perfect Parent myths for working parents. We were happy for Katrina when she gets what she wants and returns to work a year and a half later. She is satisfied and fulfilled by having a professional identity although, once again, generally exhausted.[32]

The imbalance in the division of labor, even within the Double Scaffolding structure, is not unusual. Studies of same-sex couples suggest that this is more an issue of time and value than sex or gender. Before children, same-sex couples tend to divide household work more equally than heterosexual couples.[33] Once children come into the picture, however, things change. When Ideal Worker expectations collide with the looming Perfect Parent myth, reality shifts. Parents are more likely to specialize, with one person taking on more of the household and parenting duties.[34] Ideal Worker expectations take precedence over critical domestic work such as caregiving and maintaining a home.[35]

It is a constant negotiation and struggle to make the Physical, Mental, Coordinating, and Emotional Work of scaffolding noticeable, no less shared. Yet the challenges of the myths of perfection, and the scaffolding they require, are no more apparent, and no more poignant, than among single parents.

NEEDLE SCAFFOLDING: NANCY HURON

Jessica is a sophomore in college. She has been babysitting for Nancy Huron for a year and a half—saving money to buy a motorcycle. Her classes end at 3:50 p.m. on Wednesdays, at which point she jumps in her car and goes to pick up eight-year-old Dylan and six-year-old Melody from after-school care. She is at the school by 4:20, grabs the kids, and heads straight to Melody's gymnastics class, which starts at 4:30. Jessica pulls in front of the studio and Melody runs in with her gymnastics bag banging against her side. After parking, Jessica and Dylan make their way upstairs to the parent viewing area. Jessica turns to Dylan and asks, "Do you have any homework?" Dylan says "No." Jessica isn't convinced, but Dylan is adamant: "I did it!" The two sit down among a dozen parents, siblings, and caregivers, to watch the gymnastics team practice. Dylan wanders over to a kid he recognizes and looks over his shoulder, watching him play iPad.

At 5:38 Jessica checks her phone. Nancy has texted her with the evening's dinner instructions. She sends a quick reply and goes back to watching gymnastics, her own homework on her lap. At 6:00 gymnastics is over, and the three drive to Nancy's house. Nancy sends another text clarifying that she won't be home until 7:30. Jessica isn't surprised.

By 6:25 Jessica has broccoli on the stove and frozen hamburgers in the microwave. She asks the kids for their spelling words. The kids have spelling tests every Friday, and Nancy has asked Jessica to help them study. Each kid pulls out a piece of blank paper, and Jessica quizzes them while preparing dinner: "Melody: fight. Dylan: frighten." They write their words down. At 6:31 she hands them each a plate with broccoli, a hamburger, and some cut watermelon that was in a Tupperware container in the fridge. Jessica stands at the kitchen island checking their words as they start eating.

At 6:58 the kids are done. Jessica returns their corrected spelling tests and asks them each to write the words they got wrong three times for practice. Then she sends them upstairs to take a shower. Jessica quickly clears their plates, rinses the dishes, and leaves them in the sink. Then she goes upstairs to help Melody (otherwise, according to Jessica, "she will use a half bottle of shampoo!"). A few minutes later Dylan comes downstairs, hair wet and wearing PJs. At 7:12 Melody and Jessica come downstairs as well.

At 7:24 Nancy walks in the door. Upon seeing his mom, Dylan gushes, "Mom! It's almost time for Ninjago!" Nancy lets him turn on the TV for his favorite 7:30 show, and the kids watch the last two minutes of Lego Star Wars while Jessica and Nancy stand at the counter chatting about the day. Nancy writes Jessica a check and confirms next week's plan while looking at the calendar on her phone: "Monday, Tuesday, Wednesday, overnight on Thursday, and I don't need Friday." By 7:40 Jessica is out the door.

Nancy puts the dishes into the dishwasher. It drives Nancy nuts that Jessica doesn't just load the dishwasher, and Nancy wonders if she just doesn't know better—"She's nineteen, she's young." But Nancy likes her. And she is glad that her schedule is so flexible this semester. They met when Jessica was working at the grocery store where Nancy takes the kids shopping every Saturday. One day, in response to Jessica's professional, "Can I help you?" Nancy joked, "Not unless you babysit." When Jessica said that she did, Nancy started using her for weekends, and eventually for weekly duties.

After loading the dishwasher Nancy grabs herself some cheese and crackers. They have almost no food in the house, but Nancy has no idea when she will be able to squeeze in a trip to the grocery store. Then she opens the kids' backpacks and takes out all the extra flyers and papers. Suddenly she exclaims, "Dylan! Do you have a field trip tomorrow? Oh, no! Do I have to pack you a lunch? I don't have any bread." He looks up from the TV and assures her, "No, it's only half day. We come back for lunch." She sighs, "Phew!"

At 8:00 Ninjago ends. Nancy turns off the TV. She flops down on the couch and both kids pile on top of her, laughing. They all end up sliding to the floor. Melody asks to stay up later. Nancy says no and corrals the kids upstairs for bedtime stories—on the futon in the upstairs landing. After the kids are in bed, Nancy works for two hours before heading to bed herself.

FOR SINGLE WORKING PARENT Nancy Huron, Needle Scaffolding is critical—and precarious. Nancy relies on others to help with life's perpetual juggling act. As with Single and Modular Scaffolding, all the invisible work is centralized in her. But unlike in those structures, she doesn't have a spouse that she can deploy to help. She does all the Mental Work and whatever Physical Work she doesn't pay for (in addition to childcare Nancy pays to have the house cleaned once a week). She also engages in a substantial amount of Coordinating and Emotional Work.

Nancy needs at least two babysitters at any point in time so she can call on one if the other gets sick or cancels at the last minute. Because she often uses college students for help, Nancy has to renegotiate the weekly schedule by semester as their class schedules change. She is also texting babysitters on a daily basis—updating them on dinner and her timing. All in all it is a *lot* of Coordinating Work. Nancy's life is a stark reminder of how much full-time workers rely on others to watch their children. For many, a spouse or grandparent can cover if an employed parent is running late or has an unexpected work request. Nancy doesn't have that luxury.

While babysitters might accommodate some flexibility in timing, Nancy simply cannot assume that coming home late or changing the schedule at the last minute will be tolerated.

Even though babysitters are paid help, Nancy makes sure her sitters feel heard and appreciated. She wants to keep these caregivers in her children's lives and wants them to be happy with their role in her family. Nancy treasures the "good ones," and has maintained relationships that border on friendship with several of her babysitters. If a babysitter texts her a photo of the kids, she will respond and be appreciative of the effort to keep her informed. While Jessica often leaves as soon as Nancy gets home, the previous babysitter liked to stay and chat in the evenings. Even though Nancy occasionally found this annoying (she wanted to change her clothes and spend what limited time she has at home with her kids), she always sat for a bit with the babysitter. Nancy recognizes the importance of that Emotional Work. A babysitter always has the choice to not work for her.

The after-school day care provider and summer camps that Nancy pays for offer different benefits and frustrations. There are the up-front challenges of organizing and planning: these forms of care require extensive Mental and Coordinating Work. Planning for summer camp each year is harder than forecasting a hotel. She makes a handwritten spreadsheet with rows for each child and columns for each week (she needs two possible camp locations and their costs). "It's like a maze" with different colored pens. During summer Nancy coordinates week by week. Each Sunday she verifies the location, drop-off and pickup times, and special considerations for the week; some camps want packed lunches, beach camp needs towels and bathing suits, gymnastics camp requires a clean leotard.

Then there is the money. Nancy puts the summer camps on her credit card in the spring and pays it off over the course of the summer. Even though such programs are not cheap, the costs are consistent and she is able to budget for them.[36] During the school year, formal day care is the most affordable option for her. As Nancy explains,

> I don't like it when they are in before- and after-care for so many hours. . . .
> But it is the only option I have, you know? I can't afford a babysitter all day
> long, or the hours that I need. I need someone both before and after school
> and that is tricky. I mean, babysitters would be double what I am paying.
> When I had a nanny, it was so expensive. I just can't afford that now.

Formal childcare provides a stable schedule and minimizes the daily Coordinating Work. Nancy can count on summer camps and after-school care to be stable (unless her kids are sick or they don't fit in well, like Teresa and Chip Davies's son, Max). The schedule is rigid, and pickup time does not accommodate a traffic jam or last-minute work request, but it's predictable. Truth be told, sometimes the rigid schedule is a welcome pushback to the intense Ideal Worker expectations. The day care center might not love a parent, or forgive them for being late, and they don't care that someone's boss emailed at 6:00 p.m. with one more request, but this lack of love and understanding also provides a legitimate excuse and a forcing function to get out the door, pick up the kids, and switch out of work mode (at least until the kids go to bed).

Nancy feels able to push back in small ways on the Ideal Worker expectations at SLH. This is because she's in a secure and valued position in a company that espouses these family priorities, and she works incredibly hard. She is willing to push back because it is the way she can spend quality time with her children and give them all the opportunities possible. Her babysitters scaffold her attempts to be an Ideal Worker by enabling her to put in the hours and occasionally travel while also supporting her aspirations to be a Perfect Parent (monitoring homework and escorting kids to various enrichment activities).

Nancy is always thinking ahead and making contingencies to get by. Her carefully orchestrated Needle Scaffolding feels like it is about to snap when her local grocery store moves the organic puffed cereal to a different aisle (she "just gave up and got Kix sugar cereal"). She comments, "One of the things I'm aware of with this is just how all the little things in life—the washing machine exploding, forgetting ziplock bags at the grocery store, etc.—really do . . . They are constant, but they are the things that make life seem unmanageable."

Nancy is not the person of last resort. She is the person of all resort. If after-school care calls, or the babysitter gets sick, she has to find the solution. It is true that she appreciates not having to negotiate and argue about what to do (Nancy is in charge). But Nancy has the responsibility of *always* being in charge. And while Nancy offloads as much as she can onto her babysitters, they can only do so much. She is constantly picking up the slack. If Dylan had actually needed lunch for his field trip, Nancy had a plan; they would have left early the next morning to stop by Starbucks for a turkey sandwich (and breakfast). But given that they already leave the house at 6:45 a.m. every morning, this is no small snag. The Physical Work of grocery shopping tends to put her over the top. She is planning McDonald's for dinner tomorrow because the kids will be too hungry to go to the grocery store when she picks them up from after-school care.

Although she doesn't have a grandparent in the wings, Nancy also benefits from informal support from friends. She relies heavily on her best friend and neighbor, Kelly. A stay-at-home mom with a two-year-old and a four-year-old, Kelly offers emotional support, practical support, and much-needed fun. Last year, when Melody broke her leg and Nancy had to leave work to take her to the doctor, Kelly was the one to get Dylan from school and bring him home. Kelly is there for Nancy in times of need. She is a critical addition to the paid help of after-school care and babysitters.

While Needle Scaffolding is, by definition, the most precarious, it is important to note that Nancy is keeping it all together. She is economically secure (though with the expense of childcare, saving money has proven impossible), loves her job, and ensures that her children are well cared for. Her time at home is generally calm and joyful—unlike the days when she and her ex-husband were together.[37]

SCAFFOLDING'S ROLE IN UPHOLDING THE MYTHS

Given the power of the Ideal Worker myth in U.S. society, it is tempting to assume that scaffolding operates primarily in service of the Ideal Worker—the invisible work of other people enabling one or both parents to stay at the office longer or travel at the drop of a hat. While this is definitely true, each myth on its own requires and benefits from the support of scaffolding.

The Perfect Parent needs the help of others in order to engage in the intensive parenting idealized by the myth. It is much easier to monitor homework and host the idealized family dinner if someone else is transporting kids to multiple activities, prepping food, cleaning, and doing some of the unglamorous work in the household. The Ultimate Body often needs someone to help carve out time to exercise and purchase the right ingredients for healthy meals. The more individuals strive to be Ideal Workers, Perfect Parents, or Ultimate Bodies (no less all three), the more they need the help and support of others. In an ironic turn, the more that people ascribe to the myths, the less time they have to develop and maintain the scaffolding structure that they need to pursue these dreams. Finding and maintaining scaffolding is not easy.

We witnessed the scaffolding structures employed by each of these families, but missing from this account is how families create the structures that work for them. For some, like Nancy Huron, there is no choice but to build a support structure. Others, like Lisa Phillips, prioritize the time to build a support system that works for them. Beyond that, the resounding message we've gotten from these families is that scaffolding serves a much bigger purpose than upholding the myths of perfection.

CHAPTER 9

BUILDING TOMORROW'S SCAFFOLDING

It was a crazy morning. Rebecca Stewart barely got the kids off to school. Peter didn't get up until 6:45 a.m. and Brittany not until 7:15. They HAVE to be on the road by 8:00. Rebecca was pulling her hair out. Packing lunches, getting backpacks together—everyone was late and Brittany forgot her homework folder.

By 9:06 Rebecca has dropped the big kids off at school and the little ones at morning preschool. She is only slightly late to Bible study. Both raised Catholic, Nick and Rebecca had all the kids baptized but have never really gone to church as a family. When they moved, Rebecca decided it would be a good way to meet people and find a community. At her prodding, they visited six different churches in the past few months. They recently settled on this one. Rebecca immediately signed up for the women's Bible study group.

Rebecca walks into Bible study feeling slightly ashamed that she only skimmed the passages last night, falling asleep as the words swam in front of her eyes. The women go around the room greeting each other and talking about their state of mind. Rebecca tells them about Brittany forgetting her homework folder. She describes feeling bad not taking it to her, but also she thinks it is good for Brit to learn a lesson about being responsible.

Rebecca is proud that she chose to prioritize her time at Bible study over taking the homework folder to Brit. But the women in the Bible study are not. They seem shocked and insinuate that Rebecca made the wrong choice as a mother. Clearly she should have taken Brittany the folder! The lack of support is upsetting, and Rebecca questions her parenting decision. Her guilt dissipates later when she picks Brittany up from school. Not only is Brittany fine, but she acknowledges it was her fault. Despite what the Bible study women said, maybe it really was a good lesson in responsibility?

Two weeks later Rebecca decides to quit Bible study all together. The group hasn't proven to be the support she had hoped for either emotionally or intellectually. Although she feels guilty for not following through with her commitment to the group, she would rather have one morning a week unscheduled. Frankie is only in preschool two mornings a week. One of those mornings Rebecca volunteers at the elementary school. So the Bible study morning is literally the only time she has alone all week.

REBECCA STEWART'S short engagement with the Bible study group hints at the difficulty of developing a support structure. Maybe if the Bible study women had been different (more welcoming? less judgmental? more able to see her struggles?), Rebecca would have liked to maintain her commitment to the group and gotten to know the women in it. We have to admit, though, that we were happy when she quit because the group was making her feel worse rather than better. Yet looking to institutions such as church to foster relationships makes sense. Places of worship, childcare centers, school—these are places where people meet each other and can develop the weak (and strong) ties that become scaffolding. Such institutions can provide a platform for fostering relationships and sharing practical resources.[1]

The physical environment also helps in developing scaffolding. While Lisa Phillips is friendly by nature, her ability to cultivate and maintain help is also reinforced by the layout and character of their neighborhood.[2] The forward-facing houses in their beach community are close to each other. People are regularly on their porches and in their front yards. For example, when a young heron ends up on top of someone's car for hours it becomes a neighborhood event. Several families come out of their houses to watch, chat, and take pictures; Susie, their neighbor, assures everyone that she called Animal Control. They said that the bird is just figuring out how to fly and will make its way to the nearby beach eventually. There is a sense of camaraderie in the unexpected.

Tim Andrews is not as embedded in his community as Lisa and Dave. But he also develops neighborhood connections that are both practical and gratifying. He lives at the end of a cul-de-sac where his children can rollerblade and play. His daughters, especially Olive, are ambassadors in the neighborhood. She knows everyone. Regularly out biking or riding their scooters on the block, the girls have made friends and their friendships provide Tim a source of support. Think back to Tim opening the refrigerator on burrito night only to discover that he has forgotten to buy cheese. He asks Olive's friend's dad on the block for the critical ingredient. Tim doesn't know the neighbor well, and likely would not describe them as friends, but the relationship between the children saves the evening meal.

Scaffolding is difficult to create. We observe organic friendships with neighbors, serendipitous connections with other parents, appreciative relationships with babysitters, deep obligations from family members, and long-term investments in fostering each of these relationships. People also rely on personal networks for recommendations about paid help: babysitters, cleaners, summer camps. Finding these supports requires the right mix of time, circumstance, individual inclination, and physical space. And it's never done. Everyone's lives are in flux, and those who provide scaffolding may move on (for example, get new jobs or suffer health issues) and become unable to offer support.

Beyond practical help, Rebecca is looking for friendship and connection in a community. Nick and Rebecca both recollect with fondness their life before moving to California—a life enriched by a network of close friends and family.[3] Nick reminisces about their old street, "I mean we loved our cul-de-sac.... One of her [Rebecca's] best friends had become our neighbor with similar-aged kids. . . . They were like family."

Lisa and Dave currently enjoy the informal and familial supports that bring joy and a valued sense of connection to their community. When they walk to dinner, they note who lives in which house along the way. Lisa gives a big hug to the smiling man who owns the Italian restaurant and asks about his son in college. Sitting down, she points out at least four tables of people they know in the restaurant—parents of their kids' friends, past coaches, and her brother's ex-girlfriend with whom she went to high school. Stopping at the ice cream store on the way home is no different— they run into another family whose daughter plays soccer with Lauren. It is clear that community, closeness, and neighborhood are an integral part of their matrix of worth. Dave and Lisa have integrated a different narrative into their sense of individual "success." Both regularly express gratitude for the role others play in their lives and the joy these relationships bring. They value their connection to the neighborhood as much as they do their dreams of being Ideal Workers, Perfect Parents, and Ultimate Bodies.

Lisa and Dave proudly, and without reservation, rely on a network of both practical connections and real friends as their scaffolding. They also give back to those around them—offering carpools, grabbing dinner for another child. What makes Lisa and Dave unique is not their reliance on others, but the fact that they do not take it for granted. Recall that Dave recently declined an excellent job offer in a different state because they wanted to maintain their connection to the community. Many people couldn't imagine making such a choice because the dominance of work is so taken-for-granted in U.S. culture. Many other people would not have a choice at all and, in the service of job security, would be forced to move. Dave is fortunate to have a skill-set that was desired in a large metropolitan area, so they could stay in their community.

Dave and Lisa recognize the adaptations and accommodations they make to be part of a particular community and maintain harmony with their extended family. Dave may wish he had time to vacuum the house himself rather than rely on his mother-in-law, but he is able to give up this point of pride and appreciate all that she does for the family. Lisa is jokingly ashamed that their neighbor walks their dog, but loves her for it and gives back in terms of emotional support and friendship. Roger and Linda Waldo have also made accommodations. Roger commuted two hours each way in order for his family to remain in the same community when the location of his work changed (he continued to work for SLH but was bounced between properties every couple of years). Roger managed to maintain his commitment to work, and his family had a supportive community, but it took a great toll on everyone and changed his role in the family.

There are technologies to help with the Physical Work that require less accommodation—platforms to coordinate dog-walkers, or the Roomba to vacuum. Virtual personal assistants can help with the Coordinating Work and don't expect to be appreciated for their help. But these forms of scaffolding are more impersonal, and they don't reflect the give and take of relationships. Dave and Lisa's life is an everyday example of the value of community. It is scaffolding at its best and most resilient. And they find it deeply fulfilling.

Scaffolding plays a dual role: people are simultaneously practical support and a source of connection. Families need scaffolding to help them strive for their dreams *and* for the pleasure of the relationships. But scaffolding does not just happen. As technology ramps up expectations, tightening the strings of interdependencies, people are increasingly pulled to each other. It is exhausting. The gig economy encourages a reduction of interdependencies by moving toward transactional relationships. But current fears about the loss of community and civility are partly a function of this move away from long-term embedded relationships. People continue to rely on others—just others that can more easily be discounted and devalued. One alternative is to loosen the strings of connectivity and expectation while simultaneously valuing both deep and practical relationships, and the help and joy they provide.

But let's take stock before we explore solutions.

THE BIG PICTURE

The myths shape how people understand themselves and others. Many families (including the families that we write about) reject certain aspects of the myths, but they accept other aspects without reflection. The specifics of the myths may take on different contours depending on one's culture, income, religion, background, or region.[4] The underlying feeling, however, is the same. It is never enough. The collective belief in the authority of the myths gives them a patina of truth. But these myths of perfection are just that: unattainable dreams. The only way to make headway toward the unattainable is to push back on the myths.

It is becoming harder to live up to the myths. By using technology to be more available, people have redefined what it means to engage the myths. Technologies allow everyone to do more. But the spiral of expectations also expands what people expect of themselves and others: intensifying what it means to be an Ideal Worker, Perfect Parent, and Ultimate Body. The only way to combat the ratcheting up of expectations is to loosen the strings without losing real connection.

The lives of these nine families show people living in terms of the myths and chafing against them. Individually, all are striving. But their accomplishments are in large part due to their families and communities. They call on the help of colleagues, grandparents, neighbors, babysitters, housecleaners, and friends—building, maintaining, and relying upon different structures of scaffolding in order to manage conflicting demands and expectations. Ironically, the more people buy in to the myths, the more help (unappreciated, undervalued, and often unnoticed help) they need to make it all happen. And though they succeed to an impressive degree, they can't do it all. The only way to honor all that goes into everyday life is to recognize, appreciate, and value the people who do invisible work, and in so doing, scaffold impossible dreams.

The reality of these families is shared by innumerable families across the United States and the world.[5]

In truth, enacting these myths ensures company profits more than individual wellness and success. But people take on individual responsibility and don't expect others, companies, or government to help.[6] To work. To have kids.[7] To exercise. These are all framed as individual "choices." This construction hides how the myths shape these "choices"; it hides the public policies that support (or undermine) them; and it conceals the collective and gendered efforts that support work, home, and the project of the self.

Underlying the Ideal Worker, the Perfect Parent, and the Ultimate Body is a foundational myth of individual accomplishment in American society.[8] Americans think of *individuals*, not neighborhoods or families, as achieving the "American Dream." Americans valorize the idea that individuals have complete control over their lives. This belief is tenacious. It is also misplaced.

MAKING SCAFFOLDING VISIBLE AND VALUED

People rarely notice the immense amount of invisible work that is an integral part of everyday life, and they do not notice how the people who perform that work are scaffolding the dreams of those around them. Scaffolding is critical to propping up the myths. The language of Physical, Mental, Coordinating, and Emotional Work helps people see it.[9] These terms define and delimit the kinds of work being done. Often one member of a family (a partner or grandparent) does the Mental and Physical work to scaffold other members of the family. Or one person acts as a centralized hub, doing the Mental, Coordinating, and Emotional work of planning, hiring, and managing a variety of people to help with Physical Work. Yet all of this work is invisible and often unequally distributed.

While difficult, many families take on this issue directly. Katrina Garcia sits down with Franco to explain why she was overwhelmed at the end of the day (and to ask for more help), and his awareness begins to change. We see Franco make an effort to take the baby and clean up. The sum of invisible work might be more noticeable if people had a better sense of all that is happening in the household and how this work fits into the bigger picture of their lives. When Olivia Shah leaves town for a conference, all that she does and organizes in a week becomes abundantly clear. If invisible work is spelled out and discussed, couples could decide on a division of work that is equitable given the various demands on the family. Couples will make different decisions about whose time and energy is going to be directed in which ways (making money, parenting, cooking, cleaning, coordinating).[10] But the work needs to be seen.

Next comes the need to value invisible work. Take Tim Andrews. As a single parent he is well aware of all the invisible work that needs to be done. He feels pretty competent at it, in fact. But as he considers what it would be like to stay home (regardless of the fact that he is the solo support for his family in a Single Scaffolding structure), he struggles:

> I've thought about it a lot. And I know that while I would be super good at it and be super great that the house is clean, dishes are done, laundry is done, like all this stuff, and you know, finances are all in order, and computer is great, and the music is all organized and all this stuff, I would get to a certain point where I would be like, "Hey, what am I doing?" Like really? I'm proud that all the laundry is clean? I know that I would just say, "God, there is something bigger for me to be doing in this world."

Invisible work is "real" work—just as real as finishing a forecast for SLH. Tim *should* be proud. What if invisible work was something people *were* proud of? What if people valued themselves and others by how much invisible work they do and how much they scaffold others?[11] Would people's sense of accomplishment and assessments of how they use their time change? Would Linda Waldo (or Rebecca Stewart) have a different sense of herself and her accomplishments if Roger (or Nick) saw and valued all that she does to support his exercise, his work, and their family?

Making scaffolding visible and valued should not be about gender. But of course it often is. The reality is that women (mothers, wives, grandmothers, caregivers, housecleaners) do the vast majority of invisible work that prop up the myths—both in the domain of paid help and in the informal family structures in which moms, and often grandmothers, take on the bulk of invisible work in the home.[12] Men and women alike may not see how the division of labor in the home is gendered. Or a woman may give up asking after countless arguments.[13] Gendered labor becomes an unquestioned fact. Pushing for equality in the workplace ignores the unequal division of household labor. And a gendered division of labor at home undermines women's professional successes because they need others to scaffold their work.[14]

Society and organizations amplify gendered expectations by trivializing fatherhood (for example, describing dads as babysitting, rather than parenting), glorifying men who engage in physical work (such as expressing amazement when someone's husband does laundry),[15] and noticing the family structure of working mothers but not fathers (such as asking how *she* does it all but not how *he* does it).[16] The question should be, How does *anyone* manage? And parents should be teaching boys and not just girls to write grocery lists, cook, schedule appointments, and do their own laundry. In order for scaffolding to become visible and valued *both* men and women need to notice, talk about, and celebrate the work that makes their everyday lives possible.[17]

Scaffolding is more visible when there are flexible roles within families. The ability to shift roles as needed, when circumstances change or a temporary disruption occurs, provides families more opportunities to adapt and be resilient and results in happier marriages.[18] This includes flexibility with gender roles.[19] Chip and Teresa Davies regularly take turns doing laundry or picking up Max from school. Franco Garcia will pick up groceries on his way home, and he and his wife each cover one day of childcare a week while the other works. Olivia Shah's father is the go-to person for picking up kids from activities when she is busy. Cory Finchley has taken on all of the invisible work of the household. These examples reveal some of the less gendered ways in which family members scaffold each other, and in so doing, increase the visibility of this work.

We are not the first to suggest invisible work needs to be visible and valued.[20] When women entered the workplace in larger numbers, and failed to convince their partners to take on more of this invisible work, many middle- and upper-class families turned to low-wage workers (often women) to help.[21] This left these new domestic workers in difficult positions. Who watches the children and does the housework of these low-wage workers? Furthermore, it failed to solve the problem of marginalizing domestic work. While parents or grandparents might do this work out of love and dedication, and those hired to do the work might also care deeply for the families they work for, it is clear that placing monetary value on underpaid or unpaid invisible work is one of the clearest ways to increase the visibility and value of this labor for all.[22] Current efforts to increase the value of invisible work have not been broadly successful: protections for domestic workers already exist (for example, overtime rules, social security benefits, minimum wages), but they are rarely enforced and don't extend to unpaid caregivers in the home.[23]

Scaffolding also needs to be made visible in the workplace. The fact that Cory supports Brenda's Ideal Worker efforts is notable to her colleagues because it is unusual. But Rebecca's efforts are invisible. When Nick stays late to work, no one comments on how amazing Rebecca is. It is likely that no one even thinks about the fact that she is home—cooking, monitoring homework, taking kids to activities. Nick knows, but he doesn't say anything. And in current American society he doesn't have to. What would happen if Nick put himself on the same footing as Brenda by being vocal at work about all that goes into scaffolding his dedication to SLH?[24] What would happen if he, and others like him, took it upon themselves to make that work visible and valued to the organization? When people see others value scaffolding, they are more likely to appreciate it themselves—and take advantage of policies that support them at home.[25] Peer pressure does matter.

Instead, the men at SLH are celebrated for being Ideal Workers, Perfect Parents, and Ultimate Bodies—and rarely do we see them acknowledging the work that others do to make their lives possible. The men are all provided some form of scaffolding through their wives (even Tim relies on his ex-wife for childcare) and the people their wives have enlisted, cajoled, or hired to help. We see Nancy's boss begin to recognize her everyday accomplishments when he goes through a divorce (although it shouldn't have to take divorce to make it visible). Leadership at SLH values family, yet this is not the same as valuing scaffolding and invisible work. The scaffolding support that makes Ideal Worker behavior possible is still largely invisible to SLH—even as the firm actively promotes family and encourages daily exercise.

Imagine these statements being said in the workplace, without ridicule, by men and women alike: "I have to leave early today because my spouse needs me to scaffold her so she can work late." Or "I can't do the weekly Tuesday afternoon meeting because that is my day to pick the kids up and take them to soccer and gymnastics." Or "Sorry, I can't go out to lunch, I'm going to take my lunch break to book dentist appointments, call the electrician, and do some online shopping because my kid is invited to two birthday parties this weekend and I am in charge of getting gifts." Such a thought exercise might seem ridiculous. If only women or people at lower levels of the hierarchy say them, they would likely be penalized.[26] But if people in power choose to make their scaffolding of support visible, change would likely follow. We see this when Nancy calls out the impossibility of a 7:30 a.m. daily meeting for many employees. Given her position as a relatively senior employee at SLH, Nancy is able to push back on the Ideal Worker myth. And she chooses to do so publicly and in service of others. It would be even more powerful if both men *and* women spoke up.[27]

In an interesting twist, the rise of the platform or sharing economy is, to a large extent, based on transforming invisible work into a visible market transaction. Online companies are sprouting up that offer to safely transport children to school and activities, do tasks around the house, help find babysitters and housecleaners, or deliver meals to people's door. Although these companies are certainly filling a need, this is an expensive solution, available only to those with substantial financial resources. More important, platforms that link buyers and sellers of invisible work do not substantially increase the value of this work (and often make it even more invisible) by outsourcing it to lower-paid workers without providing a living wage, job security, or benefits.[28] Further, the platform economy attempts to replace social connections with market transactions. This does little to promote the social cohesion that makes scaffolding others enjoyable and meaningful.[29]

To say that scaffolding is often not visible or valued does not negate the fact that mutual reliance on others is often a source of joy and fulfillment. The emotional, tactical, and practical moments associated with helping one's family, engaging in a community, or helping a colleague can be pleasurable. That said, the upsides of scaffolding would be more obvious if these efforts were visible and valued by all.

RETHINKING SCAFFOLDING

One problem with the systemic undervaluing of invisible work is the burden on individuals and families to create and cultivate their own structures of support. By rethinking scaffolding, people will imagine new forms of support and develop broader changes that will make living their dreams easier.

Rethinking scaffolding at home. Take for example the family. The truth is that what it means to be a family is very different than the imagined nuclear family seen in the popular press and books on the challenges of motherhood.[30] A good start is to rethink and expand the meaning of family.[31] One-quarter of all families have a single parent. Nancy Huron turns to paid help (such as babysitters, after-school care, and summer camps). Many families rely on three working adults. Franco and Katrina Garcia rely on Katrina's sister. Dave and Lisa Phillips, Jay and Olivia Shah, Teresa and Chip Davies, and occasionally Tim Andrews all rely on a grandparent to make their daily schedule work. Laws that support multiparent families would enable childcare to be shared, and allow for a sister or grandparent to sign a field trip permission slip.[32] Families rely on many people to scaffold their dreams, and families would be helped if people advocated for laws that promoted their acceptance.

Rethinking scaffolding in communities. Scaffolding often comes from one's local community. Places of worship, libraries, community centers, local city governments, and gyms can all be spaces where people meet, share resources, and develop creative and cooperative structures of support (think shared meals, cooperative childcare, exercise classes that welcome children or provide childcare).[33] In Germany, neighborhood support groups and parent centers offer family activities and support, as well as educational activities.[34] In African-American communities in the United States, the idea of community mothering has long been common practice.[35] Relatives, friends, and neighbors all regularly help in the raising of children. Help with caregiving is common in many cultures.[36] Discovering or perhaps even creating such efforts in one's community is a place to start. A broader embracing of family and community in childrearing would offer more sources of scaffolding support. Rebecca Stewart and Cory Finchley might find scaffolding their family easier if there were community or neighborhood organizations to coordinate meals, carpools, or playdates. It is clear that being embedded in a community not only provides new forms of scaffolding but can be a source of friendship and joy. However, there are any number of reasons why a family might not develop such ties, or move once they are developed. There are no "right" answers and no easy answers. Job instability and job mobility make it difficult to maintain community.[37] But these are questions for families to ask, and the trade-offs important to consider, because it is clear that community helps scaffold people's dreams and makes daily life easier.

In times of transition and crisis community efforts can be critical: a meal or carpool train for a family after the birth of a child (when neighbors or friends sign up to bring meals or assist with carpools for a set period of time), or GoFundMe campaigns to hire household help after a medical emergency (through which people offer financial resources when a family is incapacitated).[38] Taking an example from another context, people are able to age in place by access to paid and volunteer services provided through online "villages."[39] Such "villages" help connect a person who needs a ride to a doctor's appointment with an available neighbor. Or find someone looking for help around the house with a reliable handyperson. We can imagine that these villages could be modified to offer support to working parents as well—connecting people who would be interested in trading meals, babysitting, carpooling, or sharing a particular expertise. Online connections that are not supplemented with in-person connections, or other forms of trust relationships, are often not the answer for building community, but it is possible that embedding technology in local communities may help.[40]

Rethinking scaffolding at work. Another domain of scaffolding support is the workplace.[41] In 1983 Patagonia offered the first onsite childcare facility, in Ventura, California, and SAS in North Carolina is a successful company renowned for on-site childcare and healthcare benefits that support working parents.[42] Patagonia's CEO argues that yearly tax credits and the ability to deduct unrecovered costs make childcare facilities almost pay for themselves.[43] Many SLH employees could use these types of benefits. In addition, on-site exercise facilities make it easier to fit in caring for the body. Thus work scaffolds time spent on fitness without taking time away from family.[44] SLH does pay for a membership at a local gym for corporate employees, which helps if people exercise during the workday when they don't need additional scaffolding support.

The emergence of organizations that support and aggregate professional expertise in new ways (contract work and on-demand expertise) could lead to dramatic improvement in the lives of professional workers who desire flexibility and want or need to engage in care work. However, for such work to be sustainable it would need to include benefits, good salaries, clear contracts, and negotiated stability of work hours.[45]

A more significant organizational change would be reducing the incentives for people to work long hours. Tim Andrews wouldn't be concerned about getting help from his parents if he could work fewer hours. But reducing hours worked is tricky. Beyond the stigma against people who take advantage of part-time schedules, the reality is that part-time or shared jobs for managerial workers are not easy to find.[46] As another option, workplace flexibility and autonomy provide more sustainable work lives to employees.[47] But the underlying issue is that a flexible work schedule doesn't limit the *amount* of work people are expected to perform. Having the flexibility to leave when he wants (and work late at night to catch up) might help Franco come home in time to make dinner, but it doesn't solve the problem of overwork.

Organization-wide efforts are required. Two examples of workplace initiatives that attempted to redesign work and make life manageable for employees are Results Only Work Environments (ROWE) and Predictability, Teaming and Communication (PTO). ROWE was an initiative at Best Buy that provided all employees with control over their work schedules. Such scheduling control allowed employees to better align work and home schedules, thus reducing the need for scaffolding and work-family conflict.[48] By providing scheduling control for all employees, not only for those who needed it most, ROWE reduced turnover and overcame the bias often levied against people who take advantage of flexible work arrangements.[49]

Similarly, PTO was a project at Boston Consulting Group aimed at providing every member of a consulting team one predictable night off a week. Weekly communication and group scheduling exercises enabled teams to make work visible, address interdependencies, and overcome an Ideal Worker culture that shunned time off. PTO teams worked together efficiently and felt more comfortable speaking up and taking personal time.[50] Both of these initiatives were designed to structure work more effectively and had the added benefit of reducing the need for scaffolding because people gained predictability in work schedules and were less judged by face time in the office.

HOPES FOR THE FUTURE

As a nation, Americans have bristled against "solutions" that might affect taxes or take responsibility away from individuals.[51] Yet people may be at a turning point. Increasing numbers of families in the middle and upper-middle class are struggling and America may be on the brink of real change.[52] The stresses experienced by the families we studied are not unique. And these families are the lucky ones. By all sociological metrics these families are in the upper echelon—educated, employed, economically secure, middle to upper class. Yet they are exhausted, facing the impossibility of achieving their dreams, and constantly making trade-offs. Working-class families struggle more with fewer resources.[53] There may be a critical mass of people who recognize how much more they could accomplish, and how much saner their lives would be, with more help. Individuals would be able to do more and their lives would feel more sustainable if the system didn't work against them.[54]

Certainly a new conversation is in order: a conversation that notices and values how some individuals are sources of scaffolding for others would be a useful start. But such a conversation has to go beyond individual awareness and openness between partners. Advocating for organizations and the government to scaffold and value invisible work will require questioning deeply held beliefs about who should do this work, how to compensate it, and the responsibilities of employers. This is particularly important because scaffolding is not equally distributed. Those with fewer resources need scaffolding as much, if not more, than the population we studied.

We call out Dave and Lisa Phillips as examples of what can happen when contributions to a community are given priority and voiced in the context of these myths of perfection. If more people included how they contribute to scaffolding the lives of others into their metrics of self-worth, people might begin to see their lives in a different light. If more people honored and made visible the work that others do to scaffold them, this could be a step toward broader change. People are valuable in reference to others and not by standing alone. Families can teach their children not just the value of accomplishment and independence, but the value of connection and support.[55] When scaffolding is visible, valued, and shared—in pursuit of achievable aspirations—it can support dreams of a life well-lived.

STEPS FORWARD

IF WORK WAS LESS DEMANDING, parenting less intensive, and caring for the body more straightforward, would you be able to do it all? Possibly. It would require rethinking the myths as they stand today, and demanding more support from the environment in which you are operating. Here are six ideas to consider.

ASK LESS OF YOURSELF

If you dialed back on the myths of perfection that shape your decisions, what would you adjust, rethink, or give up? The myths are not inherently bad or wrong. But they ask a lot. What would it mean to do less?

What would happen if you didn't respond to an email immediately, or even told your colleagues that you weren't available? This may be an issue professionally, but it may not. It is worth taking a second to consider.

What would happen if kids were in fewer activities or didn't get all their homework done perfectly? Would they not get into college? Fail at life? Research suggests kids benefit from failure and down time.[1] Perhaps it might make everyday life a little saner and happier for everyone?

What would happen if you could enjoy "me time" in front of the TV as much as "me time" on a treadmill? Or even prioritize sleep? This is not to say that exercise isn't good for the mind and the body, but perhaps you don't need to "count" all of your physical activity.

ASK FOR VISIBILITY

What would happen if you and your partner spoke openly, responsively, and respectfully about all the forms of invisible work and who was doing this labor? Family life would likely change for many. Women may have tried and failed to get their partners to see and share in this work.[2] These conversations are not easy. Why would someone who is currently off the hook for doing invisible work want to take on these thankless tasks? If this work wasn't thankless and was instead valued, the work might be easier to share. But the taken-for-grantedness of invisible work can get in the way.

We can imagine several tactics for upending this dynamic. Perhaps a weekly check-in meeting about what's on the collective family plate for the upcoming week is in order? This is a problem for which technology might actually provide help. A spreadsheet of activities, on which couples list what they are doing (and when they feel supported), may be a useful exercise.[3] Or parents can incorporate project coordination tools designed for the workplace (such as Trello, Asana, Jira) to track to-do lists and have explicit conversations about who is doing what.[4] Less technological interventions can similarly help with articulating invisible work, negotiating values, and assigning tasks.[5] But *both* parents must engage.

ASK MORE OF YOUR DEVICES

What if you were able to use your devices to loosen the strings that have intensified the myths of perfection? Technology designers tend to assume that all users want constant, ubiquitous, seamless, and unobtrusive connectivity. But technological interventions can be designed to loosen the strings of expectation rather than tighten them. Take for example the automatic "Do Not Disturb" feature of some phones. The feature sends an automatic response while the phone is moving and assumes the recipient of the message is driving ("I am driving now and am not receiving messages. I will respond when I reach my destination"). If it is an emergency, the sender can send the message a second time and it will go through. What if people could enable automatic messages for various situations other than driving—perhaps at work, during a child's activity, or while exercising? Certainly a boss could still send a second message to reach you, but some joint agreement about what constitutes an emergency could help.

Features like this would undermine expectations of constant availability, giving individuals more predictability and control over their time, and thus more ability to plan ahead, manage scaffolding, and (maybe) fit everything in.[6] And if the strings are loosened at work, it would cascade into the home. Olivia Shah would not be "on call" to see if Jay can pick up the girls or needs to work late. Jay could simply commit to picking up the kids from swimming on Tuesdays and Thursdays. This would reduce the need for Olivia to keep her father in the wings or be ready to pick up the girls herself. Find out what your applications can already do (batch email, automate responses) and look for features that will help loosen the strings.

ASK MORE OF YOUR ORGANIZATIONS

As long as workplaces reward Ideal Worker behaviors and ignore the support people receive from others, people will have to make forced choices. Given that work is the biggest draw on people's time and energy—and thus much of the reason people need so much scaffolding support—shifting practices at work can be the basis of giant strides in making life more manageable.

If more people, and people in power, took advantage of existing policies and lobbied for more organizational supports for all employees, everyone would benefit. We urge managers to be role models, whether by adopting a flexible schedule or taking parental leave. The policies will only work if those who use them are respected. We also urge you to get to know what policies are available and, when possible, find the bravery to speak up and discuss why accommodations help both you and your organization. Finally, we urge you to support nonprofit organizations such as OpenWork.org and ideas42 that strive to help organizations creatively rethink solutions to Ideal Worker norms and create organizational cultures, policies, and ways of working that benefit individuals *and* the organizational bottom line.[7]

In service of these goals, a relatively easy technological intervention is for organizations to implement a system that queues emails and automatically holds off on delivering messages sent during off hours until the beginning of the workday.[8] If SLH had such a system, Tim Andrews wouldn't receive a 6:44 a.m. email from the CEO asking him for a report. He would get that email when he was at his desk and prepared to deal with the request. Even more important, his boss would know that the email wasn't received until Tim got to work and thus not be waiting on an early morning reply. Even without changing the corporate email system, colleagues can agree collectively to these new norms. Most email clients already have the ability to batch messages. It is just about agreeing on a norm and sticking to it. If you and your colleagues were to create norms against sending non-urgent emails in the evenings, mornings, or weekends you would disrupt the cycle of ratcheting up expectations for everyone.

Another idea for client-facing work is to restructure work to enable "on call" periods like those used by doctors. This could be done informally or via technologically enhanced scheduling systems. Designating who is on call could provide predictability and reduce workload without sacrificing external reputation.[9] It would also help to build in time at the workplace to catch up on work without interruption (thus reducing the temptation to do "real work" at home during off hours) or people could create transition days before and after scheduled vacations to help them prepare for disconnecting and then reengaging in work.[10] Organizations could also develop creative ways to compensate for jobs that require intense periods of "all hands on deck"—providing overtime for salary work, shortened days after the deadline, or paid time off for hours worked at night or on weekends.[11]

All these ideas aside, we are skeptical that organizations will lead the way in reducing the need for scaffolding or valuing invisible work. For-profit companies benefit from Ideal Worker norms—when people are willing to work beyond traditional hours without pay or recognition. SLH is a case in point. Even in such an enlightened organization, with an explicit endorsement of balancing work and home, the pressure to prioritize work dominates. Innumerable signals, both implied and overt, make this clear: late-night emails, intense focus on making quarterly numbers, and expectations that people should be able to hop on a plane to visit a property. Organizations are focused on their bottom line and constant growth. There are limits to relying on organizations to help individuals live more sustainable lives and reduce the need for scaffolding. The solutions discussed thus far mostly focus on expanding childcare to allow people to work more hours. Such is the expectation in a country that valorizes work. This needs to become a national issue.

ASK MORE OF YOUR POLITICIANS

We end with a call to support candidates and policies that would put better programs in place.[12] This lack of infrastructure is holding you back. Policies that restructure work and support working parents would make a huge difference in the sustainability of everyday life.[13] And as long as public policies abandon individuals and ask them to resolve the challenges of childcare alone, families will continue to struggle.

Understand, advocate for, and support efforts that will help you and other families. Let's start with paid family leave. If everyone had significant paid parental leave, Teresa Davies wouldn't have to worry about how to get more time when she has a baby or worry about how to pay for it. If both fathers and mothers were forced to take parental leave like in other countries, marriages and children would benefit. California, New Jersey, New York, and Rhode Island all have existing policies for paid leave. Learn from them, improve them, and expand them.[14]

Next, what about aligning the school day and workday? If the school day ended at 5:00 p.m. and not 3:00 p.m., two full-time working parents could manage to balance much easier. (Even better, the work week could be shortened to match the school day, as it is in Sweden.)[15] It would have been easier for Katrina Garcia to fulfill her dream of going back to work if the school day and workday had more comparable hours. Nancy Huron wouldn't need to pay for so much childcare or worry about leaving work early to pick up her children before dinner twice a week. Those hours wouldn't necessarily mean more "school": childcare, homework assistance, and enrichment activities could be integrated with the school system. The school facilities exist, and many organizations provide after-school assistance. Make it work for everyone.

To this end, consider universal preschool. Quality universal preschool would reduce the financial burden of the early years when families bear the entire cost of childcare. Cory Finchley might work at least part-time if there was universal preschool. Not only would such programs reduce the need for scaffolding, they would come with educational benefits for children, addressing the achievement gap between high- and lower-income students. New York City has piloted such a program, and Oklahoma has had public preschool for two decades.[16] These are successful models for large-scale or federal programs.

Universal family care could include a social insurance fund to provide all types of care; this would take the burden off individual organizations and allow needed flexibility for workers to develop the scaffolding that works for them.[17] Chip Davies might not have brought Max to his office when after-school care didn't accommodate Max if there were childcare resources that funded multiple potential solutions for after-school care. If these offerings were available to all, and from an early age, it would reduce the crunch time families experience after the birth of a child until school begins. Paid parental leave and universal preschool would make it much easier for families to juggle. A tax deduction for paid household services would also reduce the financial burden and increase the value of invisible work (housekeeping, gardening, cooking, and tutoring are household services).[18]

And finally, remove the exemption for overtime among professional salaried workers. If organizations had to pay employees for all the hours they actually worked, they might make more efficient use of their work-force and put less of a premium on work conducted during off hours.[19] It is well documented that the "overwork" mentality does not actually translate to better work.[20]

Support politicians who advocate for all of these policies.

RELAX

It is important to end this list with a reminder that it is okay to take a deep breath and give yourself a break. Give yourself permission to do nothing, spend time with friends, relax, and get some sleep.

REFLECTIONS ON THE PROJECT

Studying families in their homes for long periods of time is relatively atypical. Many have asked us about the experience—decisions we made and dilemmas we faced. We published a book chapter in 2016 about our methodology and the value for organizational research of crossing the boundaries between work and home (while we were engaged in follow-up visits and before starting the book project).[1] We refer readers to that chapter for considerations of some of the bigger-picture questions about our methodological choices. Here we provide the details on how we ended up with a book about nine families working, parenting, and living in Southern California.

The origin of our collaboration began when we were both on the faculty at University of California, Irvine. We each had the unusual experience (for our field) of talking to couples about the role of work in their personal lives. New information technologies (email, smartphones) were the motivation to ask questions of employees and their spouses. Christine wrote two papers about Navy couples experiencing deployment; Melissa completed several studies about the role of smartphones in work and home—with lawyers, private equity bankers, and salespeople in a footwear manufacturing firm. We were both struck by how often people talked about work bleeding into their home lives and how important partners were to the individual experience of work.

Very few researchers in our field had talked to couples about this topic, and fewer still investigated what happened outside of work. So we decided to embark upon a project to explore technology in the busy lives of professionals outside the workplace. With our joint expertise in qualitative research and the desire to understand the lived experience of families, we decided ethnography was the right route. We knew how people talked about the role of technology in crossing the work-home boundary, but we didn't know how those narratives lined up with everyday experience outside of work. In designing this project we read widely and drew inspiration from several prior studies of the home by respected sociologists.[2]

THE SAMPLE AND OUR TEAM

We knew we wanted to study families. But who would let us into their homes? And what would we see when we got there? Using our personal networks we started with two pilot families in 2011. Doctoral student Ellie Harmon conducted a week-long pilot engagement with each family. This helped us understand what the experience would be like for us and the families we studied. These families trusted us and were interested enough in technology that they agreed to let an unknown graduate student into their homes.

We learned through these engagements that while sometimes we could be a fly on the wall, at other times we needed to engage with people—to put them or their children at ease. We learned that asking for a daily tracking of every email they sent or received was too onerous. And we learned that families were busy hubs of activity—there was plenty going on to observe. It was nice to be able to ask in real time what they were doing or had done earlier that day and see both the activity and hear the account of that activity. Finally, we were relieved to find out that once a family got used to someone hanging around it was also okay to just sit and observe. Hence, we decided that longer engagements with families were necessary so we could ease in and become more inconspicuous over time.

Confident that immersing ourselves in families was possible and could generate worthwhile insights, we brainstormed about our research design. We decided early on that we wanted to focus on employees from a single company. We are organizational scholars, and we wanted to see how individual and family experiences were filtered through a particular organizational context. As we were contemplating options, we worked with Silver Lake Hospitality (SLH), to conduct a study of their firm. SLH is a hotel management firm that manages hotel properties for individual owners and large chains. Hotel owners hire SLH to run their properties. Every employee of the hotel thus works directly for SLH rather than the hotel owner, and the firm manages all legal, human relations, and payroll functions. Executives work from a central office, and directors either travel between a few properties in a regional role or are deployed to individual hotels to manage all of the staff in the property.

The executives at SLH were aware that we were considering SLH as a possible site for our family study, but we conducted the organizational research first and approached the family study as a separate project. SLH was interested in how technology influenced their culture, and we designed a research project that mapped onto our mutual interests. Along with Ellie Harmon, we spent six months in the organization observing and asking questions about employees' experiences using technology at work and at home. During our six months at SLH we interviewed seventy-five employees and sixteen spouses. We spent sixty days on-site at multiple hotels and the firm headquarters, shadowing employees and participating in meetings.

SLH was an interesting organization to study because they were in the midst of a strategic and cultural shift. The firm was growing aggressively, they emphasized 24/7 availability, and use of technology was becoming central to how they sold themselves to potential customers. SLH operated as a part of a family-owned company before spinning out on their own, and this informed their early culture and practices (they were acquired a few years after our engagement ended). It was a work environment where people worked hard and put in long hours (in an industry known for grueling environments). The organization was perennially understaffed, and everyone reported being overworked. But it was also an organization that valued family and health outside of work. The company appeared to walk the talk when it came to valuing family and encouraging employees to strive for balance. When we were in the organization we were struck by how much family and wellness slipped into everyday conversation. We don't know if this is still true today.

After the organizational engagement, we made a list of employees we had met during our company interviews that had at least one child under the age of twelve. In many instances (but not all) we had interviewed the spouse as part of the organizational study. These employees had different family arrangements (single and two-parent families, both single- and dual-earner families). To the best of our knowledge, all of the employees on the list were heterosexual and cisgender (though we were not looking for this demographic and would have welcomed otherwise). We emailed each of them (and their spouses when we had that information), thanking them for their participation in the organizational study and introducing them to the family study. We talked about our interest in how mobile technologies were used in the context of daily lives—for work, during personal time, and within families. We emphasized that this study was independent from the prior engagement and the company was in no way involved. We offered $1,000 financial compensation for participation. Though this amount was substantial it was not enough to make a significant difference in their finances. Our institutional IRB board agreed that it was not so high to be considered "coercive" to this population and was appropriate given the time and commitment we were asking for.

In designing the family study we decided to focus on salaried directors and executives. These were the employees we had had the most exposure to in the organizational study, and these professional workers were akin to those we had previously studied. The balance between work and home felt impossible to employees in many of the other organizations we had studied—for example, elite lawyers and management consultants—but what about here? SLH seemed to take "work-life balance" seriously. We thought employees might feel able to attain these dreams and aspirations—staying committed to work while also able to live fulfilling lives on the home front.

Our strategy was to take families that were similar on many dimensions (for example, worked in the same organization, with kids of similar age) and through examining the details of everyday life begin to see overarching patterns of similarity as well as what made them distinct.

We chose to look for families with children under twelve for several reasons. Young children are not yet independent and require extensive parental involvement. This makes the time-crunch of working families particularly acute. We thought that parents would be uniquely able to articulate the tensions between work and life at this life stage as they were learning to navigate the pressures. This does not mean that the myths are not relevant at other life stages, but the tensions between them are particularly poignant when one is managing young children. The Perfect

Parent and the Ultimate Body, in particular, might have looked different for those with older children (or no children). We saw inklings of this in families that also had children in middle and high school. It was easier for these parents to exercise because kids were more independent, but they had more challenges in monitoring their teen's technology use. The myths themselves were not less relevant for these parents.

Of the fifteen families that we emailed, nine agreed to participate. These families lived across four different counties in Southern California. Two-thirds owned their own homes, and their median household income was $170,000, ranging from $95,000 to over $400,000. Four of the spouses worked full-time and a fifth was self-employed part-time. All of the employees were college-educated, as were most of the spouses. The employees had worked at SLH between two and nineteen years, with a median of six years. The median hours worked by SLH employees was forty-five hours in the office, with another five at home. Most of the couples were Caucasian, with two Hispanic-Caucasian families and one Indian family. The median number of children was two (ranging from one to four), and the couples had been married, on average, ten years. Their median age was forty, ranging from thirty to forty-five. The age range of the children was two to seventeen. We note the ages of the participants at the time of the survey, which was completed at the end of our initial observations. We use the same ages throughout the book, even though several children celebrated birthdays during our time with them. Finally, adults obtained an average of six-and-a-half hours of sleep a night. Table A.1 summarizes the demographic details of each family.

The organizational engagement proved a useful way to gain entry into families. Our interactions with spouses, as well as our prior understanding of their work environment, proved critical to their willingness to talk to us about the family study. When families expressed interest, two members of the research team brought pizza to their home to meet the family and explain the details of the study. Although we were explicit that agreeing to pizza did not mean they were agreeing to participate in the study, every family agreed to participate in the study during the initial meeting or shortly thereafter. Family members signed consent forms and we made a plan for starting our visits. One member of our research team conducted all site visits, with two people attending the first and last visit (at the last visit to help conduct closing interviews and administer a survey to

	Parents	Children	Education
Single Parents	**Tim Andrews (36)** Divorced: Shared custody	Chloe (5) Olive (8) Hannah (9)	Tim: BA
	Nancy Huron (42) Divorced: Sole custody	Melody (6) Dylan (8)	Nancy: BA
Dual-Earner Parents	**Teresa (32) &** **Chip (36) Davies** Married	Max (7)	Teresa: BA Chip: MA
	Franco (40) & **Katrina (30) Garcia** Married	Matt (2) Charlotte (4)	Franco: BA Katrina: Some college
	Dave (45) & **Lisa (42) Phillips** Married	Harry (7) Lauren (12) Danielle (13)	Dave: BA Lisa: BA, teaching credential
	Jay (44) & **Olivia (42) Shah** Married	Tessa (9) Neelam (13)	Jay: BA Olivia: BA
	Roger (45) & **Linda (44) Waldo** Married	Ryan (12) Sadie (17)	Roger: MA Linda: Some college
Primary Worker/ Default Parent	**Brenda (35) &** **Cory (42) Finchley** Married	Tabitha (2) Kyle (4) Bobby (7)	Brenda: BA Cory: BA
	Nick (40) & **Rebecca (40) Stewart** Married	Frankie (3) Eric (5) Peter (6) Brittany (8)	Nick: BA Rebecca: MA

TABLE A.1 Demographics of the Families

SOURCE: Socioeconomic class determined by the Pew Income Calculator.
See Fry and Kochhar, "Are You in the American Middle Class?"

Employment, Tenure at SLH, and Average Hours Worked (per week)	Ethnicity	Family Income*
Tim: Executive at SLH, 8 years tenure. 55 hrs. at work, 5 hrs. at home.	Caucasian	Middle
Nancy: Senior Director at SLH, 13 years tenure. 35 hrs. at work, 15 hrs. at home.	Caucasian	Middle
Teresa: Director at SLH, 8 years tenure. 45 hrs. at work, 5 hrs. at home. Chip: Engineer. 35 hrs. at work, 0 hrs. at home.	Teresa: Hispanic Chip: Caucasian	Upper
Franco: Director at SLH, 3 years tenure. 55 hrs. at work, 5 hrs. at home. Katrina: Regional manager at a restaurant chain. 55 hrs. at work, 5 hrs. at home.	Franco: Hispanic Katrina: Caucasian	Upper
Dave: Director at SLH, 2.5 years tenure. 45 hrs. at work, 5 hrs. at home. Lisa: Middle school teacher. 40 hrs. at work, 5 hrs. at home.	Both: Caucasian	Upper
Jay: Executive at SLH, 19 years tenure. 55 hrs. at work, 15 hrs. at home. Olivia: Travel agent and small business owner. 25 hrs. at home.	Both: Indian	Upper
Roger: Director at SLH, 6 years tenure. 55 hrs. at work, 5 hrs. at home. Linda: Food service in middle school. 30 hrs. at work, 0 hrs. at home.	Both: Caucasian	Middle
Brenda: Director at SLH, 6 years tenure. 45 hrs. at work, 5 hrs. at home. Cory: Parent/homemaker.	Both: Caucasian	Middle
Nick: Executive at SLH, 2 years tenure. 35 hrs. at work, 15 hrs. at home. Rebecca: Parent/homemaker.	Both: Caucasian	Upper

each adult). In order to build rapport and gain trust it was important that one person conduct the primary ethnographic research for each family. However, having two people attend the first and last visits and get a feel for the family and their personal space ended up being very useful for our collective understanding of each family.

Our research team comprised the two of us and a graduate student, Ellie Harmon. We are all heterosexual, cisgender women at different life stages, spanning two-and-a-half decades in age. Christine and Melissa are both married. At the time we conducted the fieldwork Christine had kids on the upper end of the age spectrum of the children in the families we studied (thirteen and ten); Melissa was on the other end, with a six-year-old and a baby arriving literally as we concluded the initial engagements. Ellie was in a long-term relationship but had no children.

Our variety of experiences proved useful as we read each other's field notes, talked about our experiences, and challenged each other's interpretations. What seemed normal to one of us was often bewildering to another. We each resonated with different families, and if one of us felt the other resonated perhaps a little too much, we would raise the question and discuss our personal experiences with the families. The visits brought up feelings about our own parenting, marriages, and bodies, and we became very good at communicating these feelings and reactions to each other. As a team we checked in on everything from how to structure our field notes (we decided time stamps were helpful), to what a particular observation might mean, to simple venting after a tiring or stressful observation.

All experienced with ethnographic research, we are aware that the ways we are perceived by others matter. How we appear to those we are studying (for example, age, gender, ethnicity, attribution of certain character traits, or assumptions of what we are looking for in the project) affects what kinds of spaces we can or cannot enter and how people will engage with us during fieldwork.

Our position as educated Caucasian women was relevant in the field. It influenced our legitimacy in the space. Being women likely made parents more comfortable when we hung out with their children (sitting on a child's bed, braiding hair, reading books out loud, holding a child or having them sit in our laps). Our status in higher education was also relevant—one family wanted their children around "smart" people, another child called us "the girl who teaches at college." One couple had been communications majors in college, and they were curious to be part of something that reso-nated with their college interests. We would share both our academic and personal experiences when they were relevant: the age and personality of our children, what one did at an academic conference, or what, exactly, a sabbatical was for.

Of course, our identities shaped what we observed, how we interpreted what we saw, and what people shared. Although we try to faithfully rep-resent what we observed, this book is made up of just that—our observa-tions and interpretations. People's understanding of their own behavior may be different from our interpretation. We try to be clear when we are speaking in the language of a participant and when we are offering our own interpretations. During the engagements themselves we strove to simply take everything in and keep ourselves from making judgments or analyzing what was going on. We also observed each family at a moment in time, when their children were at a particular age and their families had a particular form, yet we know that families are dynamic and constantly changing.[3] In the intervening years we have learned about the births of multiple children, two marriages, and one divorce. The structures of scaf-folding that we observed in each family have undoubtedly changed over time, as the children grow, job demands shift, and priorities change.

We each focused on a subset of the families and shared some of the follow-up visits. Melissa conducted primary engagements with four fami-lies, Christine with three, and Ellie with two. Melissa did six follow-up visits, Christine thirteen, and Ellie two. In each instance, we entered into a social environment infused with history and relational dynamics. We were witness to moments in long-standing relationships, and our being there sparked conversations that may or may not have occurred without our presence. A conversation with us, or our mere presence, occasionally appeared to legitimate certain topics or allow for a particular expression of motive or aspiration (for example, a grandmother using our presence to express dismay at the number of activities her grandchildren participated in, or a child calling out that a sibling was caught using technology in the middle of the night).

Organic conversations with parents provided an opportunity for ten-sions, concerns, and appreciations to surface. At the beginning adults were more likely to be acting as their "best self"—but that is hard to sustain over eight weeks. We were witness to parents occasionally snapping or yelling at their children and each other. They are human after all. We served in the role of listener, by being open to conversations about health issues, stress, work, marriage, and parenting. People wanted to know if their experience was normal and if others faced similar struggles. We tried to validate their experiences without compromising the anonymity we promised all families. We would call out positive aspects of our observations and point out that every family we were with was incredibly different. We assured families that we did not know what "normal" looked like and that it likely didn't exist.

We were also lucky. All of the families were lovely: generally open and welcoming. We learned from these families and took new practices and understandings back into our own lives. We borrowed "highs and lows" from Tim's dinner table. We had new conversations with our spouses. We tried to get more sleep. Certainly there were times when we were uncomfortable or it was awkward to be in the room. A fight between spouses; a quick temper with a child; feeling that either a partner or child was being dismissed, devalued, or ignored. There were times someone made a decision that we wouldn't have made ourselves. But we felt strongly throughout this study that every single participant was a good person who was doing his or her best. It was not difficult to suspend judgment and simply meet them where they were at. In general it was easy to push our opinions aside and approach these families with openness, curiosity, generosity, and appreciation.

We are relieved to report that at no time did we feel that anyone's safety was at risk or any significant harm was being done to a participant in the study. Perhaps that makes this less exciting than other ethnographies of the day. This story is not one of horrific life circumstances, dramatic moments, or high-speed chases. This is the story of relatively secure families and the little moments, constant efforts, and tedious details of getting through the day.

That said, not everyone was initially happy to have us in their home. In one family, we were horrified to learn that the husband had not talked to his wife about what the study would entail before we showed up with pizza. After assuring her that no, we did not intend to put video cameras around the house, she relaxed. She ended the engagements feeling very comfortable with our presence and told us repeatedly that it "was so much better than expected", but it was a difficult starting point. In another family, the spouse had a difficult time ever feeling at ease. Her career experience as a social worker meant that family visits were associated with investigating potential abuse. Despite our assurances that we were not there to judge her, this was hard for her to internalize. We assured her that the family did not have to remain in the study, but she decided to continue the site visits and appeared to become more comfortable over time.

As for how we actually conducted the research, we sought to balance our stance as critical researchers and outsiders with our position in these families' most intimate spaces. We simultaneously tried to fit in and bring our real selves to the interaction. We talked about our life experiences and families when it felt relevant. For us (Christine and Melissa), our experience as moms put people at ease. We felt comfortable engaging with the children (and generally knew how to step back and not engage with them as well). Parents knew we were familiar with temper tantrums. We could knowingly nod when a child refused to eat. Or share details of our own child's eating habits. When Melissa was visibly pregnant, embedded in a family and conducting follow-up visits, children and parents alike were eager to discuss the upcoming addition to her family.

However, we strove to make the interactions about them, not us. And we were happy to tone down our own interests in the service of fitting into family life. We watched television shows we would not have watched on our own, we studied up on books that teenagers were into, we listened to unfamiliar music, and we did not call out our unfamiliarity with these activities. We drank wine with dinner if it was standard in the family but would have never asked for a glass of wine if it was not. We tried not to assert our own cultural markers; for example we did not share that our next visit would be delayed because of an international conference when we knew that the family we were observing had never left the country. It felt distancing. We figured out how to dress, take notes, and interact differently with each family.

There are undoubtedly aspects of their experience that we didn't understand or misunderstood. We do not talk about issues of race or intersectionality because we don't want to over-interpret on the basis of two Hispanic-Caucasian couples or one Indian couple and because it wasn't a topic they brought forward to us. If we had shared an ethnic background with them, perhaps those conversations would have happened. We can say that Franco Garcia and Teresa Davies both had work ethics that they described as the product of their cultural background. The Shah family's extended family and Indian community were an important part of their scaffolding, and their culture cannot be disconnected from that community. But this is not a book that explores these issues.

We followed their lead in how to interact with those outside the family over the course of our time with them. Sometimes we were introduced as friends, other times we were introduced as academics "doing a study," and in other moments we weren't referenced at all. Brenda and Cory Finchley recounted with laughter the concern expressed by a grandparent when the children kept referring by name to this woman who was spending time with them at home with their dad. No, they told the grandparents, this was not a cause for concern. We tried to answer honestly the questions posed to us (including by children) about the details of our lives and professions.

The trust families placed in us—sharing their worries, their triumphs, and most profoundly their children—was a responsibility we took seriously. We were continuously aware that we had received a gift from these families. We were allowed into a private and intimate space; thus we had a moral injunction to understand what we might possibly give back and to recognize that not everything shared or observed should be published. In particular, we provide little commentary on spousal relationships. This has been the focus of other books (for example, *The Second Shift*). Our focus is on individual relationships with the three myths of Ideal Worker, Perfect Parent, and Ultimate Body through the orienting lens of technology. Spouses were critical to supporting these ideals (hence the construct of scaffolding), but our book is not about the relationship between couples. We were not always privy to those dynamics, and when we were it felt beyond the purview of this study.

THE VISITS

Our initial engagements with each family were six to eight weeks long. Our goal was to visit each day of the week twice and to capture different periods in the day. This provided a useful structure for organizing visits. One Saturday we might arrive with everyone still in pajamas and stay until early afternoon. Another Saturday we might arrive in the afternoon and stay until bedtime. We tried to observe one weekday morning routine. Most of the weekday evening observations began before the working parent came home—with a parent at home or a babysitter. The observations generally ended with bedtime—either the children's, the parents', or our own (one family in particular were night owls). Occasionally the end of the evening found both parents dozing on the couch or one or both parents "getting back to work." Each visit was somewhere between four and six hours long (with one eleven-hour visit). We spent an average of eighty hours with each family.

At or after the final visit, we conducted individual interviews with the parent(s) and children (ages five and older). The interviews were recorded and transcribed. Each adult completed a survey asking about their family history and demographic characteristics, and we included some work-family conflict scales. Our first initial visit was in mid-2012 and our last family was observed in mid-2015. Over the year following our engagement with the family, approximately every three months, we conducted follow-up visits. Follow-up visits lasted one to two days and included interviews. In general families had two to four follow-up visits, adding eight to twenty hours of engagement. We were unable to do follow-up visits with two of the families. Our final follow-up visits ended in 2015.

It took a few visits to settle into a routine. On the first visit we asked for a "technology tour" to learn where devices were located in the house. Children often conducted those tours, and it proved useful to have set foot into all of the areas of the home at the very beginning of the study—if we didn't go into every room of the house on the first visit it felt strange to do so later.

After this initial tour we tried to fade into the background. We gave constant reminders in the beginning that they didn't need to entertain us; we wanted them to continue their lives as usual. What they worried about in the beginning was often indicative of what they felt they should be doing: family dinner, limiting children's technology, or trying not to check their iPhone. With joking reminders to treat us like a visiting family member (someone you don't have to ignore but also don't have to entertain) and the passage of time, much of this pretense faded. But we took it all in. We quickly learned that it was impossible to ignore young children in the initial visits. And if we actually got on the floor and played with the kids in the first visits, the parents relaxed and the kids themselves soon lost interest in us. It was also important to interact with older children and teenagers—who took longer to open up.

We tried to take notes as unobtrusively as possible, and what that meant varied by family. If parents were on their laptops or cell phones it was most inconspicuous for us to take notes on our devices as well. If they weren't on their devices, we put our technology aside and took shorthand notes in notebooks, being as unobtrusive as possible. Sometimes we would find a central location on the couch, or a seat at the kitchen island, and make it our observation spot. Other times we moved around.

Children occasionally asked to play a game on our phone or draw pictures in our notebook. We generally agreed to the pictures in the notebook. We followed any family rules that existed, so our willingness to let a child play with our phone varied by family. We became practiced at being just boring enough for the children that they would lose interest in us, our phones, and our notebooks (and Christine learned not to bring colored pens!). As much as we enjoyed our interactions with the children, we wanted them to act as they would without our presence.

Regardless, most of the children showered us with affection—and we developed genuine fondness for every one of them. Across the board they were open-hearted, engaging, and generally fun. Children invited us to their birthday parties, plays, and athletic events. Christine went to see Tim's production of *Annie*, but we attended sporting events only during our scheduled visits. As the children warmed to us and the parents began to trust us, we sometimes felt like a member of their extended family. We generally didn't discipline the kids, but we knew all the rules. A few times we were left alone with the kids (in the car, when parents were running errands). Those times were challenging. In a cramped and sometimes warm space, kids got cranky, amped up, or demanding, and our impartial role as observer (not parental figure) became more difficult to maintain. At our final visit we brought each child a token thank you gift (a book or small toy). We chose items that reflected what we had learned about them during our visits.

We attempted to engage with the family in ways that felt natural but to intervene as little as possible. We ate family meals, went for walks, or watched television. We cheered on the sidelines at numerous kids' sporting events—karate, swimming, soccer, baseball, and dance competitions. We shopped for groceries and prom dresses. We went to church and helped put on wedding showers. We joined people at amusement parks and daily errands. We chopped vegetables, set the table, and washed dishes. In some families it felt natural to participate in minor chores. In others it didn't. There was no universal engagement. When alone in the house with another adult and small children, some parents wanted to chat, while others preferred to be quiet. We tried to respect the rhythms of the family.

We had limited interactions with most of the families after ending the follow-up visits. We chose to distance ourselves in order to break the intimacy of the relationship and give us the space to think about and analyze these data. We reached out to each of the families and shared the first draft of the book. We will give each family a copy of the published version. Although we have "lived" with these families in our notes and in our heads for the past five-plus years, we suspect we have faded from their memories. We are sorry not to see how the children have grown and blossomed. We became attached to them. And this was the hardest part of ending the engagement. We know from social media that many of the families have new jobs, new pets, new children, new spouses. Their lives have continued to be full and busy. Even during our time with these families, something was always in transition: a new work challenge, a new activity for the kids, a new food regime, a separation, a new life partner, or a health scare. We captured only a snapshot of their lives.

Each family felt different. In some families we noted the eerie quiet. In others the energy was frenetic. It partly depended on the age and number of children, partly on who was home, and partly on the personalities of the parents and children. Our notes also reflected our feelings. We were at various times bored, distressed, or joyful. But even when our observations were uneventful, they were emotionally draining. It was a lot to absorb and observe and track. It was made harder by our efforts to continually be appropriately engaged or fade into the background.

We tracked all that we could while with these families. There were long stretches of time when no technology was being used but plenty was happening. We would write it all down. After each visit we took our in-the-moment notes and extended them into a narrative form—trying to re-create the chronology of an afternoon or evening. Needing to share our notes with two other people, and to help them see what we saw, was a forcing function that ensured our notes were comprehensive and detailed. We often used an intermediate step of expanding our notes by talking into a tape recorder as we read back over our notes at the end of an evening. Then we would have our voice recording transcribed. By narrating immediately after a visit we were able to include direct quotations and rich details that would have faded quickly with time.

As is standard in ethnographic research we did not enter this study with a clear hypothesis or specific idea about what we were studying. Our broad research focus was to understand the role of technology in the everyday lives of busy professionals. However, our focus quickly expanded. It was impossible to spend such a long time with these families without becoming aware of the multiple challenges, stressors, and joys that characterize their everyday lives—hence our eventual focus on working, parenting, and attending to the body.

That is not to say that the role of technology in everyday life was not fascinating and central to our analysis of these data. Observing technology use on mobile devices has its challenges. It was often unclear what people were doing on a device such as a smartphone or a computer. Were they checking sports scores or playing a game? Who were they communicating with—colleagues, friends, or family members? Given the difficulty of assessing not only the nature of the task but also the subjective experience, we would often ask for a quick description of what was going on in the virtual realm. Who was that? How many emails have come in since you last checked? From whom? What are you going to do? When will you respond? How do you feel about that? It helped that we were familiar with many of their co-workers and the routines of their daily work. We knew which general manager was most likely to make late-night requests and understood much of the office gossip. We often conducted an end-of-the-day check-in when we would ask parents to review the emails that had come in while we were there. Other times we would sit next to someone on the couch, essentially looking over their shoulder while they worked, answered email, surfed Facebook. Several participants started forwarding us messages or texts that came in when we weren't there that they thought we would find interesting.

People quickly became accustomed to dictating what was happening: "Oh, I just got an email from my GM" or "all junk emails," and they would recount things we had missed in an evening off: "you would have loved . . ." or "I thought of you when . . . " While other forms of recording might track keystrokes on a computer, log websites visited, or provide copies of emails, these tools would not provide insight into whether a 10:00 p.m. email to a colleague was the result of stress or friendship, or whether it was experienced as intrusion or welcome distraction. The ethnographer is unique in that he or she is able to include both observations and accounts. Thus we are able to see technology use with a nuance unavailable to other forms of data gathering.

An unexpected challenge was the question of confidentiality. We ensured confidentiality at the beginning, and we never spoke with one family about another that participated in the study. But colleagues chat. And some participants learned that co-workers were participating. Many of the families knew each other. Two families were related through marriage. Some employees had encouraged others to participate. Several SLH employees were in hierarchical relationships in the workplace (with two instances of a parent in one family being the supervisor to a parent in a different family). Although only a few people explicitly fished to see what they could learn about other participants, everyone wanted to know if they were normal and how they compared. We carry a general concern that one participant will be able to deduce the identity of another participant and match that knowledge with our pseudonyms. We think of this as the reverse identification problem, and our best solution is to not talk about the relationships between them. But we wish we had thought that through ahead of time and come to a better solution. That said, we did our best to ensure anonymity throughout this process. We have eliminated functions from job titles and didn't distinguish between the different hotels. One of the reasons we decided to share a draft of the manuscript with each family before publication was because of these layers of interconnection. People agreed as individuals to let us into their homes, but the difficulty of ensuring confidentiality because of the single research site was more daunting than we anticipated.

DATA ANALYSIS

We exited the field with a flurry of our own personal changes. Melissa had a baby and Christine moved across the country. This allowed, or forced, a period of reflection. Our notes were written but not revisited in detail. All of the field notes, photographs, interviews, and surveys were put into NVivo; we created a set for each family. We talked about the big picture and what really stood out to us. It was in these conversations that we started discussing the intersections between the pressures of work, parenting, and body that we observed in these families. These insights were related to how participants used technology, but it extended beyond it.

In the intervening years Ellie went on to write a dissertation contrasting the experience of two of these families with the use of technology by hikers on the Pacific Crest Trail. After graduating with her doctorate in 2015 Ellie left the project—we could have not done the data collection and early analysis without her. Christine and Melissa spent a multitude of hours analyzing field notes, interpreting what we had seen and written about, and making the link between the small experiences of everyday life and a sociological moment for professionals in the United States. We have straddled our role as critical interpreters, striving to see the things that people don't see about themselves (taken-for-granted norms, expectations, and assumptions that reveal the durable patterns and ontological assumptions that orient daily life) and the ethnographer who is able to become a legitimate member of a social collective and have insight into the native experience of that space.[4]

Eventually we (Christine and Melissa) moved forward with a book proposal. We each read the full set of field notes and transcripts for each family, we wrote each other memos, and we had long conversations. We coded (and double or triple coded) large sections of text—with nodes such as work, parenting, self, intersecting, health, gender, culture. This helped to organize our re-reading of notes and made for a more manageable set of documents to read when we returned to talk about work, parenting, or the body in particular. Technology was infused in all of the nodes (although we had a code for that as well). We coded what felt like "key moments" in the field notes and discussed what they revealed. Sometimes they were moments of technology enabling a seamless integration between work and family; other times they were about demands colliding. But technology was often *not* featured in the key moments of the lives of the families we studied. The field notes from our very first visit with Nancy Huron talk about the invisible work of managing the household (although we didn't call it invisible work until much later in our process):

> She started out saying that she is always multitasking and that that's hard because she doesn't sit down and engage with the kids enough. So in my head I'm thinking "multitasking with work and so forth" but really what she meant was while they are eating breakfast she is unloading the dishwasher. And right after dinner, they are playing and she is packing up their lunch for the next day. It's really just the management of the house is such that she

feels like she can't actually just sit down and be with them. So, it's not really the technology or the work stuff that is getting in the way.

Some of these key moments are reflected in the vignettes in the book. Brenda Finchley looking at the Babies 'R Us catalog, Roger Waldo needing to get out of bed to answer an email from his boss, Olive Andrews asking her dad to set a timer while she rollerblades outside so she isn't tempted to watch a TV show with her sisters. Other moments were in vignettes that we've since removed.

Writing narrative "stories" of these moments provided concrete detail that helped us examine the stresses, motivations, and challenges these families faced. Our insights about the myths of perfection emerged slowly out of this inductive analysis. We became aware of how people were living in terms of the myths and how they felt they should be acting—with colleagues, and with their children. This constant assessment of self vis-a-vis a broader idea of how "good" colleagues, parents, and bodies should act revealed itself through jokes, throw-away apologies, eye rolls, and moments of frustration and satisfaction. In examining these moments, we began to get a sense of what broader cultural discourses were resonating with these families, and we began to articulate some of the contours of the myths.

At this point we had a fuzzy idea of which orienting myths these families seemed to be living in terms of. But it was time to fully understand the cultural discourse around working, parenting, and exercise. So we spent months (years!) reading everything we could—from scholarly books and academic journal articles, to profile pieces in respected news sources, self-help books, blogs, and twitter feeds.

The ideas around what it means to be the Perfect Parent and the Ideal Worker are well-documented in scholarly and popular texts. Given the prevalence of conversations about these ideals throughout the country we felt comfortable giving them the status of myth. It may be that the Ultimate Body is particularly resonant in Southern California, the home of wellness retreats and farmers' markets. That said, these families were generally not "new age" and did not inhabit many stereotypes of Southern Californians. Still, they were all aware of cultural injunctions associated with what it means to be "healthy," and they either exercised regularly or felt guilty about not exercising regularly. The media certainly promulgates the idea of the Ultimate Body (look at the covers of magazines at the check-out counter of a grocery store), so we felt comfortable giving it the status of a myth and believe that it is not unique to this geographic location.[5]

From this analysis we synthesized the elements of each of the orienting myths as presented in scholarly works and popular media. After fleshing out our ideas about what each myth entailed, we were able to revisit our data with new eyes. This exercise helped us see how much families did or did not buy into each of the myths. For example, Brenda Finchley joked about their doctor telling them not to worry about Bobby eating vegetables ("I've never known a child to go to college without eating vegetables," Brenda recounts the doctor saying). She also scoffs at the expectations of volunteering for Bobby's baseball team ("They are not going to kick me off because I don't volunteer.") These are the types of stories that make clear the Finchley family is not deeply attached to the Perfect Parent myth—even though they fully understand its injunctions. We used these types of stories to contrast the families and develop an understanding of how each family engaged with the orienting myths—Dave Phillips's coaching of Harry's baseball team, or the Shah family's concern over Tessa's computer habits. These served as analytic counterpoints to the Finchley family.

The writing and analysis were iterative. We thought at first that we would structure the book like Hochschild or Lareau—with one family featured in each chapter.[6] But this undermined our desire to draw connections between the families. We drafted chapters with almost all of the families making an appearance but decided that was too much for the reader to parse at once. We settled on a goal of not more than four families in each chapter (with everyone making at least a brief appearance in our discussion of scaffolding in Chapter 8). We swapped couples in and out of each chapter as we sharpened our points. We chose to write in the style of vignettes to create a window into the daily lives of these families. We wanted it to feel close and immediate. But we also wanted the space to be analytic and not just descriptive.

We struggled with how to bring ourselves into the book. We were clearly there, witnessing and affecting these scenes. But we wanted this to be a story about these families and their experiences. So we intentionally kept ourselves out of the vignettes, even when something they said was to us in the room. We observed almost all of the vignettes in person. Occasionally we were told shortly after the fact. For example, we weren't in Nancy's bedroom at 4:00 a.m. when she woke up and checked her smartphone. But we were in her bedroom at other times, and she shared that story with us later that day. Occasionally we included an aside that explains our perspective of a scene when it felt relevant. But we largely abandoned the first person. We do not mean to imply that we are omniscient. We are presenting what we observed and our joint interpretations of those observations. And while it may be our interpretation, our aim was make this book about the experience of these families.

This is the story of these nine families who are all related to one organization. We try to contextualize these families wherever possible, but we do not attempt to generalize in the classic sense. We reference a great deal of academic work on many of the topics that come up in our analysis and description, and we primarily use endnotes to accomplish this conversation with the scholarly literature. We wanted the text to read smoothly (knowing that not everyone would leave a bookmark at the endnotes). Feel free to get lost in the endnotes (as we did). There is a wealth of interesting research and scholarly attention to these topics.

We continue to respect and admire our participants. They are generally happy, well-off, healthy, and satisfied. Many feel exceedingly lucky. But their lives are complicated, they are often tired and regularly overwhelmed and overworked. They often appear stretched incredibly thin—with no relief in sight. Their dreams are not as easy to reach as they might hope, or as we initially expected. This is their story.

ACKNOWLEDGMENTS

A book is always a collective effort, and no more so than a book about collective effort. This book has been the product of eight years of joint research, writing, and collaboration. We have listed our names alphabetically on the cover because lists are linear. In practice, this has been a thoroughly shared endeavor, from imagining the project to debating each endnote, and every small and large decision in between. The writing of this book has been an exercise in partnership. Each word and sentence has been touched by both of us. At this point, there is no way to distinguish who wrote what. The ideas that we put forth have similarly emerged organically—asserting themselves slowly and with increasing specificity—and we brainstormed, discussed, shared our thoughts with friends, and engaged in healthy debate. We take equal credit and responsibility for this book.

Both of us have children and hard-working husbands dedicated to their families and careers. We know intimately the conflicting desire to take care of ourselves as individuals while being good parents and productive professionals. Collectively we have relied on our parents, sisters, full-time nannies, college students, recent graduates, housecleaners, and neighbors for the innumerable logistics of working, parenting, and living. Writing this book has helped us appreciate the role of these people in our lives all the more.

We had tremendous help with the project along the way. Ellie Harmon was an excellent researcher and thought partner in the early stages. Ellie participated in designing the study and conducting fieldwork at SLH, and she was embedded in two families. She is the kind of diligent, intelligent, and passionate graduate student all academics dream of having as a collaborator. Ellie left us with excellent data and our perspectives expanded. Mary Pauline Lowry has been a friend and assistant throughout the project, doing everything from transcribing our field notes to providing feedback on the final manuscript. Her enthusiasm and support kept us going. Caroline Beckman has also been a tireless thought partner, helping us brainstorm about constructs (she came up with the term *scaffolding*!), providing feedback, and formatting endnotes. Caroline's perspective as a young feminist has helped us true our course and hone our message.

We are so thankful for the academic colleagues that we consider some of our truest friends. The intellectual prowess, patience, and good humor of Michel Anteby, Beth Bechky, Gerardo Okhuysen, Siobhan O'Mahony, and Mark Zbaracki are unparalleled. Our annual writing retreats have been a highlight of this process. May we continue to prop each other up for the rest of our academic lives.

The generosity of academic colleagues is not to be underestimated. We received excellent reviews of our book proposal and manuscript from five reviewers. They provided spot-on and generative feedback on our initial manuscript. Thank you. Several colleagues also provided advice and encouragement, and graciously commented on early drafts of the manuscript. Thank you Gillian Hayes, David Kirsch, Leslie Perlow, and Constance Steinkuehler.

We would also like to thank Margo Fleming, who was the first champion of this book project and has continued to be an encouraging supporter from the sidelines. She made us believe we could write a book. Marcela Maxfield from Stanford University Press has an excellent way with the proverbial red pen. Vera Khovanskaya's illustrations brought our time with these families to life. And thank you to Ben Platt for helping us synthesize and see the structure in this manuscript.

Last but not least, we want to recognize the employees at SLH and their families, who let us interview them, follow them around at work, and, most remarkably, come home with them. We thank you all. The moments we spent with you and your families were a gift, and thank you especially for letting us get to know your precious children. We are inspired by what you have done, day in and day out.

Christine and Melissa

CHRISTINE BECKMAN

The genesis of the project for me was reading *The Second Shift*, by Arlie Hochschild, in 1989 as an undergraduate. The ethnographic mode of research and deep dive into family life was informative to my imagined future self, and I carried with me a kernel of hope that I might engage in a project like that some day. Joanne Martin helped cultivate and sharpen these interests in graduate school, and Debra Meyerson was my role model and friend. They have both been inspirational to this work—an imagined voice in my ear. I've embarked upon many different research projects in the intervening years. Finding Melissa as a collaborator, who also wondered about work and family life in the home, provided an opportunity too good to pass up. I'm so glad she was up for it. I wouldn't and couldn't have done it alone, and it was a dream come true.

Friends provided feedback at critical junctures: Jen Coleman, Stephanie Fossan, Marnie Rocklin, Marci and Bill Weinberg, Karen Zacarías, and our amazing Book Club. With such busy lives, I know how hard it was to fit in one more thing. I am grateful for their wisdom and friendship.

I'm thankful to my sister, Kim, who spent six years scaffolding my family. There is so much that we could not have done without her. The book is but one example. She has been my grocery shopper, cook, driver of children, walker of dog, errand maven, confidante, and unflappable presence (despite an occasionally irritable sister). Kim, I am forever grateful for giving us your time and heart, and for being part of our "little" family.

And I'm thankful to my children, Caroline and Theo, who proudly, patiently, and with great generosity were part of the journey. Caroline and Theo, my love for you knows no bounds. I wish you futures in which there is infrastructure as well as people to scaffold your dreams (and in which you feel fulfillment from scaffolding others as well). I am standing by.

My children, along with Kim and my husband, Ted, have been my greatest champions. They all read parts of the book (Caroline read it twice!) and helped me work through parts of the argument. They never complained when I brought it into yet another conversation. Ted, in particular, has been talking about invisible work with me since the moment we met. Ted, I appreciate all that you do. Our negotiations around invisible work are constant, but you've been a willing and amazing intellectual partner every step of the way. I am lucky to have all of you in my corner.

MELISSA MAZMANIAN

This has been more than an academic journey. The closer we came to articulating the themes in this book, the more I recognized my own scaffolding—the people who sustain my life and make it possible.

In that spirit, I want to call out my parents, Mary and Dan Mazmanian. Not simply because they have provided love and support for many years, but because now, in my forties, they provide the practical scaffolding that saves my and my husband's life every day. My parents cared for our children until each started kindergarten and then proceeded to pick them up every afternoon from school. The invisible work my mother does for my family (such as researching schools, going to parent-teacher nights, shopping for clothes, transporting kids to activities) is remarkable—and very visible to me. I am so grateful.

I also have new appreciation for my husband, Bryon Martin, who has never begrudged my career and the demands of my research. Bryon was there to parent and keep our home going when I was spending time in other living rooms with other families. Thank you. It thrills me to support you—both as a father and as a successful public criminal defense attorney. Here's to continuing to craft our partnership.

In recognizing all that makes our lives work, I am grateful for the best neighbors and ex-neighbors imaginable. Adriana Campos Johnson and Horacio Legras, Wendy Liu and Jered Haun, Natalie and Dan Klatt, Yolanda Black Fortin, and Norbert Fortin—you and your children provide the practical and emotional support that this book celebrates.

Thank you as well to my friends and colleagues in the UC Irvine Department of Informatics. Rebecca Black, Paul Dourish, Gillian Hayes, Constance Steinkuehler, and André Van der Hoek—you put the joy in academia.

I am also blessed to have long-time friends supporting me in this project. From their respective perches (in Colorado, Michigan, Alaska, and Maine), Rebecca Berman, Amanda Coulter, Erin Hamilton, and Christine Urwin read various chapters, debated titles, and resonated with our ideas. Thank you to the technologies that have allowed us to be virtual neighbors. Together we are weathering the storms of marriage, parenting, and career.

Finally, Zabelle and Danny, I simply could not love you more. May you both grow to recognize *your* dreams, not just those that society dictates. And may our society become one that truly supports you—as workers, parents, and people.

CHAPTER I

1. We use the language of myth to invoke how valorized ideal types act as guidelines for everyday action. Mary Blair-Loy's discussion of "cultural schemas" is a similar construct, but we felt that *myth* has a broader resonance as a term. That said, we find Blair-Loy's definition of cultural schemas helpful in defining what we mean by *myth*. Cultural schemas are "cultural definitions of the conceivable, the moral, and the desirable [that] help sculpt the capitalist firm and the nuclear family." According to Blair-Loy, schemas are generally unquestioned and socially shared, and they "shape social structure, the patterns and activities of groups and individuals in institutions, firms, and families. They are also subjective and partially internalized, thereby shaping personal, aspirations, identities and desires" (*Competing Devotions*, 1–5).

The Merriam-Webster definition of *myth* also aligns well with our use of the term: "A popular belief or tradition that has grown up around something or someone; especially one embodying the ideals and institutions of a society or segment of society" (*Merriam-Webster's Collegiate Dictionary*, s.v. "myth"). More broadly, myths act in similar fashion to Michel Foucault's term *discourse*, including the practices, histories, and broad networks of association that inform how cultural objects are approached and understood. Another similar construct is James Gee's "figured worlds," or the taken-for-granted stories about how the world works that people use to code what is "normal" and "abnormal." See Foucault, *Archaeology of Knowledge*; Gee, *Introduction to Discourse Analysis*.

2. *Ideal Worker* was termed by Joan Williams. *Perfect Parent* is a variant of intensive mothering and concerted cultivation discussed by Sharon Hays and Annette Lareau. Blair-Loy talks about the tensions between the work and parent ideals. We coined *Ultimate Body* on the basis of sociological work in body studies, notably the work of Chris Shilling. See Blair-Loy, *Competing Devotions*; Hays,

Cultural Contradictions of Motherhood; Lareau, *Unequal Childhoods*; Shilling, *The Body*; Williams, *Unbending Gender*.

3. For an analysis of how displaying wealth and privilege has evolved in upper-class families, and often centers around practices of intensive parenting, see Currid-Halkett, *Sum of Small Things*. For a view of how the Perfect Parent is understood and realized in lower-class families, see Bowen, Brenton, and Elliott, *Pressure Cooker*.

4. Other scholars have focused explicitly on how these broader pressures (what we call myths) influence families across the economic spectrum. See, for example, Bowen, Brenton, and Elliott, *Pressure Cooker*; Cooper, *Cut Adrift*; Pugh, *Tumbleweed Society*; Ishizuka, "Social Class, Gender, and Contemporary Parenting Standards."

5. Anthony Giddens discusses the reflexivity that characterizes "late modern" life at the end of the twentieth and beginning of the twenty-first centuries. According to Giddens, the erosion of traditional forms of social order provided the opportunity for human beings to break free of traditional delineations of status and hierarchy. However, in so doing individuals are now more fully responsible for establishing a "lifestyle" through which they can find a sense of purpose, identity, and ontological security. In other words, "The self is seen as a reflexive project, for which the individual is responsible. We are, not what we are, but what we make of ourselves" (*Modernity and Self-Identity*, 75).

From this perspective, the myths explored in this book are created relationally and reflexively; what we see others doing, what we think others are doing, and how we relate this understanding (accurate or otherwise) to our expectations of ourselves. Critical to establishing and making sense of our lifestyle choices is the reflexive project through which people attempt to make sense of the world around them in service of establishing a place in a shifting social order. Put simply: "What to do? How to act? Who to be? These are focal questions for everyone living in circumstances of late modernity—and ones which, on some level or another, all of us answer, either discursively or through day-to-day social behavior" (Giddens, *Modernity and Self-Identity*, 70).

6. In this book we broadly speak to the experience of middle- and upper-class heteronormative professionals in the United States. We believe that the strength of the myths is widespread, but we do not claim to speak to everyone's experience.

7. Teresa points her Facebook friends to Hartley, "Women Aren't Nags."

8. The American belief in personal responsibility and the individual assumption of risk is long-standing and well-documented. Pugh uses the term "insecurity culture" to capture a belief in personal responsibility in an era of market dominance and the withdrawal of state support. Lane sees this faith in individual agency among high-tech workers laid off in the early 2000s. When people

experience insecurity as inevitable, they take on the responsibility of managing their own careers rather than questioning or trying to change the system itself. See Lane, *Company of One*; Pugh, *Tumbleweed Society*, 4.

Indeed, individualism has a long history in America. Originally writing in 1985, Bellah and colleagues discuss the negative consequences of extreme individualism in America, and its impact on our collective solidarity. They call out the dangers of individualism and highlight counter-balancing civic actions that encourage solidarity. More than thirty years after its initial publication, the book remains relevant. See Bellah, Madsen, Sullivan, Swidler, and Tipton, *Habits of the Heart*.

9. See de Tocqueville, *Democracy in America*; Durkheim, *Division of Labor*.

10. Part of the lifestyle project of the self that emerged with the erosion of traditional social orders is the transformation of the body from a biological necessity into a reflexive project. Seen in this way "health" becomes an individual and visible achievement and an arena for marketing self-fulfillment through consumerism rather than a shared problem of infrastructure and access. See Giddens, *Modernity and Self-Identity*; Lavrence and Lozanski, "'This Is Not Your Practice Life'"; Williams, "Health as Moral Performance."

11. See Kathi Weeks for a critique of how mythologies valorizing work suffuse Western culture. As Weeks suggests, "The social role of waged work has been so naturalized as to seem necessary and inevitable, something that might be tinkered with but never escaped" (*Problem with Work*, 7).

12. Many scholars discuss the ways in which devotion to certain schemas of intensive parenting and domestic care serve to keep one parent in the home and, in so doing, prop up classic imagery of the "economic man" as a fully devoted agent of the workplace. See, for example, Blair-Loy, *Competing Devotions*; Marçal, *Who Cooked Adam Smith's Dinner?*; Williams, *Unbending Gender*. That said, Anne-Marie Slaughter suggests that families often find themselves in need of a "lead parent" who works part-time or leaves the workforce temporarily. The challenge is to make sure that that decision is discussed, is planned for, and doesn't become the default expectation of the woman. See Slaughter, *Unfinished Business*.

13. When we use the word *technology* throughout the book we are referring to everyday digital information and communication technologies (ICTs) such as smartphones, tablets, and laptops, and their associated software and applications.

14. For an excellent historical overview of the promise of digital technologies to relieve time pressure and enhance productivity in the spheres of economic and domestic life, see Wajcman, *Pressed for Time*, 87–135.

15. See Mazmanian, "Avoiding the Trap of Constant Connectivity," for a theoretical overview of how the introduction of new information and communication technologies generally leads to the tightening of strings or shared expectations of availability and responsiveness in the workplace.

16. Our construct of scaffolding is related to the "web of time" outlined by Clawson and Gerstel. While we focus on the semi-stable structures of scaffolding that families craft and maintain to get through both typical and atypical days, these authors trace how "normal unpredictability" in one person's life cascades throughout a web, affecting the time of friends, family members, colleagues, and managers. These authors focus specifically on the inequalities of power across these webs and the ongoing negotiation and contestation that shape how time and unpredictability play out across webs. See Clawson and Gerstel, *Unequal Time*. For another take on how power is realized through hierarchies of time, see Sharma, *In the Meantime*.

17. Conceiving of time as a "web" of interdependencies shows how seemingly individual choices about what to do when are often constrained by the power dynamics and inequities people face in managing everyday life. See Clawsen and Gerstel, *Unequal Time*.

18. Other books speak to the dynamics of couples' relationships, from the classic book by Arlie Hochschild to more recent books about egalitarian couples. See, for example, Hochschild, *The Second Shift*; Petriglieri, *Couples That Work*.

19. Our sample of families is similar but slightly more well-off than other recent studies of middle-class families. In 2001–2004 the Center on the Everyday Lives of Families (CELF) studied middle-class families in Southern California in their mid-thirties to forties with two to three children, mostly in middle school, and a median income in Los Angeles of $115,000. They describe their families in the "loosely bounded socioeconomic category of the American middle class." For a discussion of CELF, see Ochs and Kremer-Sadlik, *Fast-Forward Family*, 55. Most of our families would not be classified as the "aspirational class" that Currid-Halkett describes, attentive to yoga and organic food, but neither have they fallen into the economic peril described by Quart or are they faced with the economic insecurity of the many Americans that Cooper studied. See Currid-Halkett, *Sum of Small Things*; Quart, *Squeezed*; Cooper, *Cut Adrift*. Low-wage workers face some similar challenges, but other challenges are unique. See Edin and Lein, *Making Ends Meet*.

20. Because the "characters" in this book are, in fact, real people, we speak only to their experience. We cannot claim to fully represent middle- and upper-class families across the United States or even Southern California. They are slightly younger than the "sandwich generation" (see Parker and Patten, "The Sandwich Generation") and not yet caring for their own aging parents. While these families enjoy diversity in family structure, they are all heterosexual cisgender parents. We did not spend time with other types of families (even though the number of same-sex couples with children doubled between 2000 and 2012 to well over a hundred thousand; see Gates, "LGBT Parenting").

LGBTQ families may experience different issues in the workplace, at home, and with respect to body image, although the broad challenges of juggling work, family, and body remain. Similarly, while we spent time with white, Hispanic, and Asian families, the ethnic breakdown of these families does not represent that of California or the nation. We do not explore how ethnicity shapes these experiences. We make no claims that the experiences of these families generalize.

For a discussion of LGBTQ families, see Anteby and Anderson, "Shifting Landscape of LGBT Organizational Research"; Orzechowicz, "The Walk-In Closet"; Gates, "LGBT Parenting"; Engeln-Maddox, Miller, and Doyle, "Tests of Objectification Theory"; Miller, "How Same-Sex Couples Divide Chores"; Farr, "Does Parental Sexual Orientation Matter?" 252.

For a discussion of intersectionality and the complicated role of race and ethnicity in family life, see Bowen, Brenton, and Elliott, *Pressure Cooker*; Collins, *Black Feminist Thought*; Dow, "Integrated Motherhood"; Elliott, Powell, and Brenton, "Being a Good Mom."

21. These SLH employees work roughly fifty hours a week (at work and at home). This describes 39 percent of all full-time employees in the United States. This "overwork" is prevalent in managerial and professional jobs and is associated with increased financial returns. See Cha and Weeden, "Overwork"; Gallup, "Work and Workplace."

22. SLH is not a "stable employer" in the sense that Pugh describes, in which employees have long-term benefits and security. But SLH makes allowances for personal circumstances: they allow workplace flexibility to go to a doctor's appointment, or attend a school performance as long as work gets done. SLH employees are grateful for that flexibility and are loyal to SLH as a result. Precariousness at SLH comes from the tumult in the industry (and a belief that the company can only do so much) as well as job mobility as employees move across hotel properties. The solution for many at SLH is a stable home but long commutes to work, and long hours at work. This increases the strain on the family. Commitments to community and extended family are presumed to be secondary to commitments to the workplace. See Pugh, *Tumbleweed Society*, 139.

23. Of course, while the roles are infused with feminine and masculine ideals, gender identities themselves can be fluid and nonbinary.

24. A number of scholars have tracked these changes and explored the consequences for individuals and society. Vincent Mosco traces the history of mythic pronouncements around technological advances and the human impulse to believe in the power of these tools. Ruth Schwartz Cowan surveys the history of American technological advances from the 1800s on and examines technological advances in light of changes in work, home, and social structure. See Mosco, *The Digital Sublime*; Cowan, *A History of American Technology*.

25. A wealth of academic work details this invisible work. See Chapter 7, note 4 for a history of this work.

26. As professional women have entered the workforce, invisible domestic work has been outsourced to poorer, immigrant women. The work remains "women's work," but it has moved (at least partly) from the shoulders of mothers to those they employ in the home. Not many of our families have outsourced this work, but it is an important phenomenon with global implications. See Ehrenreich and Hochschild, *Global Woman*; Hondagneu-Sotelo, *Doméstica*; Stack, *Women's Work*.

27. Gendered role expectations suggest that gender inequities in society will not be solved by a move beyond gender normative binaries. The work itself is gendered, and this reflects a devaluation of essential caring work. See Folbre, *For Love and Money*. To make real change, society needs to value caring work and, in so doing, simultaneously prop up all who currently do this work while encouraging and allowing men to do more. See Slaughter, *Unfinished Business*; Williams, *Unbending Gender*.

28. Blaming ourselves is uniquely American. Families struggle in other countries too, but they blame their governments or outdated cultural expectations. See Collins, *Making Motherhood Work*.

29. Unpredictable schedules have grown in number in recent decades. Schedule instability is associated with psychological distress, sleep disruption, and unhappiness. Although economic insecurity is one factor explaining these negative outcomes, the struggle to balance work with family obligations has even more explanatory power. Whether or not workplace flexibility is experienced as empowering or precarious is closely related to gender and class. See Clawson and Gerstel, *Unequal Time*; Schneider and Harknett, "Consequences of Routine Work-Schedule Instability."

30. Even among the middle- and upper-class families in this book, people would benefit from different solutions. Our aim, however, is to focus on solutions that will help all families—including those with fewer financial resources, less job stability, and more interlocking identities.

CHAPTER 2

1. The Ideal Worker as a pure type is well documented in academic research. We detail four elements of the Ideal Worker myth. First, people are expected to put in "face time" (showing one's face in the office). And they fear negative career ramifications if they don't display enough "face time" (long hours) in the office. See Elsbach, Cable, and Sherman, "Passive 'Face Time'"; Elsbach and Cable, "Why Showing Your Face at Work Matters." Second, people regularly work from home outside of traditional hours, a practice that contributes to overwork. See Schor,

The Overworked American; Cha and Weeden, "Overwork"; Wynn, "Misery Has Company." Third, a variety of work practices and new technologies encourage constant availability. See Towers, Duxbury, Higgins, and Thomas, "Time Thieves and Space Invaders"; Barley, Meyerson, and Grodal, "E-mail as a Source"; Mazmanian, Orlikowski, and Yates, "The Autonomy Paradox"; Perlow, *Sleeping with Your Smartphone*. Finally, professionals are expected to prioritize work and make it the driver of life decisions. See Bailyn, *Breaking the Mold*; Blair-Loy, *Competing Devotions*; Davies and Frink, "Origins of the Ideal Worker"; Turco, "Cultural Foundations of Tokenism"; Weisshaar, "From Opt Out to Blocked Out."

2. The lack of competing obligations is central to the Ideal Worker myth. Joan Williams describes the Ideal Worker as a person who works long hours and has someone at home to manage the household. Mary Blair-Loy describes a "devotion to work schema" to highlight the same norms and assumptions. The Ideal Worker assumes, if not demands, that people make work the sole focus of their lives. Other roles and relationships (friends, family, religion, community service) are framed as a distraction. In such an all-or-nothing schema, long work hours and availability become markers of dedication and elite status. See Williams, *Unbending Gender*; Williams, "Deconstructing Gender"; Blair-Loy, *Competing Devotions*; Dumas and Sanchez-Burks, "The Professional, the Personal, and the Ideal Worker."

3. Joan Acker noted that organizations rely on a male image of a fully devoted worker who does not have to consider the domestic domain. See Acker, "Hierarchies, Jobs, Bodies," 149. Recent calls to explore work as a "masculinity contest" in which long work hours become "the measure of the man" suggest that the gendered underpinnings of the myth still resonate. See Williams, Berdahl, and Vandello, "Beyond Work-Life 'Integration,'" 527–528. Erin Reid finds that women are less likely than men to "pass" as an Ideal Worker even when they are engaging in similar actions. That said, in today's world both men and women hold professional jobs and both enact and chafe against the expectations of an Ideal Worker. See Reid, "Embracing, Passing, Revealing"; Acker, "Hierarchies,"; Padavic, Ely, and Reid, "Explaining the Persistence of Gender Inequality"; Schulte, *Overwhelmed*; Slaughter, *Unfinished Business*.

4. Work and occupation have supplanted traditional means of status and social hierarchy, and "work is increasingly central to personal identity" (Porter and Kakabadse, "HRM Perspectives," 537).

5. See Darrah, Freeman, and English-Lueck, *Busier Than Ever!*; Sharma, *In the Meantime*; Williams, Berdahl, and Vandello, "Beyond Work-Life 'Integration,'" 527–528.

6. According to a 2017 Gallup survey, people work 44.5 hours a week on average. Overall, 39 percent of full-time employees work more than fifty hours per week. Only 8 percent of full-time employees work less than forty hours a week.

See Gallup, "Work and Workplace." Scholars have argued that the average American workday is getting longer and fewer individuals are taking their paid leave. See Schor, *Overworked American*; Fraser, *White Collar Sweat-Shop*; Fassel, *Working ourselves to death*.

7. See the Table A.1 in "Reflections on the Project" for an estimate from each SLH worker; the average number of hours was forty-seven in the office and eight at home.

8. See Elsbach, Cable, and Sherman, "Passive 'Face Time'"; Elsbach and Cabel, "Why Showing Your Face at Work Matters."

9. See Kunda, *Engineering Culture*; Perlow, "Boundary Control."

10. See Mazmanian and Erickson, "Product of Availability."

11. Research shows that constant work availability decreases feelings of calmness, mood, and energy levels. See Dettmers, Vahle-Hinz, Bamberg, Friedrich, and Keller, "Extended Work Ability."

12. The United States has high rates of labor mobility. A 2013 Gallup poll found that the U.S. was one of the most mobile counties in the world, with 24 percent of people moving within the past five years (as a contrast, fewer than 5 percent moved within China). In a recent article in *The Atlantic*, Adam Chandler reports that the average person in the United States moves eleven times in his or her lifetime (as opposed to an average of four times across European countries), primarily for work. See Chandler, "Why Do Americans"; Esipova, Pugliese, and Ray, "381 Million Adults."

13. These Ideal Worker women of SLH are not alone—57 percent of women are in the workforce. According to a 2013 Pew report, 40 percent of all U.S. households with children under the age of eighteen have mothers who are the primary or sole breadwinner. Of this group, 63 percent are single mothers, and 37 percent are married mothers who earn a higher income than their spouse. See Wang, Parker and Taylor, "Breadwinner Moms."

14. See Acker, "Hierarchies, Jobs, Bodies." Acker discusses how the premise and taken-for-granted nature of organizations are based on masculine assumptions. For further discussion of the masculine assumptions of the Ideal Worker, see Ely and Meyerson, "Theories of Gender in Organizations."

15. This trifecta of bias has been well-documented in studies of hiring. The "motherhood penalty" suggests mothers are viewed as less competent and committed than women without children, and fathers do not face a similar penalty. See Correll, Benard, and Paik, "Getting a Job." Accomplished women are less likely to be hired than men because of concerns about women's commitments to intense work expectations. See Rivera and Tilcsik, "Class Advantage." And women with high academic performance are perceived to be less likeable than lower-performing women (whereas high-achieving men are seen as more likable).

See Quadlin, "Mark of a Woman's Record." These research findings are consistent with a warmth-competence trade-off for women in which highly competent women are seen as less warm (and as Quadlin shows, less likeable). See Fiske, Cuddy, Glick, and Xu, "Model of (Often Mixed) Stereotype Competence." This trade-off is unique to women.

16. See Elsbach and Bechky, "How Observers Assess Women Who Cry."

17. In being the object of discussion and analysis, women at SLH are put in the position of "revealing" their reasons for leaving the office early (and thus revealing their competing demands) as well as "passing" on providing evidence of when or where they work. Erin Reid examines how male and female consultants manage Ideal Worker expectations and their professional identity. "Revealing" involves disclosing deviance from the expectation. "Passing" involves misrepresenting oneself in an interaction, either intentionally or accidentally, to manage one's identity. The need to pass or to reveal arises when they are being less than the Ideal Worker (see Erving Goffman). Reid finds that men are more likely than women to "pass" and mask information such as how many hours they work. See Reid, "Embracing, Passing, Revealing"; Goffman, *Stigma*.

18. Joan Williams describes the "choice" rhetoric used to describe women's behaviors. This language is used by academics, courts, and women themselves. But the choice language does not question the basic tenets of the gendered system, which include "the entitlement of employers to hire ideal workers, for men to be ideal workers, and for children to have mothers whose lives are framed around caregiving" (*Unbending Gender*, 39). Without questioning these assumptions, these "choices" are not really choices at all. Kathi Weeks goes further to suggest that the idea of waged work itself needs to be questioned. See Weeks, *The Problem with Work*.

19. Natasha Quadlin sent out fake résumés for job applicants (called an audit study), and she varied gender, GPA, and college major. Women with high GPAs were less likely to receive callbacks compared with similarly accomplished men (9 percent versus 16 percent). A follow-up study suggests this was because women with high GPAs are presumed to be less likeable. See Quadlin, "Mark of a Woman's Record."

20. See Fiske, Cuddy, Glick, and Xu, "Model of (Often Mixed) Stereotype Content."

21. The costs of Ideal Worker behaviors are significant. Ideal Worker expectations can lead to overwork and burnout, serious health issues, and negative work-life spillover and work-family struggle. See Fraser, *White Collar Sweat-Shop*; Golden, "Brief History"; Greenhaus, Allen, and Spector, "Health Consequences"; Van Steenbergen and Ellemers, "Managing the Work-Family Interface"; Bass, Butler, Grzywacz, and Linney, "Do Jobs Undermine Parenting?" It takes a strong

leader to recognize that the ability to take real vacations, care for family when needed, and not always put work first leads to more committed, more effective, and more focused employees at work. See Slaughter, *Unfinished Business*.

22. When organizations are structured around images of career success that only take into account long hours and visibility of commitment, work suffers. See Bailyn, *Breaking the Mold*, Chapter 2, 21–32.

23. See Williams, Berdahl, and Vandello, "Beyond Work-Life 'Integration,'" 527–528.

24. The relationship between Ideal Worker behavior and career progression has been well documented. See Bailyn, *Breaking the Mold*; Reid, "Embracing, Passing, Revealing."

25. Those who work part-time or flextime find their careers suffer when they take advantage of the very resources put in place to help them. These people are marginalized and stigmatized, face low wage growth, are awarded fewer promotions, and receive lower performance reviews than those who engage in Ideal Worker behaviors. See Coltrane, Miller, DeHaan, and Stewart, "Fathers"; Epstein, Seron, Oglensky, and Saute, *Part-Time Paradox*; Leslie, Manchester, Park, and Mehng, "Flexible Work Practices"; Judiesch and Lyness, "Left Behind?"

26. In prior work we discuss how the intense work environment of SLH supports an organizational culture in which people who succeed are deeply committed to the organization. See Mazmanian and Beckman, "'Making' Your Numbers."

27. SLH employees move for the company (or commute long distances), and partial commitment is not an option (in other words, people don't work part-time). Industry instability is expected, and workers respond with Ideal Worker intensity. In this latter sense, SLH employees are dedicated in similar fashion to those with stable employers discussed in Pugh's work. See Pugh, *Tumbleweed Society*. See also Cooper, *Cut Adrift*.

28. Companies encourage employees to incorporate their personal selves into the workplace in ways that reinforce the primacy of work. See Dumas and Sanchez-Burks, "The Professional, the Personal, and the Ideal Worker," 824.

29. Theorizing about how work friendships can undermine the ability to gather diverse opinions, capitalize on diversity, and engage in effective work practices, Pillemer and Rothbard provide a succinct account of the strain in work friendships. These authors spell out the ramifications of the fact that, in their words, "The four defining features of friendship (informality, voluntariness, communal norms, and socio-emotional goals) are in tension with four fundamental elements of organizational life (formal roles, involuntary constraints, exchange norms, and instrumental goals)" ("Friends Without Benefits," 635).

30. In contrast, low-income workers often struggle with getting enough hours. See Jacobs and Gerson, *The Time Divide*.

31. The seminal work of Lotte Bailyn introduces the notion of the "dual agenda" or possibility that work can be redesigned in service of a "win-win" for both organizations and individuals. This scholarship is premised on the conviction that it is possible for organizations to thrive and remain profitable while meeting the needs of all employees as humans with multifaceted lives. In fact, Bailyn argues that if workplaces are unable to shift perspective away from the ideology of separate domains (that work is separate from, and primary to, other aspects of life) they will not remain competitive. This perspective is mirrored and championed in the more recent popular call to arms by Anne-Marie Slaughter. Although this may be possible, we worry that pressures for corporate growth and leadership changes make this difficult to sustain. See Bailyn, *Breaking the Mold*; Slaughter, *Unfinished Business*. See Mazmanian and Beckman, "'Making' Your Numbers" for a discussion of these issues at SLH.

32. Elaine Kossek and her colleagues have produced an impressive research stream that repeatedly makes the "business case" for policies that foster workplace flexibility and counter Ideal Worker norms. See Kossek, Hammer, Thompson, and Burke, *Leveraging Workplace Flexibility*; Kossek, Baltes, and Matthews, "How Work-Family Research." Providing employees more control over time and schedules results in concrete business benefits. See Kelly, Moen, and Tranby, "Changing Workplaces"; Kelly et al., "Changing Work"; Perlow, "The Time Famine." Yet organizations have either not been convinced by these findings or are unable to implement long-term change, often abandoning "successful" change efforts in service of reinstating Ideal Worker norms. See Rapoport, Bailyn, Fletcher, and Pruitt, *Beyond Work-Family Balance*; Kelly, Moen, and Tranby, "Changing Workplaces."

33. In a Q&A between *New York Times* editor Tim Herrera and career advice author Alison Green, Green makes a compelling case for being wary of organizations that say they are "like a family." In her words, "It often means that boundaries get violated and people are expected to show inappropriate amounts of commitment and loyalty, even when it's not in their self-interest" (Herrera, "Workplace Isn't Your Family").

34. See Blair-Loy, *Competing Devotions*; Lamont, *Money, Morals and Manners*; Williams, *Unbending Gender*.

CHAPTER 3

1. Brenda likely saw a product advertised to accelerate a baby's brain development and also reduce a mother's risk of postpartum depression. The attachment shirt is a nod to attachment parenting, a parenting philosophy based on a 2001 book by William and Martha Sears that advocates for a substantial amount of skin-to-skin contact. This philosophy positions the mother as the primary

caregiver who devotes herself to raising children. See Sears and Sears, *Attachment Parenting Book*.

Sharon Hays has called these devotional and attachment trends "the ideology of intensive mothering" (*Cultural Contradictions of Motherhood*, 9). In her book, Hays outlines how mothers—even working mothers—are generally responsible for the bulk of childrearing. It is expected that such mothering is child-centered, guided by expert information, emotionally and financially intensive, and time intensive. Such social expectations have led to an overall increase in the time and attention directed toward children, with working mothers today spending more time with their children than did nonemployed mothers in the 1970s. These ideas play centrally into the myth of the Perfect Parent (and in fact the perfect mother). See also Ciabattari, *Sociology of Families*.

The benefits of intensive parenting are not backed by research; a recent longitudinal study of children ages three to eleven shows that the amount of time parents spent with children has no correlation with children's well-being—including behavioral, emotional, and academic outcomes. Yet one study author, sociologist Kei Nomaguchi, is quoted as saying, "Mothers' stress [not time], especially when mothers are stressed because of the juggling with work and trying to find time with kids, that may actually be affecting their kids poorly" (Schulte, "Making Time for Kids?"). See Milkie, Nomaguchi, and Denny, "Does the Amount of Time Mothers Spend."

2. Estimates of fathers as full-time caregivers range from 3.4 percent to 16 percent of at-home parents (or two million dads). Some of these estimates include involuntary staying home, because of unemployment, when men are actively looking for work. The number of families making an active decision about parental roles, like Cory and Brenda Finchley, is much lower. Although the Perfect Parent myth is a feminine construction, Ruddick argues that motherhood is not about sex but about caregiving. Anyone who takes on the primary responsibility for responding to children's demands has maternal thoughts. Further, fathers are just as capable of taking on the "lead parent" role. We focus on the Perfect Parent to acknowledge the reality of this role as sex-neutral. See Ruddick, *Maternal Thinking*; Harrington, Van Deusen, and Mazar, *The New Dad*; Slaughter, *Unfinished Business*.

3. Despite a lack of evidence, the expectations of total devotion to children and parenting have become widely accepted in U.S. society. We see this myth presented (and its impossibility recognized) in mainstream media, in part because it provides power to mothers and in part because it pushes women out of the economic sphere. In the 2016 film *Bad Moms*, Mila Kunis plays a mom who works, cares for her children, and manages the household (all with a spouse who doesn't help). When she eventually "snaps," she learns to gleefully flout the norms with two other moms. The humor of the movie is directly related to the extreme

portrayal of motherhood as an endeavor fraught with ideals of perfection and mothers judged harshly by each other. See Milkie, Nomaguchi, and Denny, "Does the Amount of Time Mothers Spend"; Schulte, "Making Time for Kids"; Pugh, *Tumbleweed Society*; *Bad Moms*; Blair-Loy, *Competing Devotions*; Douglas and Michaels, *The Mommy Myth*.

4. This construction is a white, heterosexual, middle-class myth. Yet the reach of the Perfect Parent myth extends far beyond upper-middle-class families, even though it is a privileged construction. Poor families uphold many aspects of this myth despite fewer job opportunities and limited childcare options. However, Dow argues that African-American mothers have rejected and historically have been excluded from practicing aspects of the Perfect Parent myth (intensive mothering and concerted cultivation); they have instead adopted a community rather than mother-centered approach. Mothers needed to work to support their families, so the assumption of intensive mothering was not available to them and working outside the home was both normal and natural. See Dow, "Integrated Motherhood"; Cooper, *Cut Adrift*; Ishizuka, "Social Class, Gender and Contemporary Parenting Standards"; Lareau, *Unequal Childhoods*.

5. Family dinner has been a place for conversation and socialization since the mid 1800s. See Griffin, "No Place for Discontent." In his recent book, *Our Kids: The American Dream in Crisis*, Robert Putnam focuses on absence of family dinners as a signal of the crisis in America. He discusses how the differences between the top one-third of U.S. society (as defined by either education or income) and bottom two-thirds of society can be explained through the degree to which the top echelon "invest" in their children through a focus on engaging in family togetherness, building community networks, and modeling civic activities. Putnam argues that family dinners act as one "indicator of the subtle but powerful investments that parents make in their kids (or fail to make)" (Putnam, *Our Kids*, 123).

That said, family dinner is also a difficult time when both parents and children can be tired, frazzled, or cranky. The image of the idealized family dinner is one in which food is plentiful and one parent has the time and will to prepare a full meal (or even better, domestic servants to do it for them). With more food insecurity, dual-working parents, and the decline of full-time domestic help, this is not the reality in the vast majority of contemporary families. See Bowen, Brenton, and Elliott, *Pressure Cooker*, 10–11.

6. Family Dinner Project. A few of the other organized efforts to promote family dinner include The Scramble Family Dinner Challenge, and The Billion Family Dinners Challenge. Similarly, Common Sense Media's campaign for a device-free dinner markets itself as a "movement for happier, healthier kids" (Common Sense Media, "Device Free Dinner"). The marketing for these challenges calls on recent studies that link regular family meals with behaviors that parents want for

their children: higher grade-point averages; resilience and self-esteem; and lower rates of substance abuse, teen pregnancy, eating disorders, and depression. See Scramble Family Dinner Challenge, "Take the Family Dinner Challenge"; Paolicchi, "Importance of Family Dinner"; Anderson and Doherty, "Democratic Community Initiatives"; Fulkerson et al., "Family Dinner Meal Frequency"; Goldfarb, Tarver, Locher, Preskitt, and Sen, "A Systematic Review"; Lawrence and Plisco, "Family Mealtimes and Family Functioning."

7. Numerous media articles have heralded the fundamental skills that children receive from arts, sports, and music (including fine-motor skills, creativity, perseverance, confidence, and collaboration). For an overview of this argument see Phillips, *The Artistic Edge*. For an articulation of this "concerted cultivation" style of parenting among middle-class parents, see Lareau, *Unequal Childhoods*. For examples of media pieces on the topic, see Strauss, "Top 10 Skills"; Neighmond, "Benefits of Sports."

8. There is a very real sense of economic insecurity among the middle-class parents that opportunities increasingly accrue to a select few and their children will be left behind unless they push hard for their success. Cooper talks about the upscaling of needs that creates anxiety for children's futures. Lythcott-Haims describes a type of overparenting that keeps kids from learning resilience and making mistakes. See Cooper, *Cut Adrift*; Lythcott-Haims, *How to Raise an Adult*; Lareau, *Unequal Childhoods*; Miller, "Relentlessness of Modern Parenting."

9. When entering the field, ethnographers observe moments and places when and where people seem self-conscious or uncertain. We were particularly attuned to this in people's homes, and these moments reveal people's assumptions of what their family lives *should* look like. In one case, after a lovely but slightly awkward salmon dinner on the first evening, it became abundantly clear that family dinner really wasn't a regular occurrence. In this family, people mostly snacked when they were hungry. With our reassurances, they quickly reverted to their regular routines (and we packed snacks). The fact that passing as a "normal" family meant having a family dinner reveals the power of the trope.

10. There have been public service campaigns such as #DANCELIKEADAD and Play Catch with Her. Advertisers have joined in as well. See National Responsible Fatherhood Clearinghouse, "About Us."

11. Susan Douglas and Meredith Michaels humorously document the media championing "new momism" beginning in the mid-1980s. It's also important to note that this puts responsibility on individuals (mothers) and not families, communities, or the state. This is a uniquely American construction. See Douglas and Michaels, *The Mommy Myth*; Collins, *Making Motherhood Work*.

12. We first became aware of the term "default parent" from an online blog. See M. Blazoned, "Default Parent." Anne-Marie Slaughter uses the language of

"lead" parent in order to give this person more agency and value. See Slaughter, *Unfinished Business*.

13. In most versions of the Perfect Parent myth among our families, family dinner was about getting a balanced meal on the table, a meal that often included frozen food, salad in a bag, or a jar of spaghetti sauce. They worried about food groups, often asking, "Is there a fruit or vegetable on the plate?" As income increases, the Perfect Parent ideal may include organic food choices, farmer's markets, and breast-feeding. See Currid-Halkett, *Sum of Small Things*; Greene, *Feeding Baby Green*. For economically insecure families, the goal of providing healthy food is no less pressing. But limited access to fresh produce, the unpredictability of options provided by food banks, and the challenges of storing food for long time periods in between shopping trips makes such ideals impossible to fulfill. See Bowen, Brenton, and Elliott, *Pressure Cooker*.

14. Family dinner messages are everywhere. On the Disney channel one evening in the Finchley family, the kids watched an animated short. Two kids walk into the room and sit down at the dinner table. A boy and a girl: smiling, scrubbed clean, big cheeks. Mom comes in and puts steaming plates of food in front of them and there is a salad bowl already on the table. The plate has chicken and some vegetables on it. The Dad walks in and taps his son's shoulder, like, "Nice to see you. Good to be here." Dad sits down and then Mom brings two more plates in and puts them in front of the adults. The parents sit at the ends of the table and they all clink their glasses. This looks like a 1950s dinner table in *Leave It to Beaver*.

15. The term "concerted cultivation" was coined by Annette Lareau in her 2003 book, *Unequal Childhoods*. This parenting style, common among the middle-class parents in her study, has parents engaging their children in multiple activities. It is contrasted with the natural growth style of parenting more common among working-class families in her sample. In Lareau's study, the middle-class parents have their children enrolled in 4.9 organized activities (compared with 2.5 activities among the working class). Participation in extracurricular activities rises with income and education. But the belief in concerted cultivation is increasingly seen across social classes. See Lareau, *Unequal Childhoods*; Cooper, *Cut Adrift*; Ishizuka, "Social Class, Gender, and Contemporary Parenting Standards"; Pew Research Center, "Children's Extracurricular Activities"; Stone and Lovejoy, *Opting Back In*.

16. Many sports teams also require parental volunteers. For example, AYSO is a volunteer soccer organization, with volunteers as coaches and referees. Expectations to volunteer at school are common as well.

17. Despite its increased prevalence, the utility of homework is questionable. See Bennett and Kalish, *Case Against Homework*; Kralovec and Buell, *End of Homework*.

18. The disconnect between schools and working parents starts with a school day that is two to three hours shorter than a typical workday; continues to include an average of twenty-nine days of the year on which schools are closed (not including summer vacation); and ends with parent-teacher conferences, school performances, and mandatory "volunteer" requests during the workday. Fewer than half of public schools offer before- and after-school care to address the gap, and when available it is unaffordable for many. The offerings are fewer for low-income schools where needs are higher. See Brown, Boser, and Baffour, "Workin' 9 to 5"; Afterschool Alliance, "America After 3PM."

19. The 2019 World Health Organization guidelines call for limiting screen time for children under the age of five (no screens under two; not more than one hour a day for children ages two to five). They also include recommendations for sleep and physical activity. See World Health Organization, "Guidelines." However, a 2016 media policy brief put out by the London School of Economics suggests that the evidence on quantity of "screen time" is misleading and does not engage the context of digital media use or the possible connections and relationships that are being facilitated through interaction with screens. See Blum-Ross and Livingston, "Families and Screen Time."

20. Pells, "Giving Your Child a Smartphone."

21. See Lanette and Mazmanian, "Smartphone Addiction Narrative."

22. Findings from the Pew Research Center suggest cell phones have become nearly ubiquitous; 89 percent of U.S. adults between the ages of 30 and 49 owned a smartphone in 2018. In addition, 73 percent of U.S. adults own desktop or laptop computers, and 53 percent own tablet computers. Common Sense Media reports that a third of children's screen time from zero to eight is mobile, with forty-eight minutes the average amount of mobile screen time a day. See Pew Research Center, "Mobile Fact Sheet"; Common Sense Media, "Evolution of Media Use by Kids Age 8 and Under 2011–2017."

23. American Academy of Pediatrics, "New Recommendations"; See also Odgers, "Smartphones Are Bad for Some"; Squire and Steinkuehler, "The Problem with Screen Time."

24. Natasha Dow Schüll writes about how certain digital technologies are designed to capture attention. Such work mimics the argument made by Tristan Harris (former "design ethicist" for Google and co-founder of the Center for Humane Technology). According to the Center, this "invisible problem is affecting all of society" and is caused by top tech companies using "increasingly persuasive techniques to keep us glued." Techniques include AI technologies that personalize information feeds and autoplay of videos on many streaming sites. See Schüll, *Addiction by Design*; Center for Humane Technology, "Problem."

25. See Mazmanian and Lanette, "'Okay, One More Episode.'"

26. Just over 2 percent of American workers moved for a job-related reason in 2016. See U.S. Census Bureau, "Americans Moving at Historically Low Rates."

27. Although educated women are more likely to be employed, there has been a drop in labor force participation for women married to educated, high-earning men. This is partially because of the increased Ideal Worker expectations of long hours that rely on someone else to cover the home front. But it also comes from the Perfect Parent myth in which "privileged domesticity" keeps higher-income women from returning to the workplace in order to impart their values and encourage academic success in their children. Ten percent of highly educated women with financially successful husbands dedicate themselves to full-time motherhood; another option is part-time work. See Cha and Weeden, "Overwork"; Livingston, "Opting Out?"; Stone and Lovejoy, *Opting Back In*, 46.

28. Rebecca is not unique in her conviction that she should take care of her children. She loves them and wants to make sure they are cared for in the manner she desires. But the fact that this is an emotion most often reserved for mothers is due to gendered constructions of parenting and intense cultural pressures on women to play this role. See Douglas and Michaels, *The Mommy Myth*; Slaughter, *Unfinished Business*.

Further, the conviction that in order to fulfill her goal of caring for her children she cannot work outside the home is evidence of the "false choice" that pits parenting and work against each other. Many stay-at-home parents would not choose to leave the workplace entirely if organizations were more accommodating to diverse career trajectories and less beholden to male assumptions of ideal worker demands. For analysis of the false "choice" narrative, see Williams, *Unbending Gender*. For a discussion of redesigning workplaces to support less linear career trajectories, see Bailyn, *Breaking the Mold*; Slaughter, *Unfinished Business*.

29. Wills, "Man Who Has It All."

30. The expectation that this is a mother at home remains, even though a majority of people say children should have a *parent* at home (not necessarily a mother). Ideal Worker demands, combined with the premise that a parent should be at home, often lead to the default assumption of a mother at home. See Blair-Loy, *Competing Devotions*; Douglas and Michaels, *The Mommy Myth*; Gerson, *Unfinished Revolution*; Hays, *Cultural Contradictions*; Hochschild, *The Second Shift*; Walzer, *Thinking About the Baby*.

31. When men can redefine masculinity to include caregiving, it provides a buffer from economic insecurity and a way forward in valuing all care work. See Pugh, *Tumbleweed Society*, 103–107; Slaughter, *Unfinished Business*.

32. As Walzer reminds us, people are not born with a clear understanding of "good" parenting. Rather, "it is their community of like-minded mothers rather

than genes that create and affirm devoted motherhood" (Walzer, *Thinking About the Baby*, 87).

33. Ammari and Schoenebeck, "Understanding and Supporting Fathers"; Ammari and Schoenbeck, "Thanks for Your Interest.'"

34. Blair-Loy, *Competing Devotions*. Mary Blair-Loy discusses how the choices of different groups of mothers (working moms on the one hand and stay-at-home mothers on the other) are reinforced by sharing stories with others like them. See also Kobrynowicz and Biernat, "Decoding Subjective Evaluations."

35. See Senior, *All Joy and No Fun*.

36. Sports lend themselves to this accomplishment orientation, and American children play a lot of sports. A 2015 Pew Poll reported that sports are by far the most popular extracurricular activity for school-aged children in the United States. Seventy-three percent of parents with at least one child age six to seventeen say that their children participated in sports or athletic activities in the twelve months prior to the survey. Amanda Ripley, in her 2013 piece in *The Atlantic*, questioned the emphasis on sports in the United States, particularly in high school. She wrote, "Even in eighth grade, American kids spend more than twice the time Korean kids spend playing sports. But in 2012, only 17 percent of the school's juniors and seniors took at least one Advanced Placement test—compared with the 50 percent of students who played school sports" (Ripley, "The Case Against High-School Sports"). See Pew Research Center, "Children's Extracurricular Activities."

37. This stream of research began with Walter Mischel's Marshmallow study and a follow-up study demonstrating that self-regulation—preschoolers who waited to eat a marshmallow until Mischel returned—is associated with positive outcomes including educational attainment and physical health. The successful techniques of self-regulation involve distraction, just like Olive does with her rollerblading. See Mischel, Shoda, and Peake, "Nature of Adolescent Competencies."

38. Strict technology monitoring can have negative consequences as well, although there is not conclusive data. See Yardi and Bruckman, "Social and Technical Challenges." However, there may be a parallel with other behaviors. We know restrictive parental behaviors toward obese children have negative consequences, such as overeating or eating unhealthy food. For more on this see Pesche, Miller, Appugliese, Rosenblum, and Lumeng, "Affective Tone." This literature suggests that inhibiting food intake—whether imposed by oneself or by others—has negative consequences including eating binges and psychological issues such as preoccupation with food and eating. See Polivy, "Psychological Consequences."

39. Another potential element of the Perfect Parent myth that is seen in the media, but not consistently among our families, is the call for creative and unstructured play. Tim Andrews had the book *Playful Parenting* on his bookshelf, in which encouraging play is trumpeted as the "secret" that encourages creativity.

It's just something else to add to the list for raising a successful child. Nancy Huron wryly recounts, "I was reading an article about this: 'remember to play with your children.' . . . I'm not always doing stuff with them. Like I don't watch if the TV is on, I don't actually sit down with them. It's because I'm always trying to get something else done." She pauses, "I mean, you can criticize yourself ten thousand ways, you know?" See Cohen, *Playful Parenting*; O'Connor, "The Secret Power of Play"; Paul, "Let Children Get Bored Again."

40. Douglas and Michaels, *The Mommy Myth*, 4.

CHAPTER 4

1. See Widdows, *Perfect Me*; Dworkin and Messner, "Just Do . . . What?"

2. The current physical activity guidelines put out by a coalition of governmental health groups in 2013 calls for adults to obtain 150 minutes of moderate intensity aerobic physical activity each week, in increments of at least ten minutes, and strength training at least two days a week. See Office of Disease Prevention and Health Promotion, "Active Adults." But recommendations have varied over time; see Blair, LaMonte, and Nichaman, "Evolution of Physical Activity Recommendations."

3. Reynolds, "Scientific 7-Minute Workout."

4. Gunnars, "6 Reasons."

5. Taraday, "Great Egg Debate."

6. Zelman, "Good Eggs."

7. Link, "What Are Superfoods?"; Magee, "Say Goodbye to Kale."

8. See Smith, "Acai"; Gustafson, "How Kale Became Cool."

9. Integral to his treatise on modernity, Giddens discusses the role of expertise in societies no longer grounded by tradition. Modern and late modern societies require trust in abstract systems (symbolic systems such as money, and expert systems tasked with monitoring and regulating complex systems such as the environment, food, and health) in order to function predictably and manage psychological resistance to uncertainty. However, in relying on scientific knowledge as the ultimate source of certainty over tradition, modern societies are left vulnerable by the fact that any and all facts are open to revision. As Giddens says in a nod to the body, "it is extremely difficult for individuals to know how far to vest trust in particular prescriptions or systems, and how far to suspend it. How can one manage to eat 'healthily,' for example, when all kinds of food are said to have toxic qualities of one sort or another and when what is held to be 'good for you' by nutritional experts varies with the shifting state of scientific knowledge?" (*Consequences of Modernity*, 148).

10. Although SLH had recently spun off from the parent company, at the beginning of our study they shared space and practices. The monthly health and wellness meeting was a proud tradition.

11. Forks Over Knives, "Getting Started"; Ornish Lifestyle Medicine, "The Proven Lifestyle."

12. We realize that this level of organizational discussion of health and wellness may come across as intrusive. However, in all of our discussions with SLH employees (not just the families discussed here), people expressed this corporate attention as beneficial and aligned with their own interests. Any vocalized frustration was at how difficult it is to "get it right," but that was not about SLH but about the expectations of the Ultimate Body myth. This may partly be a function of being in Southern California, where wellness is a popular topic, and partly a function of the intensity of the overall company culture. But companies in other places have corporate wellness initiatives: co-workers run, track steps, or do zumba or yoga together. So an attention to health per se is not unusual.

13. Exercise provides a feeling of concrete accomplishment. See Conrad, "Wellness as Virtue."

14. See Conrad, "Wellness as Virtue."

15. One survey includes twenty "life-saving must-haves" for working moms, including iPads, kids' TV shows, Netflix, grandparents, reliable babysitters, and wine. See Santos, "When You Factor in Family Duties."

16. "Needs reduction" is a common strategy to reduce stress in two-income households. By needing less, they can manage. See Hochschild, *The Time Bind*.

17. This reframing of "me time" in service of work serves to prioritize work over the body or the self. See Happify, "Why 'Me' Time Matters."

18. Our assessment is that three of these families are firmly committed to the Ultimate Body, but everyone buys into the myth to some extent. Most try to regularly exercise and eat healthy. In two families we see attention to food, but not exercise (but in those two families, they joke about their inability to find time to exercise); in one family, we see attention to exercise but not food.

19. A *Time* magazine headline asks, "Are You Among the 'Sleepless Elite'—Or Just Sleep Deprived?" The article begins with the line, "For many Americans, sleeplessness is a matter of pride. Many is the hard-charging corporate climber who claims to thrive on four or five hours a night, while the rest of us weaklings wallow in our beauty sleep" (Melnick, "Are You Among the 'Sleepless Elite'"). The *Wall Street Journal* reports that a "Sleepless Elite" does exist but only in about 1–3 percent of the population. Sleeplessness is heralded as a heroic state. Take the mantra "I'll sleep when I'm dead" that is the basis of innumerable memes; an anthology by Warren Zevon; a Bon Jovi song; and a 2016 documentary about electronic musician, producer, and "dance artist" Steve Aoki. See Beck, "The Sleepless Elite"; *I'll Sleep When I'm Dead*.

20. See Walker, *Why We Sleep*; Huffington, *Sleep Revolution*; Friar, "Why Do Rich Women Keep Telling Me to Sleep?"

21. Walker, *Why We Sleep.*

22. Jen Pylypa reminds us that personal responsibility for the state of the body reflects and perpetuates the American Dream ideology and faith in the power of hard work and equal opportunity: "Everyone can be in good shape and thin, if they just try hard enough" ("Power and Bodily Practice," 28). Lavrence and Lozanski further point to individual responsibility for "wellness" as the product of "good choices made by morally autonomous and efficacious citizens" ("'This Is Not Your Practice Life'," 80). This leads to intense anxiety over preserving an inherently fallible vessel.

23. Chris Shilling has spent the last two decades exploring the social, biological, and historical forces that shape how we understand, inhabit, and manipulate our physical selves. Shilling discusses how people have become increasingly reflexive about the body. With the development of consumer culture in the second half of the twentieth century, the body served as an "object for display" in media and advertising. This attention to the body as a site of consumption intensified manipulation of physicality (through dress, diet, exercise, and surgical intervention) and perpetuated the idea that class could be transcended via body manipulation. Rather than a biological imperative, the body became a "malleable manifestation of personality rather than a fixed marker of social position" (Shilling, *The Body,* 11). See also Shilling, "Rise of Body Studies"; Williams, "Health as Moral Performance."

Lavrence and Lozanski take the desire to govern the self to broader political concerns. These authors compellingly articulate how the branding of athletic clothing giant lululemon promotes a discourse of empowerment and choice that emphasizes the responsibility of individuals to govern the self in a manner aligned with neoliberal ideology of free markets, economic deregulation, and individualism. In an analysis of popular diet books, Jovanovski similarly calls out how a veneer of feminist empowerment hides claims for personal responsibility, body-policing, and disciplinary practices around cultivating "skinny" bodies. See Lavrence and Lozanski, "'This Is Not Your Practice Life'"; Jovanovski, "Femininities-Lite,'" 63.

24. In his later years Michel Foucault discussed this individualistic orientation to the project of the body through the language of "biopower" or the ways in which power manifests itself in the form of daily practices and routines that are the site of self-surveillance and self-discipline. *Biopower* is a term for describing how "political order is maintained through the production of 'docile bodies'— passive, subjugated, and productive individuals" (Pylpa, "Power and Bodily Practice," 22).

Given the complexity of these ideas it is worth quoting Foucault at some length:

The obsession with the fit, thin, and healthy body (three ideas that have come to be entangled and treated as equivalent) has resulted from the creation of two types of discourse. The first is a health discourse, which includes both knowledge produced by the medical profession and the popular discourse of health which takes on a scientific tone. This discourse presents the fit and thin body as healthy, and treats the overweight or unfit body as unhealthy and deviant. The second type of discourse is the product of the media and advertising industry. This discourse portrays the fit and thin body as not only healthy, but also beautiful and sexy. The unfit body is ugly, unsexy, and unpopular. Although frequently presented in "scientific" and "objective" terms, talk about health is not value-free; it is a moral discourse. The unfit and overweight body is deviant. It is associated with personal irresponsibility and immorality. Lack of fitness is the individual's own fault—she maintains an unhealthy "lifestyle"; she is lazy, gluttonous, idle, unvirtuous (*Power/Knowledge*, 25).

25. As Dworkin and Messner point out, this message also ignores the racial, class, and gender exploitation of women in developing countries. It celebrates female empowerment and depoliticizes feminism. See Dworkin and Messner, "Just Do . . . What?" 22.

26. See Conrad, "Wellness as Virtue"; Widdows, *Perfect Me*; Lavrence and Lozanski, "'This Is Not Your Practice Life.'"

27. According to Shilling, the bodily stakes are high: "For [the] privileged this means voluntary cultivation for social status, work prospects, marriage prospects. For not privileged it means enslavement of the body for profit (organ harvesting, sex slaves, physical and dangerous work)" (Schilling, *The Body*, 80). For a discussion of the role of appearance (particularly female appearance) in labor markets, see Featherstone, "Body in Consumer Culture"; Ehrenreich, *Fear of Falling*.

28. Pylypa further discusses the moral discourse around "health" in which a body that is not fit is seen as deviant and reflective of personal "irresponsibility and immorality" ("Power and Bodily Practice," 25); see also Conrad, "Wellness as Virtue."

29. Conrad, "Wellness as Virtue."

30. Beauty as an ethical ideal is prevalent across the globe and is often associated with thinness and sculpting of the body. See Widdows, *Perfect Me*.

31. Widdows compellingly describes the depth of the fear of failing as "a preoccupation of daily conversation, and increasingly dominating of our thoughts and habits." We are living in terms of a myth that both has become core to how we structure our lives and sense of self and will, ultimately, betray us: "We sag, bulge, wrinkle, and crumple. NO matter what we do, thinness, firmness, smoothness, and youth cannot be maintained" (*Perfect Me*, 254).

32. Michel, "Transcending Socialization," 343.

33. Giddens, *Modernity and Self-Identity*.

CHAPTER 5

1. See Wajcman, *Pressed for Time*, and Cowan, *More Work for Mother*, for excellent histories of domestic technologies in western contexts.

2. A 2009 Windows Mobile ad with the tag line "Consider your life juggled" is a particularly striking example. The ad suggests that with a smartphone you can take a work call from the car, check a map for a meeting location, text your daughter, and email a birthday greeting to a friend, all in the span of thirty seconds (in other words be a colleague, parent, and friend all at the same time). Advertisements for mobile communication devices suggest technologies allow one to accomplish the impossible. See Harmon and Mazmanian, "Stories of the Smartphone."

3. See Mazmanian, "Worker/Smartphone Hybrids," for a discussion of how the worker with a smartphone becomes a particular kind of worker who sees time as an individual resource and technological "tools" as under individual control. Contemporary capitalism has come to rely upon this always available worker.

4. See Ling, *Mobile Connection*, "Chapter 4: The Coordination of Everyday Life."

5. A 2016 Gallup Poll of ICT-enabled mobile work in the European Union and five additional countries reported that 37 percent of all U.S. workers claim some amount of telecommuting; 20 percent of U.S. workers reported using technology to work from home at least one day a week on the 2012 General Social Survey. This is approximately the same percentage as found in the EU, with an average of 17 percent reporting working from home at least one day a week (from 37 percent in Finland to 7.5 percent in Italy). See Messenger et al., "Working Anytime, Anywhere."

6. Sociologists such as Eviatar Zerubavel have long shown that the high social status of professionals is associated with temporal freedom and flexibility over when and how much one works. Paradoxically, symbolic displays of professional commitment entail a lack of temporal boundaries and a willingness to be accessible. See Zerubavel, "Private Time and Public Time." More recently, the introduction of mobile communication devices has been shown to intensify the association between temporal flexibility and status in knowledge professions. When professional identity revolves around temporal autonomy, and handheld mobile devices promote a sense of control over incoming communication, professionals subtly shift their shared expectations of availability and collectively erode the temporal autonomy awarded their social position. See Mazmanian, Orlikowski, and Yates, "The Autonomy Paradox."

7. It is no surprise that parents are confused and often fearful about the effect of social media and smartphones on adolescents. There is substantial debate among psychologists about the effect of these technologies on the mental health and well-being of adolescents. Some scholars suggest that smartphones are the

key cause of reported increases in unhappiness and depression among adolescents. See, for example, Twenge, *iGen*. Others claim that more vulnerable teenagers may find existing mental health issues exacerbated by the overuse of screens, but this is not the case for all teenagers. See Odgers, "Smartphones Are Bad for Some."

8. Watching Lisa and Dave interact with their girls reveals the small ways in which parents are put in the position of media experts—even though they did not grow up with these tools and are not educated about the shifting landscape of how adolescents use online tools. Recent Pew research shows that while adolescents are experts at using social media, they do not think broadly about the privacy implications of their actions. See Madden et al., "Teens, Social Media, and Privacy."

9. In helping their children be reflective of their social media experience, Dave and Lisa are skirting around the potentially negative effects of social comparison on social media among teenagers and encouraging them to be thoughtful about their social media presence. See Freitas, *The Happiness Effect*.

10. Recent surveys and news articles bolster each of these claims. In addition, these sources suggest that parents believe they are far more savvy and able to keep up with their teenagers' behavior than they actually are. See Homayoun, "What Teens Wish"; Madden et al., "Teens, Social Media, and Privacy"; Robb, "Think You Know."

11. All the injunctions mentioned here are regularly touted as necessary for good parenting in the digital age. See Hofman, *iRules*; Nicol, "Best Parental Control Apps."

12. For a thoughtful reflection on how parents can think about the role of digital devices in their family, see Patterson and Patterson, "Take Charge."

13. Sherry Turkle makes a compelling argument that the "tethered self" engendered by ubiquitous technologies undermines the ability of adolescents to develop a unique identity—a process that traditionally happened as children separated from the family and crossed a "threshold of independence." Once upon a time teenagers were required to navigate a city, drive alone, and figure out what to do if a car broke down or they got lost. These adolescents were forced to face freedom and responsibility—and to navigate the world's possibilities and threats. According to Turkle, "The cell phone buffers this moment; the parent is 'on tap.' With the on-tap parent, tethered children think differently about their own responsibilities and capacities. These remain potential, not proven" (Turkle, "Always-On/Always-On-You," 127).

14. The term "quantified self" (QS) is credited to Kevin Kelly and Gary Wolf at *Wired* magazine. The quantified self refers to the practice of regularly recording data about oneself. It has been spurred by technologies that enable us to easily and often automatically collect data on a wide range of possible personal data

points, such as food, weight, exercise, heart rate, blood pressure, sleep, mood, and productivity. The Quantified Self movement website described itself as an "[i]nternational community of users and makers of self-tracking tools who share an interest in 'self-knowledge through numbers'" (Quantified Self, "What Is Quantified Self?").

15. The underlying promise of the QS movement is that the body is malleable and always open to improvement. Further, the rhetoric implies that measuring numerous bodily functions will lead to greater self-knowledge, and, with this knowledge, to any number of elusive goals such as health, happiness, and productivity. See Wolf, "Know Thyself."

Deborah Lupton eloquently discusses how the urge and capacity to quantify health practices is a complicated endeavor with wide-ranging implications. Lupton points to how data can undermine one's sense of self and to the exploitation of personal data for profit. The insight that quantified self practices lead to the expectation that there exists "an Optimal Human Being" is particularly related to the myth of the Ultimate Body. See Lupton, *The Quantified Self.*

16. Lupton provides a thorough overview of how people can use digital technologies to track and measure the body. First there are the digital cameras, smartphones, and tablets. Then there are wristbands, headbands, and patches that have technology embedded into the fabric and can measure bodily functions or movement and upload data wirelessly. There are sensors in toothbrushes and pajamas. GPS devices and accelerometers track movement. Apps and other devices can monitor blood pressure and weight and ask about mood. There seem to be unlimited possibilities to measure, monitor, and quantify the body. See Lupton, "Quantified Self Movement."

17. Expansive collection of health-related data from targeted populations, and the possibility of micro health intervention at the level of the individual, shift responsibility for care from clinician to patient. Using the language of patient empowerment and cost-effectiveness, these trends further place the burden on the individual to be responsible for health-related behaviors and outcomes. Aggregate comparisons can be used to look for signs of distress, promote healthy behavior, or engage in illness prevention as data are collected on large populations (either voluntarily or passively), though the lingering concerns about what else the data are used for exist as well. The unknowns about what happens to these data and how they will be used to monitor and target populations are plentiful. See Lupton, "M-Health and Health Promotion"; Lyon, *Surveillance Society.*

In addition, while tracking can provide a sense of agency over the project of the self, it is also a practice that can provide a false and exaggerated sense of control over health outcomes. See Lupton, *The Quantified Self.* Empirical studies reveal how the disconnect between cause and effect exacerbated by tracking technologies can have negative ramifications on self-image and emotional stability. For example, fertility self-tracking applications are associated with intense emotional experiences of infertility when applications suggest a greater control over outcomes than is possible for such a complex issue. See Figueiredo, Caldeira, Eikey, Mazmanian, and Chen, "Engaging with Health Data." The quantification of food consumption and calorie visualizations in weight loss applications fuels obsessive behavior in women with eating disorders by promoting techniques of control over calorie consumption. See Eikey and Reddy, "It's Definitely Been a Journey."

18. See Odgers, "Smartphones Are Bad for Some."

CHAPTER 6

1. See Mazmanian, Orlikowski, and Yates, "The Autonomy Paradox," and Gregg, *Work's Intimacy*, for empirical work on the role of smartphones in the lives of busy professionals. Both of these studies discuss how, in an environment of always-on connectivity, the inability to check email quickly is simultaneously stress relieving and stress inducing.

2. Giddens describes the erosion of barriers that divide when and where we are naturally forced to engage with people from different domains of life with the phrase "time-space distanciation," in which time and space are indefinite and no longer link together to frame interactions. See Giddens, *Modernity and Self Identity*, 21–23.

3. For an excellent history on the discourse of time management and the social implications of a collective attention to productivity applications, see Gregg, "Getting Things Done." See also Gregg, *Counterproductive*.

4. The spiral of expectations is a modified and expanded version of the dynamics of escalating engagement and diminishing autonomy outlined by Mazmanian and colleagues in 2013. In a paper on the introduction of BlackBerry mobile email devices in elite knowledge work settings, these authors described how individual use of the devices initially appealed to professionals' sense of self as committed but autonomous workers, while collective use transformed how individuals displayed commitment and experienced autonomy. In other words, mobile communication devices paradoxically helped individuals navigate the tension between autonomy and commitment, while undermining their collective ability to preserve autonomy over where and when they were expected to be available. See Mazmanian, Orlikowski, and Yates, "The Autonomy Paradox."

5. Roger Waldo posts his exercise on Facebook; Lisa Phillips tracks her runs; Katrina Garcia has her Fitbit. But we do not see the spiral of expectations for the Ultimate Body in these families as clearly as we do for Ideal Worker and Perfect Parent. We can see how it could happen, and we explain what it would look like.

But we have not yet seen intensified patterns of use for the Ultimate Body in these families, and only time will tell if it happens more broadly. The "Quantified Self" movement suggests it's likely. See Lupton, *The Quantified Self*.

6. In 1989 Ben Agger suggested that increasing speed, or "fast capitalism," ensured that control over populations would be dispersed and unobtrusive. In 2004 he translated his theoretical insights into an expansive and critical portrait of how speed, and the desire for speed, shapes internet culture, work, childhood, family life, and the manifestation of the body in the digital age. See Agger, *Fast Capitalism*; Agger, *Speeding Up Fast Capitalism*; Hassan, *24/7*.

7. Several scholars provide overviews of how design plays a role in drawing people in and keeping them hooked to social media, smartphones, and slot machines. The design of technology certainly helps explain the intense relationships people have with digital devices. See Alter, *Irresistible*; Schüll, *Addiction by Design*. However, the language of "addiction" focuses attention on individual pathology rather than on a collective dynamic. Further, current measures that are used to assess "addiction" in internet research are problematic. See Lanette and Mazmanian, "Smartphone Addiction Narrative," 1–6; Lanette, Chua, Hayes, and Mazmanian, "How Much Is 'Too Much'?"

8. The suggestion that people can, and should, take individual action to disconnect from communication technologies is more or less implied and encouraged in major books of the past decade. For example, see Turkle, *Alone Together*; Turkle, *Reclaiming Conversation*.

9. See Morandin, Russo, and Ollier-Malaterre, "Put Down That Phone!," for a scholarly provocation suggesting that individuals need to become more aware of the risks of communication technologies and reevaluate the costs and benefits of such devices.

While these injunctions to individuals to reevaluate their relationship to technologies that enable constant connectivity are not without merit, we call attention to the power hierarchies involved in who feels they can or cannot ignore their email and the collective dynamics that are the core of rising expectations of availability and accessibility. See Slaughter, *Unfinished Business*, 269.

10. Ziptopia, "Don't Touch That Phone"; Baek, "At Tech-Free Camps."

11. Mary (Ellie) Harmon, the graduate student who aided with this research, explored how experiences are coded as "connected" or "disconnected." Harmon contrasted some of the families in this book, Silicon Valley–run camps designed for a technological detox, and hikers on the Pacific Crest Trail (who used digital technologies regularly but did not experience the expectations and obligations associated with such devices while on the trail). She wrote an insightful dissertation detailing how the accessibility and availability that people have come to associate with technological devices are not the fault of the devices themselves.

By exploring how computing has become the *context* for social life and human action, Harmon argues that people currently engage with the capacities of digital technologies in ways that reframe what it means to "connect" and "disconnect." In other words, it is not devices themselves that engender the experience of constant connectivity but the expectations of availability and responsiveness associated with being "plugged in" that lead to the experience of "constant connectivity"—even when use of such devices is punctuated and strikingly not "constant." See Harmon, "Computing as Context."

12. See Perlow, "The Time Famine"; Perlow and Porter, "Making Time Off Predictable."

13. We did not set out to write a book about children and technology; we were interested in working adults and how they use technology to navigate their lives. We observed parents struggling with how to monitor their children's technology, as we describe in the parenting chapter. We did observe one family with intensive technology use by both parents and children that shaped interactions within the family. But it was one of nine families, so we tread lightly. And this is not our area of focus. See also Mazmanian and Lanette, "'Okay, One More Episode'."

14. For a critical assessment of how CEOs are portrayed in the media, see Nelson, "Myth of CEO Work-Life Balance."

15. For a thorough overview of the impossible visions of motherhood as portrayed in the media, see Douglas and Michaels, *The Mommy Myth*.

16. See Jovanovski, "Femininities-Lite."

17. For an incisive overview of the argument that giving people perceived control over work-life schedules manifests as an individualization of work-life conflict, see Wynn and Rao, "Failures of Flexibility."

CHAPTER 7

1. The Shah family relies on paid domestic help, in addition to Olivia's parents. While domestic workers are not the subject of this book, important scholarship examines the experiences of immigrant domestic workers and raises questions about how this redistribution of labor has shaped female migration globally. Many women need to leave children behind in their own countries and find work caring for children in wealthier countries. This displaces but doesn't solve the problem of devaluing and often not seeing the extent of domestic work. See Ehrenreich and Hochschild, *Global Woman*; Hondagneu-Sotelo, *Doméstica*.

2. Jay's life is a less extreme version of the one that Amy Nelson humorously calls out in her takedown of the "myth of CEO work-life balance." After reading a profile of Evernote CEO Chris O'Neill in the *New York Times*, Nelson bristles at the reverent tone in which the author describes O'Neill's "masterfully balanced" life of workouts, meditation, work travel, and fatherhood. She points out how it

takes an army of support to make this life even remotely possible. See Nelson, "Myth of CEO Work-Life Balance."

3. Arlene Kaplan Daniels first described these various activities as *work* and noted that the women who perform this work are undervalued by themselves and others. Daniels called for reconceptualizing work to include all forms of paid and unpaid labor that make up the fabric of our lives. See Daniels, "Invisible Work."

4. A wealth of academic scholarship describes this invisible work. Hochschild details the "second shift" as the time that working mothers spend outside of formal employment engaging in childcare and housework. DeVault defines caring work as the physical and mental work of feeding and caring for a family. Walzer describes the mental and feeling work that follows the birth of a baby. Blair-Loy similarly describes the physical and mental work of the family schema described by women who had given up full-time work. Emens describes "admin" work as the managerial and secretarial office work of the household: scheduling doctor appointments, completing paperwork, and coordinating care. Wade continues these themes in a 2016 piece for *Time* magazine about the "invisible workload" of women. She wrote about the work of "noticing"—noticing that the toilet paper is running out and knowing the family's preferred peanut butter.

More recently, Allison Daminger describes cognitive labor as the work of anticipating, identifying, deciding, and monitoring work. We explicitly draw apart these types of work to explore the different patterns of scaffolding that we see in Chapter 8. See Hochschild, *The Second Shift*; DeVault, *Feeding the Family*; Walzer, *Thinking About the Baby*; Blair-Loy, *Competing Devotions*; Emens, "Admin"; Wade, "Invisible Workload"; Daminger, "Cognitive Dimension"; Daniels, "Invisible Work."

5. Our conception of Emotional Work is about managing the emotions of *others* who are aiding and assisting in the invisible work. The concept builds off the idea of an "economy of gratitude" in which men and women provide gratitude for what the other provides (which helps facilitate the other continuing to engage in those actions). See Hochschild, *The Second Shift*, 156. We observe the same asymmetry observed by Hochschild between men and women in the economy of gratitude almost thirty years later. Women still express more gratitude for husbands who do something around the house than the reverse. Now, however, women have found more people outside the home to help. Managing this help, however, requires new forms of invisible work: work to coordinate this outside help, and more work to be aware of and sensitive to the emotions of all those who help with invisible work. See also Walzer, *Thinking About the Baby*, 32–45; Daminger, "Cognitive Dimension." This all builds from Hochschild's classic labeling of "emotional labor" in the workplace, in which people (particularly in service industries) are expected to manage and subjugate their emotions as part of the job. See Hochschild, *The Managed Heart*.

6. Regular confessionals from blogs and the popular media suggest that this work is still largely invisible, much to the frustration of those who do it. M. Blazoned blogged about the exhaustion of being the parent "responsible for the emotional, physical and logistic needs of children." The French cartoonist Emma sketches pointed comics. Gemma Hartley created a buzz with her article in *Harper's Bazaar* in which she agonizes over managing household tasks (such as hiring a cleaning service). She highlights the Physical Work of household tasks as well as the Mental Work of organizing them. Lockman points out that while women may be able to deploy men to do some Physical Work they remain in charge of the Mental, Coordinating, and Emotional Work. See M. Blazoned, "The Default Parent"; Emma, *The Mental Load*; Hartley, "Women Aren't Nags"; Lockman, *All the Rage*.

7. Men do more housework and parenting today but they have more leisure time; women still do more of the invisible work in the household. See Kamp Dush, Yavorsky, and Schoppe-Sullivan, "What Are Men Doing?" Katrine Marçal writes engagingly about how the invisible work of care does not "count" but is necessary to make our economic system work. And as she points out, "it's true that the conversation about balancing a career and a child is often about women who have a career. It's less frequently about men, which it should be" (Marçal, *Who Cooked Adam Smith's Dinner?* 195). We look both to women who prioritize work and to men who prioritize home, and this reveals the challenges both face in their counter-normative roles. We agree with Joan Williams and Anne-Marie Slaughter that challenging norms of domesticity is critical for men and women alike; we need to support men who may want to take on domestic roles and share invisible work but do not see it as financially or culturally viable. See Williams, *Unbending Gender*; Slaughter, *Unfinished Business*.

8. See Daniels, "Invisible Work"; Daminger, "Cognitive Dimension." Although beyond the scope of this work, research also suggests women do the often invisible "office housework" in the workplace, taking notes, mentoring, and other non-career-enhancing administrative tasks. See Fletcher, *Disappearing Acts*; Kanter, "Men and Women," 89. Also, see Grant and Sandberg, "Madam C.E.O.," for a brief summary of this research.

9. Accounting for this second shift, women worked fifteen hours more than men in the 1960s and 1970s, with that gap shrinking by half in 2009. See Hochschild, *The Second Shift*. For the primary data Hochschild relies on, see Milkie, Raley, and Bianchi, "Taking On the Second Shift." If we include activities done simultaneously (for example, feeding kids and emptying the dishwasher), the gap has shrunk to a quarter. See Pew Research Center, "Raising Kids."

10. The gender gap in the division of labor has narrowed over time, but even within dual-income couples when work is shared most equally, 54 percent of couples say women manage more of the children's schedules and 31 percent say

women handle more of the household chores and responsibilities. See Pew Research Center, "Raising Kids."

11. See Wajcman, *Pressed for Time*; Cowan, *More Work for Mother*.

12. See Bittman, Rice, and Wajcman, "Appliances and Their Impact"; Cowan, *More Work for Mother*.

13. Samsung's smart refrigerator line markets itself with the following tagline: "It's more than a fridge. It's the Family Hub: Make your kitchen the center of your home. With the Family Hub, you can shop for food, organize your family's schedules and even entertain—all from your fridge." See Samsung, "Family Hub."

14. In discussing the profound degree to which what were once considered intimate services have become market transactions, Hochschild argues that the "answer" to dilemmas posed by this outsourcing is not more access to the market but a reinvestment in community and social cohesion. See Hochschild, *The Outsourced Self.*

CHAPTER 8

1. Scaffolding has been referenced in many other literatures. We use the word *scaffolding* to capture the doing of invisible work in order to support the efforts of individuals striving for the myths of perfection. Using terms from construction, we find the metaphor holds up when one thinks through the various forms of scaffolding available to builders. In construction, *single row scaffolding* is simple and easy to build, with one row of scaffolding anchored to the ground and secured to the house. It does not rely on other supports. *Modular Scaffolding* consists of ready made parts that can be brought together and rebuilt in different configurations. It is expensive to construct, but once built is resilient and provides flexibility to different needs. *Double row scaffolding* has two rows of scaffolding in balance with each other and anchored to the ground. Stability comes from equal tension between the rows. *Needle scaffolding* is cantilevered from the house and does not touch the ground; the scaffolding is fully supported by needles coming out from the house.

2. Single Scaffolding is the structure of an American family easily imagined in any Norman Rockwell, 1950s-style suburban vision, and it is the most familiar in American discourse. The cultural belief that one parent should stay home to manage the household is baked into long-standing assumptions about the separation between public and private spheres that emerged in the industrial era. But the vast majority of families today do not choose or cannot afford this model.

Currently, 27 percent of all mothers and 7 percent of all fathers stay at home. This is similar to the overall rates twenty-five years ago. It is important to note that this category of "stay-at-home" parent includes people who cannot find work, are disabled, or are in school. Despite the prevalence of the narrative, a working father and stay-at-home mother has never accounted for more than 40 percent of American families (in the 1970s). See Cohn, Livingston, and Wang, "After Decades"; Livingston, "Stay-at-Home Moms and Dads."

3. Forty-six percent of married or cohabiting couples with at least one child under eighteen were both engaged in full-time work in 2015. The percentage increases to over 60 percent once part-time work is included. See Pew Research Center, "Raising Kids"; U.S. Census Bureau, "Majority of Children."

A large portion of these families are likely to engage Modular Scaffolding. A Modular Scaffolding structure generally privileges the career of the person who is not the hub and thus is relieved of much of the invisible work. If the hub doesn't have an excellent lattice of support, true work flexibility, or a schedule that aligns with the needs of the family, the model can become untenable. If work demands are too much, the hub may end up dialing back on work or the family may change the structure of scaffolding.

Outsourcing perpetuates the devaluation of invisible work, and such work is often outsourced to poorer immigrant women. See Hondagneu-Sotelo, *Doméstica*. We discuss the problems with this solution in Chapter 9.

4. The frustration and resentment felt by professional women who expected equality in their marriages and have ended up as the hub for a Modular Scaffolding structure are well-documented by Darcy Lockman. See Lockman, *All the Rage*.

5. In this model we see both parents working without one career taking precedence. It is possible that many of the 46 percent of U.S. two-parent households with two full-time jobs enact this structure; this was the most common household structure in the United States in 2016. That said, it is well-documented that even among dual-earner families in which invisible work is shared, it is often not equal. Roughly 60 percent of households with two full-time working parents share equally the household chores and activities for children (Physical Work). However, 54 percent of mothers do more to manage children's schedules and activities (Mental and Coordinating Work). See Pew Research Center, "Raising Kids." Numerous studies find that when fathers are more involved in childrearing and household chores marriages are more stable and both partners are more likely to report marital satisfaction. See Lockman, *All the Rage*; Geiger, "Sharing Chores."

6. Just over 25 percent of American households with children at home rely on single parents to do it all (21 percent of children live with a single mother; 4 percent live with a single father). By definition, all of these households rely on Needle Scaffolding. Roughly three-quarters of those single parents are working, and over a quarter of all single parents live below the poverty line. See Livingston, "Changing Profile of Unmarried Parents"; Pew Research Center, "Raising Kids"; U.S. Census Bureau, "Majority of Children."

7. Stay-at-home dads are increasing in number but still account for at most

17 percent of all stay-at-home parents in 2016. About 7 percent of families have a stay-at-home father (although not always by choice, and not necessarily with a working spouse). See Livingston, "Growing Number of Dads"; Livingston, "Stay-at-Home Moms and Dads"; Cohn, Livingston, and Wang, "After Decades."

8. Emotional Work includes showing appreciation for another as well as being considerate in what not to share. Technology makes it easy to share every detail. But balanced couples deliberate over what to share as well as what to withhold, and this provides couples with resilience. See Beckman and Stanko, "It Takes Three."

9. Thirty-four percent of stay-at-home mothers were in poverty in 2012, although most of that is driven by single or cohabitating mothers, or mothers with nonworking husbands (15 percent of mothers with working husbands are in poverty). Despite increased financial insecurity, not all stay-at-home parents yearn for a professional identity. About 85 percent of stay-at-home mothers with working husbands say they stay home to care for their family (thus constituting about 17 percent of all households). See Cohn and Caumont, "7 Key Findings." However, only 5 percent of stay-at-home mothers are as educated as Rebecca and have a family income above $75,000. See Cohn, Livingston, and Wang, "After Decades." Cory Finchley and Rebecca Stewart are not actively looking for work, and each has embraced the idea of full-time family devotion, even while they both slightly mourn the loss of a professional identity. See Blair-Loy, *Competing Devotions*.

10. Despite the limited Coordinating and Emotional Work in Single Scaffolding, a look to mom blogs and popular books reveals plenty of frustration. Women express resentment at the Coordinating Work of trying to enlist husbands in the chores of invisible work and feeling like they have to offer appreciation and gratitude for those efforts (which counts as Emotional Work). They also complain about not being appreciated (suggesting their husbands are not doing Emotional Work in support of their efforts with the invisible work). See Hartley, "Women Aren't Nags"; Seidman, "I Am the Person"; Lockman, *All the Rage*; Stack, *Women's Work*.

11. The financial security provided by Nick's job makes this arrangement work. If Rebecca didn't miss her job as a social worker, and if her aspirations for parenting were not so high, Rebecca might be more satisfied. It is not uncommon, however, for the stay-at-home parent to express feelings of isolation and insecurity. See Gerson, *Unfinished Revolution*, 49–50.

12. Managerial workers increasingly receive a wage premium for working long hours (at least fifty hours a week, true of all of these SLH employees), and this accounts for about 10 percent of the gender wage gap in managerial jobs. Because these high-income workers need more support at home (given their long work hours), it is more difficult to sustain two careers. In the context of scaffolding, this

means that the primary worker requires more scaffolding from others. Because women often have less support at home and are thus unable to work long hours, they often scale back on their own work in order to scaffold their husband's Ideal Worker behavior. See Miller, "Women Did Everything Right"; Cha and Weeden, "Overwork"; Weeden, Cha, and Bucca, "Long Work Hours"; Yavorsky, Keister, Qian, and Nau, "Women in the One Percent"; Slaughter, *Unfinished Business.*

13. Indeed, gender flexibility helps couples navigate the unexpected changes to breadwinning and caregiving responsibilities. See Gerson, *Unfinished Revolution*, 10.

14. It should be noted that same-sex couples do tend toward specialization of duties once they have children even if the division of those responsibilities is more deliberate and less characterized by resentment. This speaks to the structural incompatibilities between the workplace and home duties more than gender per se. See Goldberg and Perry-Jenkins, "Division of Labor"; Miller, "How Same-Sex Couples Divide Chores"; Lockman, *All the Rage.*

15. Eighty-nine percent of the highly educated parents, like Rebecca Stewart, intend to return to the workforce, and 70 percent do so within two-and-a-half years. See Livingston, "Opting Out?"

16. This network of support may also provide parental stand-ins for children who can help in times of difficulty or transition. Gerson finds paid help to be more typical for middle-class families (with kin more prevalent in lower-income families), but we find families and friends to be critical for these middle- and upper-class families as well. See Gerson, *Unfinished Revolution*, 64–66.

17. While the Phillips family does not engage paid help, the Shah family does. Olivia Shah, also the center of a Modular Scaffolding structure, relies not only on her parents but also on two different house helpers and a personal trainer. The Shah family's mix of paid and unpaid help reflects their higher income bracket.

18. Granovetter's seminal work on the cohesive power of weak ties outlines how knowing those around you, not as close friends but as familiar faces, leads to stronger social cohesion. See Granovetter, "Strength of Weak Ties"; Granovetter, "A Network Theory Revisited."

19. Petriglieri finds that dual working couples go through different phases, and some couples shift who's in the lead over time. The key is an explicit set of conversations in each transition, about their interdependencies and needs for individuation. See Petriglieri, *Couples That Work.* Petriglieri's double-primary model, in which couples prioritize both careers, may be more difficult in some fields given the rewards for overwork. See note 12 for a discussion of the gendered implications of overwork.

20. Allison Daminger's dissertation work examines this work, labeling it "cognitive labor." She describes four aspects of this work: anticipating family needs,

identifying the options, deciding what to do, and monitoring or tracking after the fact. Daminger finds that although interviewees do not offer gender as the explanation for the division of labor, women are more likely to anticipate needs and monitor behavior. See Daminger, "Cognitive Dimension." Consistent with this and other work, we see Lisa Phillips anticipating and coordinating the daily schedule and monitoring homework completion in the evening. See also DeVault, *Feeding the Family*; Walzer, *Thinking About the Baby*.

21. In the popular press, invisible work is negotiated in a marriage partnership, usually with the woman taking on more. Ellen Seidman in "Love That Max" blogged about being the person who does everything from noticing when the toilet paper is running out to paying the bills. The blog post ends with, "It doesn't take a village, it takes *me.* . . . And, therefore, I rock" ("I Am the Person"). Many women have bought into the cultural narrative of motherhood valorized as an individual accomplishment: "[I]t's every mom for herself. It only takes a village if you, Mom, aren't doing enough by yourself" (Douglas and Michaels, *The Mommy Myth*, 308). See also Hartley, "Women Aren't Nags."

The problem with this individual ownership is that mothers don't have enough help to manage the unreasonable demands and they fault themselves for any (inevitable) failure. And it encourages maternal gatekeeping in which mothers hold partners to their standards when asking for assistance; in essence asking for help rather than joint ownership.

22. See Ehrenreich and Hochschild, *Global Woman*; Hondagneu-Sotelo, *Doméstica*; Stack, *Women's Work*.

23. For a discussion of temporal politics around whose time is used in service of making time for others, see Sharma, *In the Meantime*.

24. Petriglieri finds that couples who tackle the logistical challenges of dividing invisible work deliberately, even when not equally, are happier with their division of labor (*Couples That Work*). Rodsky provides a practical "how to" of initiating and structuring such conversations (*Fair Play*).

25. Two of our families have children with Individualized Education Programs (IEPs); these plans, supported by the federal Individuals with Disabilities Education Act, are required for children needing any special education services. Beyond the extensive effort necessary to get and maintain an IEP in a school district, it's important to point out that this support does not extend to after-school programs. Although after-school programs are places of public accommodation, how programs deal with special needs kids is not clear. So some portion of the 13 percent of public school children with IEPs are in paid childcare outside of school, but how well that works likely varies enormously. See Digest of Education Statistics, "Table 204.30."

26. Chip's unusual situation means that he doesn't bring a laptop home like

Teresa, and he only works when he's in the office. Thus he can be a good worker but he is not subject to the Ideal Worker expectations that Teresa lives by (despite making 50 percent more than Teresa). Teresa is an exempt employee (like the majority of professional workers), and exempt workers have no limits to the number of hours they are expected to work in a week. These jobs are the basis of intensive work cultures in which long hours become the norm and childcare is stretched to the limit.

In contrast, non-exempt hourly workers simply aren't paid if they have to leave early (and may in fact put their job at risk if they can't work as scheduled). The income volatility of work has grown particularly in the retail and service sectors, where employers use dynamic staffing policies. See Morduch and Schneider, "We Tracked Every Dollar." Chip's technical job and needed expertise means that these problems don't apply to him.

27. There is a vast academic and popular literature on the challenges of working moms: Sharon Hays's description of intensive mothering, Arlie Hochschild's coining of the second shift, Joan Williams's analysis of how the tension between Ideal Worker and caring work discriminates against women and working moms, Mary Blair-Loy's articulation of the work or family devotion schemas chosen by executive women, and Brigid Schulte's popular 2015 book, *Overwhelmed*. See Hays, *Cultural Contradictions*; Hochschild, *The Second Shift*; Williams, *Unbending Gender*; Blair-Loy, *Competing Devotions*; Schulte, *Overwhelmed*.

Thus Katrina Garcia is not unusual. But notably, increasingly men *and* women experience these stresses. Describing this as a work-family issue (and then a gender issue) displaces the underlying causes of the problem onto individuals and hides the myths as a fundamental factor. Unreasonable expectations of work and of parenting create the challenges described in this book. Joan Williams explains, "[W]e need to redefine equality as changing the relationship of market and family work so that all adults—men as well as women—can meet both family and work ideal" (*Unbending Gender*, 42). See also Padavic, Ely, and Reid, "Explaining the Persistence of Gender Inequality."

28. Keeping the house clean is yet another expectation that Katrina takes on. We observe her forever tidying and picking up after the kids. One could imagine a myth of a spotless home. Rebecca Stewart puts out seasonal decorations. Olivia Shah's home exudes calm with its uncluttered surfaces. Brenda and Cory Finchley have the evening ritual of having the kids put toys away. Teresa and Chip Davies acknowledged they put off participating in the study until they had tidied the apartment. Although the families didn't verbalize an idealized version of what home should look like, upkeep of their homes and their collection of material possessions would have been another interesting investigation. See Arnold, Graesch, Ragazzini, and Ochs, *Life at Home*.

29. Katrina's decision to put her career on hold has a significant financial cost. According the Center for American Progress calculator, someone of Katrina's age (thirty) and income level ($80,000 per year) loses $209,000 over her lifetime by stopping out of work for the 1.5 years that she stays home. This number is a combination of lost wages (40 percent), lost wage growth (30 percent), and lost retirement assets and benefits (20 percent). See Madowitz, Rowell, and Hamm, "Hidden Cost." And for many, it is a feeling of being pushed rather than opting out. See Stone, *Opting Out?*; Stone and Lovejoy, *Opting Back In*.

30. An audit study of hypothetical resumes sent to employers finds a significantly lower rate of callbacks among resumes when the applicant has opted out of the labor force (even more of a penalty than a period of forced unemployment). See Weisshaar, "From Opt Out to Blocked Out." This punishment for violating a key tenet of the Ideal Worker myth (prioritizing work) applies to men and women. In fact, men face a steeper penalty for stepping out. Men who opt out of the labor force for a period are stigmatized and seen as highly uncommitted to work. See Rudman and Mescher, "Penalizing Men." Men who take advantage of flexible work policies in the workplace are similarly punished. See Bailyn, *Breaking the Mold*, 31.

31. See Williams, *Unbending Gender*. This "choice rhetoric" describes women as choosing to stay home not because of the hierarchical priority of a husband's career (an old-school idea) but because the choice allows for a more manageable, fulfilling life. But it's a false choice. Katrina would never choose to stay home if the demands of work were not so intense and the demands of domesticity not in conflict and by default her responsibility. For others, the "choice" to maintain two full-time careers requires other concessions in the partnership, often relating to a lopsided division of the invisible work. See Pugh, *Tumbleweed Society*.

Of course there are people who would prefer to stay home with children than have a professional identity (even if it were easier to do both). We should appreciate the diversity of family arrangements that work for families rather than promote one over another. And many families make the decision to have one parent act as "lead parent" and the other as "primary worker" for a period of time for practical reasons. We hope that these decisions are discussed, planned for, and made explicit between a couple—rather than happen as a gendered default assumption that a woman's career will always take the back seat. See Slaughter, *Unfinished Business*. Further, the choice to have one parent either not work or work part-time is not available to most families without significant financial strain. For an in-depth discussion of the narratives of stay-at-home parents, see Blair-Loy, *Competing Devotions*.

32. The kinds of exhaustion *and* fulfillment Katrina experiences are well described by Susan Douglas and Meredith Michaels: "[E]ven though stress and

self-doubt are facts of life for most of us precisely because of these multiple, conflicting demands, we also do harbor some pride over the fact that we were told 'do it all' and a lot of us did—a whole lot of it. We are used to the contradictions, comfortable in them, despite the pressure" (*The Mommy Myth*, 326). Katrina is happier juggling the unrealistic myths than she was giving up the thrill of her professional life.

33. For a review of studies of lesbian couples, see Brewster, "Lesbian Women"; for a study of gay fathers, see Tornello, Sonnenberg, and Patterson, "Division of Labor," 365; and for a general review of LGBTQ research on families, see Moore and Stambolis-Ruhstorfer, "LGBT Sexuality." The little work on transgender families suggests the division of labor may be divided according to more masculine and feminine stereotypes. See Pfeffer, "'Women's Work'?" More research is needed on invisible work beyond the heterosexual, cisgender people studied here. This work has the potential to enrich our understandings and develop new theories of household work. See Geist and Ruppanner, "Mission Impossible?"; Miller, "Women Did Everything Right."

34. Work expectations appear to drive specialization in household work. See Miller, "How Same-Sex Couples Divide Chores"; Sweeney, Goldberg, and Garcia, "Not a 'Mom Thing'"; Moberg, "Gender Composition in Couples"; Schneebaum, "Economics of Same-Sex Couple Households."

35. Capitalist societies tend to place outsized value on professional work and economic productivity. See Marçal, *Who Cooked Adam Smith's Dinner?*

36. The Economic Policy Institute reports that the annual cost of childcare for a four-year-old is $8,230. Childcare is one of the biggest expenses for families and unaffordable (more than 10 percent of income) for the vast majority. Infant care is more expensive than public college in California. A typical family needs to spend 31.5 percent of their income on childcare for two young children. For low-wage workers, childcare for an infant requires one-half of their income. See Economic Policy Institute, "Cost of Childcare in California."

In addition, childcare has an impact on people's careers, according to a cost-of-care survey by care.com. Seventy-five percent said their job has been affected when childcare plans fall through while 78 percent have had to use a sick day, 37 percent have fallen behind on work, and 28 percent have lost a day's pay.

The suggestion to cut back as a way to manage the demands of parenting and work is economically unrealistic for many. In addition to the loss of income, recent research shows that reducing time, or taking time off, is a permanent setback for career trajectories, and earnings never recover. See Weisshaar, "From Opt Out to Blocked Out" for the impacts of parental leave on career. See also Care.com, "This Is How Much Child Care Costs"; Afterschool Alliance, "America After 3PM."

37. It is important to recognize that single parents can have stable family lives because they have paid work and are not in conflict-ridden relationships that bring financial or emotional instability. See Gerson, *Unfinished Revolution.*

CHAPTER 9

1. Day care center parents may not have deep ties to one another, but they can be helpful and supportive nonetheless. See Small, *Unanticipated Gains.*

2. New urbanism, a construct that gained popularity in the 1980s and 1990s, asserts that we can foster a sense of community through focused attention on the built environment and the relationship between public and private space. See Katz, Scully, and Bressi, *New Urbanism.* Although initial excitement about the ability to construct community has faltered and new urbanism has faced critique, the built environment can increase the probability of interaction and neighborhood cohesion. See Ellis, "The New Urbanism"; Podobnik, "New Urbanism."

3. Liane Cole describes the search for her "village"—the same journey that people like Rebecca Stewart are on and many of our families have discovered. See Cole, "Searching for My Village." Melissa Gregg calls out the support team in the wings of the workplace. See Gregg, "False Dichotomy."

4. The experiences of work and parenting are different across ethnicity and income but there are shared insecurities and expectations as well. See Cooper, *Cut Adrift*; Dow, "Integrated Motherhood"; Ishizuka, "Social Class, Gender and Contemporary Parenting Standards"; Lareau, *Unequal Childhoods;* Pugh, *Tumbleweed Society.* The belief in eating healthy and the pressure to do so are even more difficult to uphold in lower-income families. See Bowen, Brenton, and Elliott, *Pressure Cooker.*

5. These challenges reach beyond the United States as well, but the cultural narratives and public policies that shape the experience and interpretation of that experience differ across countries. See Collins, *Making Motherhood Work*, for a comparison of mothers in Sweden, Germany, Italy, and the U.S.

6. This is a very American construction of work-life responsibility. See Collins, *Making Motherhood Work.*

7. Certainly society also benefits when parents raise children for the next generation of jobs—providing the future doctors, caregivers, and workers. Calling the decision to have children a "choice" ignores the societal benefit and the many ways in which American culture undermines or makes that choice difficult. Crittenden, *The Price of Motherhood.*

8. See Bellah, Madsen, Sullivan, Swidler, and Tipton, *Habits of the Heart*; Durkheim, *Division of Labor*; Marçal, *Who Cooked Adam Smith's Dinner?*

9. Language matters. Cooper finds that people manage the emotions associated with this relentless striving by relabeling their emotions (for example, I am

stressed not economically anxious) and redirecting their attention (for example, it must be me, it's not the organization or society in which I live). Emotion management is an important tool for reinforcing the status quo. See Cooper, *Cut Adrift*.

10. Among others, both Mary Blair-Loy and Katrine Marçal discuss the ways in which devotion to certain schemas of intensive parenting and the devaluing of domestic care serve to keep one parent in the home and, in so doing, prop up classic imagery of the "economic man" as a fully devoted agent of the workplace. See Blair-Loy, *Competing Devotions*; Marçal, *Who Cooked Adam Smith's Dinner?*

Here we want to be very clear that our suggestions seek to bridge the gulf between parents (often mothers) who stay home to do domestic work and working parents who outsource this work to others. The goal is to challenge the norms of domesticity, instilling value in that work regardless of who provides it. Succeeding in the quest for caregiving as a functional category rather than a maternal presumption will benefit all people doing this work regardless of whether they are currently paid or unpaid—mothers or other caregivers. In this, we subscribe to the strategy of "domesticity in drag" described by Joan Williams and the importance of an "infrastructure of care" called for by Anne-Marie Slaughter. See Williams, *Unbending Gender*, 245; Slaughter, *Unfinished Business*, 279.

11. This is Katrine Marçal's call for the field of economics—as a counterpoint rather than a replacement to the one-sided focus on competition and self-interest. See Marçal, *Who Cooked Adam Smith's Dinner?* 188.

12. Research on the gendered nature of care work abounds. See Ehrenreich and Hochschild, *Global Woman*; Federici, *Revolution at Point Zero*; Folbre, *For Love and Money*; Bowen, Brenton, and Elliott, *Pressure Cooker*, for examples. That said, fatherhood is changing. Recent findings suggest that men are more involved in childcare and cite parenting as central to their identity. Scholars question whether this involvement, however, will spread to invisible work as well. See Livingston and Parker, "8 Facts."

13. Couples explain their gendered division of labor as a result of personality (for example, she's just a planner or he just can't remember). Some suggest it's about "maternal gatekeeping," which is the idea that women have unreasonably high expectations men do not subscribe to. But a close look at this reveals a whole set of basic activities that couples generally agree on (such as having clean clothes, children getting fed, getting children to sleep and to school on time). This keeps gender as an underground (although visibly apparent to a researcher) explanation for the division of labor. See Daminger, "Cognitive Dimension"; Lockman, *All the Rage*.

14. We acknowledge that this is not just a question of gender. Our analysis completely ignores intersectionality and the racial and economic demographics

of those engaged in caring work. As we acknowledge, immigrant and nonwhite women are hired to do the invisible work of the economically privileged. The invisibility and devaluing of this work are not altered by hiring this work out. See Duffy, *Making Caring Count*; Ehrenreich and Hochschild, *Global Woman*; Hondagneu-Sotelo, *Doméstica*; Folbre, *For Love and Money*.

15. Recounted by an American mother about her friends' reactions to the fact that her husband did his own laundry in Collins, *Making Motherhood Work*, 216.

16. As just one example of many, Jennifer Garner spoke out about this double standard in 2014. Talking about comparing notes with her then husband Ben Affleck, after a day of respective press junkets, she noted,

> We got home at night and we compared notes. And I told him every single person who interviewed me, I mean every single one . . . asked me, "How do you balance work and family?" . . . he said no one asked him about it that day. As a matter of fact, no one had ever asked him about it. And we do share the same family. Isn't it time to kinda change that conversation? (Beaumont-Thomas, "Change the Conversation").

See also Midkiff, "Lauren Groff Gives the Perfect Response"; Nelson, "The Myth of CEO Work-Life Balance"; Slaughter, *Unfinished Business*; Stack, *Women's Work*.

17. Arlie Hochschild discusses the gendered "economy of gratitude" within heterosexual couples and the ways in which women appreciate men participating in domestic duties as a "gift," while men are taught that women doing domestic duties is to be assumed and therefore does not need to be acknowledged or thanked. We suggest that the articulation of different types of invisible work within the context of marriage could lead to not only new expressions of gratitude but actual redistribution of the work itself. We acknowledge, however, that Hochschild wrote this in 1989 and it remains true today. Individual solutions like we have discussed thus far are not likely to be enough. See Hochschild, *The Second Shift*.

18. More than half of married U.S. adults (56 percent)—both with and without children—say sharing household chores is "very important" to a successful marriage (even though mothers are likely to report that they do more around the house). See Geiger, "Sharing Chores."

19. Gender flexibility describes couples with more fluid boundaries between breadwinning and caregiving, and couples with this type of flexibility are more able to share and value both roles. Gerson, *Unfinished Revolution*, 10. Williams discusses "gender flux" as the way toward "destabilizing domesticity's gender roles." More generally, flexibility in a relationship is associated with resilience. See Williams, *Unbending Gender*, 227; Beckman and Stanko, "It Takes Three."

20. When Sweden was faced with a population decline and sought to encourage childrearing in 1941, Alva Myrdal proposed state compensation for having children. She recognized that this economic support of motherhood would enable

women to engage more fully in wage labor. Wages for housework was a movement that began in New York in 1972 (with roots in Italy). The idea that housework is real work that requires remuneration to be seen as visible was seen as radical in 1972 (even more so in 1941), even within the feminist movement. Greater attention among feminists was given to improving access to (and reducing discrimination in) the workplace. See Myrdal, *Nation and Family*; Federici, *Revolution at Point Zero*; Federici and Austin, *Wages for Housework*.

21. The hiring of lower-income women has simply redistributed the work among a new set of women. Furthermore, the dismantling of welfare means that low-income women have even less support for their own families (how can you work if you don't have childcare?). The intricacies of how to pay for this work are complicated. We like the idea of a social insurance fund that pays in-home domestic workers and provides resources to improve wages. State or employer support would enable better wages for domestic work without further burdening individual families. More broadly, including paid and unpaid household labor in the GDP would put a quantifiable value on invisible work. See Crittenden, *The Price of Motherhood*; Collins and Mayer, *Both Hands Tied*; Ehrenreich and Hochschild, *Global Woman*; Federici, *Revolution at Point Zero*; Hondagneu-Sotelo, *Doméstica*; Stack, *Women's Work*; Folbre, *For Love and Money*; Hilgers, "Out of the Shadows."

22. In her comprehensive overview of care work in the United States, Folbre highlights the role of intrinsic motivation, altruism, and human dignity in performing care work. However, she also emphasizes, "Even the highest levels of intrinsic motivation will erode over time without adequate compensation and support" (*For Love and Money*, 188). See also Hughes, "Good People and Dirty Work and "Work and Self."

23. The National Domestic Workers Alliance is working to organize domestic care workers (for example, ensuring that housekeepers and nannies receive benefits and fair wages); similarly, the Domestic Workers' Association has worked to educate domestic workers about their rights in Los Angeles. See Hilgers, "Out of the Shadows"; Hondagneu-Sotelo, *Doméstica*.

24. While men and women both chafe at Ideal Worker expectations in many workplaces, research finds that men are able to "pass" and appear to embrace this work identity while women are far more likely to reveal the tension caused by Ideal Worker expectations and suffer consequences in terms of performance evaluations and being passed over for promotion. What would happen if more men refused to "pass"? See Reid "Embracing, Passing, Revealing."

25. See Pedulla and Thébaud, "Can We Finish the Revolution?"; Thébaud and Pedulla, "Masculinity and the Stalled Revolution."

26. While such discrimination is not uncommon, a sign of hope is the recent and dramatic increase in the number of family responsibilities discrimination

cases being filed and won in the court of law (for example, caregiver discrimination, such as when parents of young children or those with aging parents are denied promotions or stigmatized for taking family leave). This is not simply a women's problem. Men are increasingly likely to file discrimination cases (although they are still less likely to win these cases than women and in many instances are more stigmatized). Family responsibilities discrimination has been a key area of focus for the WorkLife Law Center at UC Hastings, work pioneered by Joan Williams. See WorkLife Law, "What Is FRD?"; Calvert, "Caregivers in the Workplace"; Rudman and Mescher, "Penalizing Men"; Williams and Bornstein, "Evolution of FReD."

27. It is powerful when people act as "tempered radicals" in their organizations to promote change. Language matters, and small acts of speaking up can make a real difference. Both men and women can play this role. Work-family conflict has become a narrative that organizations rely on to uphold expectations of a 24/7 work culture. This narrative turns the issue of Ideal Worker expectations into a female problem even though men *and* women push back in an attempt to make life manageable for everyone. See Meyerson, *Tempered Radicals*; Padavic, Ely, and Reid, "Explaining the Persistence of Gender Inequality;" Slaughter, *Unfinished Business*.

Further, while egalitarian work-family preferences are preferred by both men and women when those options are available, institutional constraints often get in the way. If both men and women were to more publicly push back against Ideal Worker norms and acknowledge the invisible work that makes their working lives possible, this would go a long way in changing that dynamic. See Pedulla and Thébaud, "Can We Finish the Revolution?"

28. If jobs in the gig economy were to pay a living wage and provide benefits, they could be a tremendous opportunity for flexible work that could better accommodate people's schedules. See *Hochschild, The Outsourced Self*; Slaughter, *Unfinished Business*.

29. Arlie Hochschild eloquently discusses the promises and challenges of turning to the market for every aspect of personal life and what happens to sense of self, altruism, joy in connection, and value in relationships that aren't marketable. A critical issue with the privatization of personal life is the lack of access to much needed goods and services by the poor. See Hochschild, *The Outsourced Self*.

30. As noted in earlier chapters, many familes are not two parents or have a mother at home in the United States. And in the global context, extended family and community support are the norm. In fact, this is what enables migrant women to come to the U.S. to watch other's children. See Ehrenreich and Hochschild, *Global Woman*.

31. Recognizing the diversity of families is an important step toward invalidating the culturally dominant mythology of a male breadwinner and female

caregiver. That mythology has never comprised more than 40 percent of American households (and is today about 20 percent). Moving beyond the families studied here to add in the diversity of race, class, and sexual orientation of families today would help in evaluating solutions with a wider variety of actual families in mind. See Pugh, *Tumbleweed Society*, 183–196.

32. These laws provide important legal rights to LGBTQ families as well as have more mundane benefits for families like those in this book. Massachusetts and California law recognize that children can have more than two parents. See Pugh, *Tumbleweed Society*, 194–195.

33. For example, the industrial kitchens in churches and schools can help fill the cooking gap. These institutions have the capacity to organize large meals that could be eaten collectively or enjoyed in a community—an opportunity to save money (meals could be provided on a sliding scale), equalize access to healthy food, and promote community engagement. See Bowen, Brenton, and Elliott, *Pressure Cooker*. Childcare centers and other institutions can also be places for networks of support to develop with the right institutional conditions. See Small, *Unanticipated Gains*.

34. Collins, *Making Motherhood Work*, 84.

35. Community mothering emerged less from desire than need. With the history of slavery and the need for mothers to work outside the home, the African-American community has long embraced a shared perspective on mothering. Even today, black mothers work more hours than any other group of mothers. We suggest that community mothering be embraced more broadly as a way to combat the individualistic expectations of Perfect Parenting while giving children the stability, care, and love they need. See Collins, *Black Feminist Thought*; Dow, "Integrated Motherhood."

36. Schulte points out that women being the sole caregivers is unusual. People need "alloparents," a word Sara Blaffer Hardy uses to describe the other adults who help mothers take care of children in a hunter-gatherer tribe in Africa. See Schulte, *Overwhelmed*, 190–196.

37. For many, community connections are undermined by job instability. Low-wage workers may be forced to move to find jobs. In higher-wage professional work, companies expect job mobility. This points to the difficulty of solving issues around community and social cohesion without attention to the structures of work. Pugh, *Tumbleweed Society*.

38. Sadly, food swaps can fall apart when judgments of what is appropriate food undermine the power of sharing food. See Fitzmaurice and Schor, "Homemade Matters," for an examination of a food swap that disintegrated because of different beliefs about what constitutes a valued swap. This seems tied to the Perfect Parent and Ultimate Body myths and what is deemed worthy for children and

people's bodies, and it shows yet another way that the myths of perfection get in the way of navigating everyday life.

39. One example is the Village to Village Network that has spawned over two hundred villages in the United States. See Village to Village Network, "Village Model."

40. Research shows that when the sharing economy relies only on technological platforms to facilitate transactions it can reproduce inequality and racism rather than promote egalitarian opportunities for exchange. There is a distinction between technology being used to enhance and facilitate social connection and technology displacing trust relationships with market transactions. Whether digital "villages" that use platforms to facilitate interaction within local communities would exacerbate social and cultural differences and promote inequality is an open question that has not been examined, to our knowledge. See Schor and Attwood-Charles, "The 'Sharing' Economy"; Schor, Fitzmaurice, Carfagna, Attwood-Charles, and Poteat, "Paradoxes of Openness."

41. Aligning individual and organizational needs is the premise of Bailyn's "Dual Agenda." While this language is now common in scholarship on "work/life balance," few for-profit organizations have been able to embrace a win-win perspective on workers' lives and the bottom line. See Bailyn, *Breaking the Mold*.

42. Employee benefits have helped SAS land on the *Forbes* "100 Best Companies to Work For" list for twenty-two years.

43. The Patagonia CEO has written about the economics of their childcare facilities (now also in Reno, Nevada). See Marcario, "Patagonia's CEO Explains."

44. One concern with organizations providing exercise facilities or "perks" such as yoga classes in the workplace is that these efforts are less about enhancing individual wellness than conditioning people to sit still, focus longer, and become more productive workers. Although this does not seem to be the case at SAS, where reasonable work hours are the norm, this is clearly a question in many organizations. See Sharma, *In the Meantime*.

45. Anne-Marie Slaughter provides several examples of companies that act as central hubs for contract lawyers, freelance software coders, and managers for hire for specific projects. See Slaughter, *Unfinished Business*, 256.

46. Collins, *Making Motherhood Work*, 233.

47. See Pedulla and Thébaud, "Can We Finish the Revolution?"; Perlow and Kelly, "Toward a Model."

48. Kelly, Moen, and Tranby, "Changing Workplaces." Although ROWE was discontinued at Best Buy in 2013 when a new CEO came aboard, it has been implemented in over thirty other organizations by trainers from CultureRx. See CultureRx, "The Results-Only Work Environment."

49. Although research found that employees in the sandwich-generation and

those with less supportive supervisors benefited most from ROWE, the power of such interventions is that they apply to all employees. See Kelly et al., "Changing Work." Further, ROWE reduced intentions to leave as well as turnover across all employees. See Moen, Kelly, and Hill, "Enhancing Work-Time Control."

Kelly and colleagues also analyze another workplace redesign called STAR (Support. Transform. Achieve. Results.). This redesign also increased schedule control with positive effects, and it provided benefits for all employees regardless of their family situation. We also encourage you to read Erin Kelly and Phyllis Moen's new book about their work on the STAR initiative. See Kelly and Moen, *Overload.*

50. Perlow, *Sleeping with Your Smartphone.*

51. Fifty-seven percent of American families believe families should primarily provide care until school age, and three-quarters think families should cover the costs of childcare themselves. This may be why universal preschool is receiving more support by extending what is considered school age. The problem is that this leaves no clear solution between birth and the age of five for the most prevalent family structures in America—dual-earner households and single-parent households. See Collins, *Making Motherhood Work,* 215; International Social Survey Program, "Family and Changing Gender Roles."

52. Political advocacy groups like MomsRising are growing in number as more middle- and upper-middle-class families struggle to balance work and family. See Collins, *Making Motherhood Work*; Stone, *Opting Out?*

53. It is important to note that households at the lower end of the economic spectrum struggle for different reasons than the families described here. Underwork rather than overwork is often the problem. People may work two jobs to try to make ends meet. Flexibility as it is practiced by many organizations is associated with schedule unpredictability and uncertainty. See Kalleberg, "Precarious Work." These households also require scaffolding to make all the various aspects of life work, and some of the solutions we describe would help these families, but other solutions tailored to this population should be explored.

54. For example, Elizabeth Emens outlines the degree to which state and federal agencies add to the administrative burden on families and individuals through elaborate forms, disaggregated information, and wait times. She calls for a comprehensive rethinking of how these entities could reduce and streamline such "admin work." Emens's suggestions include reducing the complexity of forms for marriage and adoption, building "one-stop" platforms that streamline legal and social work services, and providing aggregated access to information (from summer camp information to immunization records) that would save individuals the time required to do such tasks themselves ("Admin").

55. The values many Americans teach their children, of independence over

commitment to others, perpetuate individualism. In the realm of self-help, the "Oprah effect" emphasizes self-empowerment that also encourages people to eschew connection and reliance on others. See Jolles, "Knowing for Sure"; Pugh, *Tumbleweed Society*.

EPILOGUE: STEPS FORWARD

1. A plethora of parenting books suggest that intrusive, intensive, and over-parenting tactics are hurting children by stunting their individual development and stripping them of resilience. We are not child psychologists, but we do think it is a good idea for parents to ask themselves what they are hoping that enacting the myth will achieve (for their children, themselves, and their families) and what would happen if they ratcheted down on the expectations of perfection. See Skenazy, *Free-Range Kids*; Levine, *Price of Privilege*; Lythcott-Haims, *How to Raise an Adult*.

2. See Lockman, *All the Rage*.

3. See Westervelt, "Surprising Benefits."

4. The use of workplace technologies to coordinate home activities is on the rise, even as people struggle with the feeling that such strategies strip away the messiness, unstructured time, and emotion that "should" characterize family life. See Lorenz and Pinsker, "The Slackification of the American Home."

We are not saying that homes should be run like a business, rather that such tools might help couples negotiate and make visible the household work that is persistently undervalued and unequally distributed. Ignoring invisible work can lead to resentment, frustration, and the dissolution of marriages. See Lockman, *All the Rage*.

5. Eve Rodsky suggests dividing household tasks by playing a card game according to the specificities of the relationship and the family (*Fair Play*). Jennifer Petriglieri similarly outlines a set of "logistic survival strategies" that includes making lists, deciding what you can drop from the list, and sharing or outsourcing the rest. Petriglieri finds that deep discussions around how to make it work and around what couples really want is key to resolving resentment (*Couples That Work*, 58).

6. One of the key issues with constant availability is that a last-minute change in one person's schedule has a cascading effect on numerous others (those people whom the individual relies on and those who rely on them) in a "web of time." See Clawson and Gerstel, *Unequal Time*. For example, while Perlow's experiments with "Predictable Time Off" didn't aim to reduce the number of hours worked, it created predictability for individual schedules that enabled workers to plan ahead and become more engaged in family life—thus, in a small way, reducing the need for scaffolding. See Perlow, *Sleeping with Your Smartphone*.

7. OpenWork shares success stories, aggregates data, and profiles

organizations that are experimenting with unique solutions to Ideal Worker norms and policies. In so doing, they make the case for new ways of organizing and measuring work in service of employees and organizational success. ideas42, a nonprofit that uses research to do projects with social impact, is testing out different behavioral "nudges" that encourage workers to recalibrate Ideal Worker expectations. These include technology reminders to schedule vacations and managers acting as role models by leaving the office on time. See Schulte, "Preventing Busyness from Becoming Burnout"; Slaughter, *Unfinished Business*.

8. At multiple points over the last couple of decades, companies have banned weekend and late-night emails in the attempt to retain women, improve productivity, or increase well-being. For a recent iteration, see Gee, "Sunday Night." Research has also shown that when email is removed for extended periods from the workplace people multitask less, have a longer task focus, and have lower heart rate variability (which is associated with stress). See Mark, Voida, and Cardello, "A Pace Not Dictated by Electrons."

9. See Mazmanian and Erickson, "The Product of Availability."

10. See Perlow, "The Time Famine"; Schulte, "Preventing Busyness from Becoming Burnout."

11. See Slaughter, *Unfinished Business*, 262.

12. Anne-Marie Slaughter makes a compelling case for addressing the underrepresentation of women in legislative bodies. She asserts that simply having more women in the position to make policy would have dramatic implications for the kinds of initiatives imagined, brought forward, and passed into law. See Slaughter, *Unfinished Business*.

Slaughter also makes an impassioned call for developing an "infrastructure of care." In her words, "We used to have an infrastructure of care: it was called women at home. But with almost 60 percent of those women in the workforce, that infrastructure has crumbled and it's not coming back. We need to build a new infrastructure of care for the twenty-first century, one that meets the demands of our society and our economy" (*Unfinished Business*, 279).

13. Many scholars have called for the restructuring of work and caregiving responsibility; this would involve high-quality childcare provided by parents and properly compensated nonparental caregivers. We share ideas from across a range of authors. See Clawson and Gerstel, *Unequal Time*; Collins, *Making Motherhood Work*; Crittenden, *The Price of Motherhood*; Folbre, *For Love and Money*; Gerson, *Unfinished Revolution*; Gornick and Meyers, *Families That Work*; Hochschild, *The Second Shift*; Hochschild, *The Time Bind*; Schulte, *Overwhelmed*, Slaughter, *Unfinished Business*; Williams, *Unbending Gender*.

14. Because Teresa Davies lives in California, she has it better than many new parents. But people need more. In California the policy guarantees up to six weeks of partial pay (55 percent of a person's usual earnings, with a $1,000-per-week

cap), funded by employees with contributions to a state temporary disability fund. California employers report the policy improves morale and has no negative effects on productivity. The federal Family and Medical Leave Act (FMLA) provides job protection when employees take up to twelve weeks of unpaid leave. As a contrast, Sweden offers 80 percent of pay for sixteen months for couples (with three months each dedicated to the mother and father and the rest to be used flexibly; it can be used in the first eight years of a child's life). Germany guarantees up to twelve months for couples at up to two-thirds of their salary, mostly funded by employers. The challenge of employer-funded leave is that organizations can put pressure on employees not to take leave (and discriminate against employees who might have children to lessen their costs). In Sweden, they have a "use it or lose it" policy for men and women—each parent is eligible for a certain amount of leave, and if one doesn't take it, the other doesn't get it instead. This makes it economically advantageous for men to take leave and reduces the stigma. See Collins, *Making Motherhood Work*; Schulte, *Overwhelmed*. See Bergmann, "Long Leaves," for a discussion of some of the unintended consequences of promoting paid parental leave and part-time work.

15. See Collins, *Making Motherhood Work*; Crittenden, *The Price of Motherhood*, 260–261.

16. See Shapiro, "Bright Spot for N.Y.'s Struggling Schools"; Sanchez, "Does Preschool Pay Off?"

17. Caring Across Generations advocates for universal family care, and it is the type of policy that would provide flexibility and new forms of scaffolding support to families. It includes provisions for childcare, long-term care, and paid family leave. There is precedent in the United States for this type of support. During World War II, the U.S. subsidized childcare to facilitate women in the workplace by partnering with cities and community organizations to care for roughly 130,000 children in 1944. Although the federal support ended, the number of women in the workplace has been on an upward trend since 1947. See Caring Across Generations, "Universal Family Care"; Westervelt, *Forget "Having It All."*

18. Sweden offers a 50 percent tax deduction for the cost of household services. Others have called for employers to pay for household work, in order to support their employees. See Collins, *Making Motherhood Work*; Schiebinger and Gilmartin, "Housework Is an Academic Issue."

19. Requiring pay for overtime work has led to less work and more schedule instability for some workers, so some caution is warranted. See Gerstel and Clawson, "Control Over Time."

20. Death by overwork is a problem in Japan, China, and South Korea (the phenomenon is common enough in Japan and China that they even have a word for it). These are countries with weak labor protections and where employees work more hours than American workers. The South Korean government has

mandated a shorter work week (with a fifty-two-hour cap) in an effort to address the problem. Japan, with a worse infrastructure for childcare than the United States, is realizing that efforts to bring women into the workplace are hindered by the burden shouldered by women at home. See Lee and May, "Go Home, South Korea Tells Workers"; Rich, "Japan's Working Mothers."

REFLECTIONS ON THE PROJECT

1. Mazmanian, Beckman, and Harmon, "Ethnography Across the Work Boundary."

2. See Darrah, Freeman, and English-Lueck, *Busier Than Ever!*; Hochschild, *The Second Shift*; Hochschild, *The Time Bind*; Lareau, *Unequal Childhoods*; Ochs and Kremer-Sadlik, *Fast-Forward Family*.

3. Gerson finds that it is not the family structure that matters but how well families respond to changing economic and caregiving situations. Couples often share ideals for how family life will work, but when faced with unexpected challenges men and women differ in their fallback positions. See Gerson, *Unfinished Revolution*.

4. Sociologist C. Wright Mills provides an eloquent description of the task of the social scientist—to foster a "sociological imagination" or the ability to "understand the larger historical scene in terms of its meaning for the inner life and the external career of a variety of individuals" (*The Sociological Imagination*, 5).

5. People have asked us about other myths that might resonate for different families or at different points in a person's life. This is an interesting thought exercise. Is there a myth of a Dedicated Child, with older children caring for aging parents? Is there a myth of an Impeccable House, with people focused on cleanliness and their physical spaces? There may be, although we did not see such myths affecting the lives of these families. See DeRigne and Ferrante, "The Sandwich Generation"; Arnold, Graesch, Ragazzini, and Ochs, *Life at Home*.

6. See Hochschild, *The Second Shift*; Lareau, *Unequal Childhoods*.

BIBLIOGRAPHY

Acker, Joan. "Hierarchies, Jobs, Bodies: A Theory of Gendered Organizations." *Gender & Society* 4, no. 2 (1990): 139–158.

Afterschool Alliance. "America After 3PM: The Most In-Depth Study of How America's Children Spend Their Afternoons." *Afterschool Alliance*, October 2009. http://www.afterschoolalliance.org/AA3_Full_Report.pdf.

Agger, Ben. *Fast Capitalism: A Critical Theory of Significance*. Champaign: University of Illinois Press, 1989.

——. *Speeding Up Fast Capitalism: Cultures, Jobs, Families, Schools, Bodies*. Boulder, CO: Paradigm, 2004.

Alter, Adam. *Irresistible: The Rise of Addictive Technology and the Business of Keeping Us Hooked*. New York: Penguin Books, 2018.

American Academy of Pediatrics. "American Academy of Pediatrics Announces New Recommendations for Children's Media Use." *American Academy of Pediatrics*, October 21, 2016. https://www.aap.org/en-us/about-the-aap/aap-press-room/pages/american-academy-of-pediatrics-announces-new-recommendations-for-childrens-media-use.aspx.

Ammari, Tawfiq, and Sarita Schoenebeck. "'Thanks for Your Interest in Our Facebook Group, but It's Only for Dads': Social Roles of Stay-at-Home Dads." *Proceedings of the 19th ACM Conference on Computer-Supported Cooperative Work & Social Computing* (2016): 1363–1375.

——. "Understanding and Supporting Fathers and Fatherhood on Social Media Sites." *Proceedings of the 33rd Annual ACM Conference on Human Factors in Computing Systems* (2015): 1905–1914.

Anderson, Jared R., and William J. Doherty. "Democratic Community Initiatives: The Case of Overscheduled Children." *Family Relations* 54, no. 5 (2005): 654–665.

Anteby, Michel, and Caitlin Anderson. "The Shifting Landscape of LGBT Organizational Research." *Research in Organizational Behavior* 34 (2014): 3–25.

Arnold, Jeanne E., Anthony P. Graesch, Enzo Ragazzini, and Elinor Ochs. *Life at Home in the Twenty-First Century: 32 Families Open Their Doors*. Los Angeles: Cotsen Institute of Archaeology Press, 2012.

Bad Moms. Directed by Jon Lucas and Scott Moore. Produced by Bill Block and Suzanne Todd. STXfilms, 2016. Film.

Baek, Raphaella. "At Tech-Free Camps, People Pay Hundreds to Unplug." *All Tech Considered, National Public Radio*, July 5, 2013. https://www.npr.org/sections/alltechconsidered/2013/07/05/198402213/at-tech-free-camps-people-pay-hundreds-to-unplug.

Bailyn, Lotte. *Breaking the Mold: Redesigning Work for Productive and Satisfying Lives*, 2nd ed. Ithaca, NY: Cornell University Press, 2006.

Barley, Stephen R., Debra E. Meyerson, and Stine Grodal. "E-mail as a Source and Symbol of Stress." *Organization Science* 22, no. 4 (2011): 887–906.

Bass, B. L., A. B. Butler, J. G. Grzywacz, and K. D. Linney. "Do Job Demands Undermine Parenting? A Daily Analysis of Spillover and Crossover Effects." *Family Relations* 58, no. 2 (2009): 201–215.

Beaumont-Thomas, Ben. "Change the Conversation: Jennifer Garner Hits Out at Sexism in Media." *The Guardian*, October 23, 2014. https://www.theguardian.com/film/2014/oct/23/jennifer-garner-sexism-media-hollywood.

Beck, Melinda. "The Sleepless Elite." *Wall Street Journal*, April 5, 2011. https://www.wsj.com/articles/SB10001424052748703712504576242701752957910.

Beckman, Christine M., and Taryn L. Stanko. "It Takes Three: Relational Boundary Work, Resilience and Commitment Among Navy Couples." *Academy of Management Journal*, 2020.

Bellah, Robert N., Richard Madsen, William M. Sullivan, Ann Swidler, and Steven M. Tipton. *Habits of the Heart: Individualism and Commitment in American Life*, 3rd ed. Berkeley: University of California Press, 2008.

Bennett, Sara, and Nancy Kalish. *The Case Against Homework: How Homework Is Hurting Children and What Parents Can Do About It*. New York: Crown, 2006.

Bergmann, Barbara R. "Long Leaves, Child Well-Being, and Gender Equality." *Politics and Society* 36 (2008): 350–359.

Bittman, Michaell, James M. Rice, and Judy Wajcman. "Appliances and Their Impact: The Ownership of Domestic Technology and Time Spent on Household Work." *British Journal of Sociology* 55, no. 3 (2004): 401–423.

Blair, Steven M., Michael J. LaMonte, and Milton Z. Nichaman. "The Evolution of Physical Activity Recommendations: How Much Is Enough?" *American Journal of Clinical Nutrition* 79, no. 5 (2004): 913–920.

Blair-Loy, Mary. *Competing Devotions: Career and Family Among Women Executives*. Cambridge, MA: Harvard University Press, 2009.

M. Blazoned [pseud.]. "The Default Parent." *Huffington Post*, October 28, 2014. https://www.huffingtonpost.com/m-blazoned/the-default-parent_b_6031128.html.

Blum-Ross, Alicia, and Sonia Livingstone. "Families and Screen Time: Current Advice and Emerging Research." *Media Policy Brief 17*. London: Media Policy Project, London School of Economics and Political Science, 2016.

Bowen, Sarah, Joslyn Brenton, and Sinikka Elliott. *Pressure Cooker: Why Home Cooking Won't Solve Our Problems and What We Can Do About It*. New York: Oxford University Press, 2019.

Brewster, Melanie E. "Lesbian Women and Household Labor Division: A Systematic Review of Scholarly Research from 2000 to 2015." *Journal of Lesbian Studies* 21, no. 1 (2017): 47–69.

Brown, Catherine, Ulrich Boser, and Perpetual Baffour. "Workin' 9 to 5." *Center for American Progress*, October 11, 2016. https://www.americanprogress.org/issues/education-k-12/reports/2016/10/11/145084/workin-9-to-5-2.

Calvert, Cynthia Thomas. "Caregivers in the Workplace: Family Responsibilities Discrimination Litigation Update 2016." *WorkLife Law*, University of California Hastings College of the Law, 2016. https://worklifelaw.org/publications/Caregivers-in-the-Workplace-FRD-update-2016.pdf.

Care.com. "This Is How Much Child Care Costs in 2018." Care.com, July 17, 2018. https://www.care.com/c/stories/2423/how-much-does-child-care-cost.

Caring Across Generations. "Universal Family Care," May 8, 2019. https://caringacross.org/policy-agenda/universal-family-care.

Center for Humane Technology. "Problem." Center for Humane Technology, 2018. http://humanetech.com/problem.

Cha, Youngjoo, and Kim A. Weeden. "Overwork and the Slow Convergence in the Gender Gap in Wages." *American Sociological Review* 79 (2014): 457–484.

Chandler, Adam. "Why Do Americans Move So Much More Than Europeans?" *The Atlantic*, October 21, 2016. https://www.theatlantic.com/business/archive/2016/10/us-geographic-mobility/504968.

Ciabattari, Teresa. *Sociology of Families: Change, Continuity, and Diversity*. Thousand Oaks, CA: SAGE, 2016.

Clawson, Dan, and Naomi Gerstel. *Unequal Time: Gender, Class and Family in Employment Schedules*. New York: Russell Sage Foundation, 2014.

Cohen, Lawrence J. *Playful Parenting: An Exciting New Approach to Raising Children That Will Help You Nurture Close Connections, Solve Behavior Problems, and Encourage Confidence*. New York: Ballantine, 2008.

Cohn, D'Vera, and Andrea Caumont. "7 Key Findings About Stay-at-Home Moms." *Pew Research Center*, April 8, 2014. http://www.pewresearch.org/fact-tank/2014/04/08/7-key-findings-about-stay-at-home-moms.

Cohn, D'Vera, Gretchen Livingston, and Wendy Wang. "After Decades of Decline, A Rise in Stay-at-Home Mothers." *Pew Research Center*, April 8, 2014. http://www.pewsocialtrends.org/2014/04/08/after-decades-of-decline-a-rise-in-stay-at-home-mothers.

Cole, Liane. "Searching for My Village." *Scary Mommy*. https://www.scary-mommy.com/searching-for-my-village.

Collins, Caitlyn. *Making Motherhood Work: How Women Manage Careers and Caregiving*. Princeton University Press, 2019.

Collins, Jane L., and Victoria Mayer. *Both Hands Tied: Welfare Reform and the Race to the Bottom of the Low-Wage Labor Market*. Chicago: University of Chicago Press, 2010.

Collins, Patricia Hill. *Black Feminist Thought: Knowledge, Consciousness, and the Politics of Empowerment*, 2nd ed. New York: Routledge, 2000.

Coltrane, S., E. C. Miller, T. DeHaan, and L. Stewart. "Fathers and the Flexibility Stigma." *Journal of Social Issues* 69, no. 2 (2013): 279–302.

Common Sense Media, "Device Free Dinner." Common Sense Media, 2018. https://www.commonsensemedia.org/device-free-dinner#.

——. "Evolution of Media Use By Kids Age 8 and Under 2011–2017." Common Sense Media, October 18, 2017. https://www.commonsensemedia.org/zero-to-eight-census-infographic.

Conrad, Peter. "Wellness as Virtue: Morality and the Pursuit of Health." *Culture, Medicine, and Psychiatry* 18, no. 3 (1994): 385–401.

Cooper, Marianne. *Cut Adrift: Families in Insecure Times*. Oakland, CA: University of California Press, 2014.

Correll, Shelley J., Stephen Benard, and In Paik. "Getting a Job: Is There a Motherhood Penalty?" *American Journal of Sociology* 112, no. 5 (2007): 1297–1338.

Cowan, Ruth S. *More Work for Mother: The Ironies of Household Technology from the Open Hearth to the Microwave*. New York: Basic Books, 1983.

——. *A Social History of American Technology*. Oxford: Oxford University Press, 1997.

Crittenden, Ann. *The Price of Motherhood: Why the Most Important Job in the World Is Still the Least Valued*. New York: Henry Holt, 2001.

CultureRx. "The Results-Only Work Environment," 2019. https://gorowe.com.

Currid-Halkett, Elizabeth. *The Sum of Small Things: A Theory of the Aspirational Class*. Princeton, NJ: Princeton University Press, 2017.

Daminger, Allison. "The Cognitive Dimension of Household Labor." *American Sociological Review*, 84, no. 4 (2019): 609–633.

Daniels, Arlene Kaplan. "Invisible Work." *Social Problems* 34, no. 5 (1987): 403–415.

Darrah, Charles N., James M. Freeman, and J. A. English-Lueck. *Busier Than Ever! Why American Families Can't Slow Down*. Stanford, CA: Stanford University Press, 2007.

Davies, Andrea Rees, and Brenda D. Frink. "The Origins of the Ideal Worker: The Separation of Work and Home in the United States from the Market Revolution to 1950." *Work and Occupations* 41, no. 1 (2014): 18–39.

DeRigne, LeaAnne, and Stephen Ferrante. "The Sandwich Generation: A Review of the Literature." *Florida Public Health Review* 9, no. 1 (2012): 12.

de Tocqueville, Alexis. *Democracy in America*. Translated by Arthur Goldhammer. New York: Library of America, 2004.

Dettmers, Jan, Tim Vahle-Hinz, Eva Bamberg, Niklas Friedrich, and Monika Keller. "Extended Work Availability and Its Relation with Start-of-Day Mood and Cortisol." *Journal of Occupational Health Psychology* 21, no. 1 (2016): 105–118.

DeVault, Marjorie L. *Feeding the Family: The Social Organization of Caring as Gendered Work*. Chicago: University of Chicago Press, 1991.

Digest of Education Statistics. "Table 204.30." National Center for Education Statistics, 2016. https://nces.ed.gov/programs/digest/d16/tables/dt16_204.30.asp.

Douglas, Susan J., and Meredith W. Michaels. *The Mommy Myth: The Idealization of Motherhood and How It Has Undermined All Women*. New York: Free Press, 2005.

Dow, Dawn Marie. "Integrated Motherhood: Beyond Hegemonic Ideologies of Motherhood." *Journal of Marriage and Family*, 78 (2016): 180–196.

Duffy, Mignon. *Making Caring Count: A Century of Gender, Race, and Paid Care Work*. New Brunswick, NJ: Rutgers University Press, 2011.

Dumas, Tracy L., and Jeffrey Sanchez-Burks. "The Professional, the Personal, and the Ideal Worker: Pressures and Objectives Shaping the Boundary Between Life Domains." *Academy of Management Annals* 9, no. 1 (2015): 803–843.

Durkheim, Émile. *The Division of Labor in Society*. New York: Simon & Schuster, 2014.

Dworkin, Shari L., and Michael A. Messner. "Just Do . . . What? Sport, Bodies, Gender." In *Gender and Sport: A Reader*, eds. Sheila Scraton and Anne Flintoff, 17–29. New York: Routledge, 2002.

Economic Policy Institute. "The Cost of Child Care in California." April 2016. https://www.epi.org/child-care-costs-in-the-united-states/#/CA.

Edin, Kathryn, and Laura Lein. *Making Ends Meet: How Single Mothers Survive Welfare and Low-Wage Work*. New York: Russell Sage Foundation, 1997.

Ehrenreich, Barbara. *Fear of Falling: The Inner Life of the Middle Class*. New York: Pantheon, 1989.

Ehrenreich, Barbara, and Arlie Russell Hochschild. *Global Woman: Nannies, Maids, and Sex Workers in the New Economy*. New York: Macmillan, 2003.

Eikey, Elizabeth V., and Madhu C. Reddy. "It's Definitely Been a Journey: A Qualitative Study on How Women with Eating Disorders Use Weight Loss Apps."

In *Proceedings of the SIGCHI Conference on Human Factors in Computing Systems*, 642–654. New York: Associaton for Computing Machinery, 2017. https://dl.acm.org/citation.cfm?id=3025591.

Elliott, Sinikka, Rachel Powell, and Joslyn Brenton. "Being a Good Mom: Low-Income, Black Single Mothers Negotiate Intensive Mothering." *Journal of Family Issues* 36, no. 3 (2015): 351–370.

Ellis, Cliff. "The New Urbanism: Critiques and Rebuttals." *Journal of Urban Design* 7, no. 3 (2002): 261–291.

Elsbach, Kimberly D., and Beth A. Bechky. "How Observers Assess Women Who Cry in Professional Work Contexts." *Academy of Management Discoveries* 4, no. 2 (2018): 127–154.

Elsbach, Kimberly, and Daniel Cable. "Why Showing Your Face at Work Matters." *MIT Sloan Management Review* 53, no. 4 (2012): 10.

Elsbach, Kimberly D., Dan M. Cable, and Jeffrey W. Sherman. "How Passive 'Face Time' Affects Perceptions of Employees: Evidence of Spontaneous Trait Inference." *Human Relations* 63, no. 6 (2010): 735–760.

Ely, R. J., and D. E. Meyerson. "Theories of Gender in Organizations: A New Approach to Organizational Analysis and Change." *Research in Organizational Behavior* 22 (2000): 103–151.

Emens, Elizabeth F. "Admin." *Georgetown Law Journal* 103 (2014): 1409–1482.

Emma. *The Mental Load: A Feminist Comic*. New York: Seven Stories Press, 2017.

Engeln-Maddox, Renee, Steven A. Miller, and David Matthew Doyle. "Tests of Objectification Theory in Gay, Lesbian, and Heterosexual Community Samples: Mixed Evidence for Proposed Pathways." *Sex Roles* 65, no. 7–8 (2011): 518–532.

Epstein C. F., C. Seron, B. Oglensky, R. Saute. *The Part-Time Paradox: Time Norms, Professional Life, Family and Gender*. London: Routledge, 1999.

Esipova, Neli, Anita Pugliese, and Julie Ray. "381 Million Adults Worldwide Move Within Countries." Gallup, May 15, 2013. https://news.gallup.com/poll/162488/381-million-adults-worldwide-migrate-within-countries.aspx?utm_source=alert&utm_medium=email&utm_campaign=syndication&utm_content=morelink&utm_term=All%20Gallup%20Headlines.

Family Dinner Project. "The Family Dinner Project." 2018. https://thefamilydinnerproject.org.

Farr, Rachel H. "Does Parental Sexual Orientation Matter? A Longitudinal Follow-Up of Adoptive Families with School-Age Children." *Developmental Psychology* 53, no. 2 (2017): 252–264.

Fassel, Diane. *Working Ourselves to Death: The High Cost of Workaholism, and the Rewards of Recovery*. New York: HarperCollins, 1990.

Featherstone, Mike. "The Body in Consumer Culture." *Theory, Culture and Society* 1 (1982): 18–33.

Federici, Silvia. *Revolution at Point Zero: Housework, Reproduction, and Feminist Struggle*. Oakland, CA: PM Press, 2012.

Federici, Silvia, and Arlen Austin. *Wages for Housework: The New York Committee 1972–1977: History, Theory, Documents*. Brooklyn, NY: Autonomedia, 2018.

Figueiredo, M. C., C. Caldeira, V. Eikey, M. Mazmanian, and Y. Chen. "Engaging with Health Data: The Interplay Between Self-Tracking Activities and Emotions in Fertility Struggles." *Proceedings of ACM Conference Computer Supported Cooperative Work* (CSCW) 2, no. 40 (2018).

Fiske, Susan T., Amy Cuddy, Peter Glick, and Jun Xu. "A Model of (Often Mixed) Stereotype Content: Competence and Warmth Respectively Follow from Perceived Status and Competition." In *Social Cognition: Selected Works of Susan Fiske*, 171–222. London: Routledge, 2018.

Fitzmaurice, Connor, and Juliet B. Schor. "Homemade Matters: Logics of Opposition in a Failed Food Swap." *Social Problems* 66, no. 1 (2018): 144–161.

Fletcher, Joyce K., *Disappearing Acts: Gender, Power, and Relational Practice at Work*. Cambridge, MA: MIT Press, 1999.

Folbre, Nancy, ed. *For Love and Money: Care Provision in the United States*. New York: Russell Sage Foundation, 2012.

Forks Over Knives. "Getting Started." Forks Over Knives, 2018. https://www.forksoverknives.com/getting-started/#gs.QcrVtP8.

Foucault, Michel. *The Archaeology of Knowledge*, 2nd ed. London: Routledge, 2002.

———. *Power/Knowledge: Selected Interviews and Other Writings 1972–1977*. Edited by Colin Gordon. Brighton: Harvester, 1980.

Fraser, Jill A. *White Collar Sweat-Shop: The Deterioration of Work and Its Rewards in Corporate America*. New York: W.W. Norton, 2001.

Freitas, Donna. *The Happiness Effect: How Social Media Is Driving a Generation to Appear Perfect at Any Cost*. Oxford: Oxford University Press, 2017.

Friar, Christine. "Why Do Rich Women Keep Telling Me to Sleep?" *The Awl*, December 19, 2016. https://www.theawl.com/2016/12/why-do-rich-women-keep-telling-me-to-sleep.

Fry, Richard, and Rakesh Kochhar. "Are You in the American Middle Class?" *Pew Research Center*, May 11, 2016. http://www.pewresearch.org/fact-tank/2016/05/11/are-you-in-the-american-middle-class.

Fulkerson, Jayne A., et al. "Family Dinner Meal Frequency and Adolescent Development: Relationships with Developmental Assets and High-Risk Behaviors." *Journal of Adolescent Health* 39, no. 3 (2006): 337–345.

Gallup. "Work and Workplace." Gallup, August 8, 2005. https://news.gallup.com/poll/1720/work-work-place.aspx.

Gates, Gary J. "LGBT Parenting in the United States." UCLA: The Williams Institute, 2013. https://escholarship.org/uc/item/9xs6g8xx.

Gee, James Paul. *An Introduction to Discourse Analysis: Theory and Method*, 3rd ed. London: Routledge, 2005.

Gee, Kelsey. "Sunday Night Is the New Monday Morning, and Workers Are Miserable." *Wall Street Journal*, July 7, 2019. https://www.wsj.com/articles/sunday-night-is-the-new-monday-morning-and-workers-are-miserable-11562497212.

Geiger, A. W. "Sharing Chores a Key to Good Marriage, Say Majority of Married Adults." Pew Research Center, November 30, 2016. https://www.pewresearch.org/fact-tank/2016/11/30/sharing-chores-a-key-to-good-marriage-say-majority-of-married-adults.

Geist, Claudia, and Leah Ruppanner. "Mission Impossible? New Housework Theories for Changing Families." *Journal of Family Theory & Review* 10, no. 1 (2018): 242–262.

Gerson, Kathleen. *The Unfinished Revolution: Coming of Age in a New Era of Gender, Work, and Family*. Oxford: Oxford University Press, 2010.

Gerstel, Naomi, and Dan Clawson. "Control Over Time: Employers, Workers, and Families Shaping Work Schedules." *Annual Review of Sociology* 44 (2018): 77–97.

Giddens, Anthony. *The Consequences of Modernity*. Stanford, CA: Stanford University Press, 1990.

———. *Modernity and Self-Identity: Self and Society in the Late Modern Age*. Stanford, CA: Stanford University Press, 1991.

Goffman, Erving. *Stigma: Notes on the Management of Spoiled Identity*. New York: Simon & Schuster, 1963.

Goldberg, Abbie E., and Maureen Perry-Jenkins. "The Division of Labor and Perceptions of Parental Roles: Lesbian Couples Across the Transition to Parenthood." *Journal of Social and Personal Relationships* 24 (2007): 297–318.

Golden, L. "A Brief History of Long Work Time and the Contemporary Sources of Overwork." *Journal of Business Ethics* 84, no. 2 (2009): 217–227.

Goldfarb, Samantha S., Will L. Tarver, Julie L. Locher, Julie Preskitt, and Bisakha Sen. "A Systematic Review of the Association Between Family Meals and Adolescent Risk Outcomes." *Journal of Adolescence* 44 (2015): 134–149.

Gornick, Janet C., and Marcia K. Meyers. *Families That Work: Policies for Reconciling Parenthood and Employment*. New York: Russell Sage Foundation, 2003.

Granovetter, Mark S. "The Strength of Weak Ties." *American Journal of Sociology* 78, no. 6 (1973): 1360–1380.

———. "The Strength of Weak Ties: A Network Theory Revisited." *Sociological Theory* 1 (1983): 201–233.

Grant, Adam, and Sandberg, Sheryl. "Madam C.E.O., Get Me a Coffee." *New York Times*, February 6, 2015. https://www.nytimes.com/2015/02/08/opinion/sunday/sheryl-sandberg-and-adam-grant-on-women-doing-office-housework.html.

Greene, Alan R. *Feeding Baby Green: The Earth Friendly Program for Healthy, Safe Nutrition During Pregnancy, Childhood and Beyond*. San Francisco: Jossey-Bass, 2009.

Greenhaus, J. H., T. D. Allen, and P. E. Spector. "Health Consequences of Work-Family Conflict: The Dark Side of the Work-Family Interface." In *Research in Occupational Stress and Well-Being*, 61–98. Bingley, UK: Emerald Group, 2006.

Gregg, Melissa. *Counterproductive*. Durham, NC: Duke University Press, 2018.

———. "The False Dichotomy of Work and Care." *The Atlantic*, October 2015. https://www.theatlantic.com/business/archive/2015/10/care-work/409999.

———. "Getting Things Done: Productivity, Self-Management, and the Order of Things." In *Networked Affect*, eds. Ken Hillis, Susanna Paasonen, and Michael Petit, 187–202. Cambridge, MA: MIT Press, 2015.

———. *Work's Intimacy*. New York: Wiley, 2011.

Griffin, Melanie. "'No Place for Discontent': A History of the Family Dinner in America." February 26, 2016. NPR The Salt. https://www.npr.org/sections/thesalt/2016/02/16/459693979/no-place-for-discontent-a-history-of-the-family-dinner-in-america.

Gunnars, Kris. "6 Reasons Why Eggs Are the Healthiest Food on the Planet." *Healthline*, April 26, 2018. https://www.healthline.com/nutrition/6-reasons-why-eggs-are-the-healthiest-food-on-the-planet.

Gustafson, Ellen. "How Kale Became Cool." *Self*, March 27, 2015. https://www.self.com/story/how-kale-became-cool.

Hassan, Robert. *24/7: Time and Temporality in the Network Society*. Stanford, CA: Stanford University Press, 2007.

Happify. "Why 'Me' Time Matters When It Comes to Your Happiness." Happify Daily, 2018. https://www.happify.com/hd/why-me-time-is-important-for-happiness-infographic.

Harmon, Ellie, and Melissa Mazmanian. "Stories of the Smartphone in Everyday Discourse: Conflict, Tension & Instability." *Proceedings*. SCGHI Conference on Human Factors in Computing Systems. Paris, 2013, 1051–1060. https://doi.org/10.1145/2470654.2466134.

Harmon, Mary E. "Computing as Context: Experiences of Dis/Connection Beyond the Moment of Non/Use." PhD diss., University of California, Irvine, 2015. eScholarship, https://escholarship.org/uc/item/1dx9060p.

Harrington, Brad, Fred Van Deusen, and Iyar Mazar. *The New Dad: Right at Home*.

Boston: Boston College Center for Work & Family, 2012. https://www.bc.edu /content/dam/files/centers/cwf/research/publications/researchreports /The%20New%20Dad%202012_Right%20at%20Home.

Hartley, Gemma. "Women Aren't Nags—We're Just Fed Up." *Harper's Bazaar*, September 27, 2017. https://www.harpersbazaar.com/culture/features /a12063822/emotional-labor-gender-equality.

Hays, Sharon. *The Cultural Contradictions of Motherhood*. New Haven, CT: Yale University Press, 1998.

Herrera, Tim. "Your Workplace Isn't Your Family (and That's O.K.!)." *New York Times*, August 13, 2018. https://www.nytimes.com/2018/08/13/smarter-living/your-workplace-isnt-your-family-and-thats-ok.html.

Hilgers, Lauren. "Out of the Shadows." *New York Times Magazine*, February 24, 2019, 28–37. https://www.nytimes.com/interactive/2019/02/21/magazine/ national-domestic-workers-alliance.html.

Hochschild, Arlie Russell. "Emotion Work, Feeling Rules and Social Structure." *American Journal of Sociology* 85, no. 3 (1979): 551–575.

——. *The Managed Heart: Commercialization of Human Feeling*. Berkeley: University of California Press, 2012.

——. *The Outsourced Self: What Happens When We Pay Others to Live Our Lives for Us*. New York: Metropolitan Books, 2012.

——. *The Second Shift: Working Families and the Revolution at Home*, 2nd ed. New York: Penguin Books, 2012.

——. *The Time Bind: When Home Becomes Work and Work Becomes Home*. Basingstoke, UK: Macmillan, 1997.

Hofmann, Janell Burley. *iRules: What Every Tech-Healthy Family Needs to Know About Selfies, Sexting, Gaming, and Growing Up*. Emmatus, PA: Rodale, 2014.

Homayoun, Ana. "What Teens Wish Their Parents Knew About Social Media." *On Parenting, The Washington Post*, January 9, 2018. https://www.washingtonpost.com/news/parenting/wp/2018/01/09/what-teens-wish-their-parentsknew-about-social-media/?utm_term=.2d0c0bcf767b.

Hondagneu-Sotelo, Pierrette. *Doméstica: Immigrant Workers Cleaning and Caring in the Shadows of Affluence*. Berkeley: University of California Press, 2001.

Huffington, Arianna. *The Sleep Revolution: Transforming Your Life One Night at a Time*. New York: Harmony, 2016.

Hughes, Everett C. "Good People and Dirty Work" and "Work and Self." Chapters 7 and 34, respectively, in *The Sociological Eye: Selected Papers*, 87–97, 338–347. New Brunswick, NJ: Transaction, 1971 (1984).

I'll Sleep When I'm Dead. Directed by Justin Krook. Netflix, 2016.

International Social Survey Program (ISSP). "Family and Changing Gender Roles." Module of the International Social Survey Program, 2012. http://zacat .gesis.org.

Ishizuka, Patrick. "Social Class, Gender, and Contemporary Parenting Standards in the United States: Evidence from a National Survey Experiment." *Social Forces*, 2018. https://doi.org/10.1093/sf/soy107.

Jacobs, Jerry A., and Kathleen Gerson. *The Time Divide: Work, Family, and Gender Inequality*. Cambridge, MA: Harvard University Press, 2004.

Jolles, Marjorie. "Knowing for Sure: Epistemologies of the Autonomous Self in *O, The Oprah Magazine*." In *The Oprah Phenomenon*. Edited by Jennifer Harris and Elwood Watson, 259–276. Lexington: University Press of Kentucky, 2007.

Jovanovski, Natalie. "Femininities-Lite: Diet Culture, Feminism, and Body Policing." In *Digesting Femininities*, 59–101. Basingstoke, UK: Palgrave Macmillan, 2017.

Judiesch, M. K., and K. S. Lyness. "Left Behind? The Impact of Leaves of Absence on Managers' Career Success." *Academy of Management Journal* 42, no. 6 (1999): 641–651.

Kalleberg, Arne L. "Precarious Work, Insecure Workers: Employment Relations in Transition." *American Sociological Review* 74, no. 1 (2009): 1–22.

Kamp Dush, Claire M., Jill E. Yavorsky, and Sarah J. Schoppe-Sullivan. "What Are Men Doing While Women Perform Extra Unpaid Labor? Leisure and Specialization at the Transitions to Parenthood." *Sex Roles* 78, no. 11 (2018): 715–730.

Kanter, Rosabeth Moss. "Men and Women of the Corporation." New York: Basic Books, 1977.

Katz, Peter, Vincent Scully, and Todd W. Bressi. *The New Urbanism: Toward an Architecture of Community*, vol. 10. New York: McGraw-Hill, 1994.

Kelly, Erin L., and Phyllis Moen. *Overload: How Good Jobs Went Bad and What We Can Do About It*. Princeton, NJ: Princeton University Press, 2020.

Kelly, Erin L., P. Moen, and E. Tranby. "Changing Workplaces to Reduce Work-Family Conflict: Schedule Control in a White-Collar Organization." *American Sociological Review* 76, no. 2 (2011): 265–290.

Kelly, Erin L., et al. "Changing Work and Work-Family Conflict: Evidence from the Work, Family, and Health Network." *American Sociological Review* 79, no. 3 (2012): 485–516.

Kobrynowicz, D., and M. Biernat. "Decoding Subjective Evaluations: How Stereotypes Provide Shifting Standards." *Journal of Experimental Social Psychology* 33, no. 6 (1997): 579–601.

Kossek E. E., B. B. Baltes, and R. A. Matthews. "How Work-Family Research Can Finally Have an Impact in Organizations." *Industrial Organizational Psychology* 4, no. 3 (2011): 352–369.

Kossek E. E., L. B. Hammer, R. J. Thompson, and L. B. Burke. *Leveraging Workplace Flexibility for Engagement and Productivity*. SHRM Foundation's Effective Practice Guidelines Series. Alexandria, VA: SHRM Foundation, 2014.

Kralovec, Etta, and John Buell. *The End of Homework: How Homework Disrupts*

Families, Overburdens Children, and Limits Learning. Boston: Beacon Press, 2001.

Kunda, Gideon. *Engineering Culture: Control and Commitment in a High-Tech Corporation*. London: Sage, 2002.

Lamont, M. *Money, Morals, and Manners: The Culture of the French and American Upper-Middle Class*. Chicago: University of Chicago Press, 2012.

Lane, Carrie M. *A Company of One: Insecurity, Independence, and the New World of White-Collar Unemployment*. Ithaca, NY: Cornell University Press, 2011.

Lanette, Simone, Phoebe K. Chua, Gillian Hayes, and Melissa Mazmanian. "How Much Is 'Too Much'?: The Role of a Smartphone Addiction Narrative in Individuals' Experience of Use." *Proceedings of the ACM Conference on Human-Computer Interaction* 2, CSCW, article no. 101 (November 2018): 2–22. https://doi.org/10.1145/3274370.

Lanette, Simone, and Melissa Mazmanian. "The Smartphone Addiction Narrative Is Compelling, but Largely Unfounded." *Extended Abstracts of the 2018 CHI Conference on Human Factors in Computing Systems*, paper LBW023, 2018, 1–6. https://doi.org/10.1145/3170427.3188584.

Lareau, Annette. *Unequal Childhoods: Class, Race and Family Life*. Berkeley: University of California Press, 2003.

Lavrence, Christine, and Kristin Lozanski. "'This Is Not Your Practice Life': lululemon and the Neoliberal Governance of Self." *Canadian Review of Sociology* 51, no. 1 (February 2014): 76–94.

Lawrence, Sharon D., and Mary K. Plisco. "Family Mealtimes and Family Functioning." *American Journal of Family Therapy* 45, no. 4 (2017): 195–205.

Lee, Su-Hyun, and Tiffany May. "Go Home, South Korea Tells Workers, as Stress Takes Its Toll." *New York Times*, July 28, 2018. https://nyti.ms/2K3wXXd.

Leslie, L. M., C. F. Manchester, T. Park, and S. A. Mehng. "Flexible Work Practices: A Source of Career Premiums or Penalties?" *Academy of Management Journal* 55, no. 6 (2012): 1407–1428.

Levine, Madeline. *The Price of Privilege: How Parental Pressure and Material Advantage Are Creating a Generation of Disconnected and Unhappy Kids*. New York: HarperCollins, 2006.

Ling, Rich. *The Mobile Connection: The Cell Phone's Impact on Society*. New York: Elsevier, 2004.

Link, Rachael. "What Are Superfoods? 15 Top Superfoods to Get into Your Diet." *Dr. Axe*. https://draxe.com/what-are-superfoods.

Livingston, Gretchen. "The Changing Profile of Unmarried Parents." Pew Research Center, April 25, 2018. https://www.pewsocialtrends.org/2018/04/25/the-changing-profile-of-unmarried-parents.

———. "Growing Number of Dads Home with the Kids." Pew Research Center,

June 5, 2014. http://www.pewsocialtrends.org/2014/06/05/growing-number-of-dads-home-with-the-kids.

——. "Opting Out? About 10% of Highly Educated Moms Are Staying at Home." Pew Research Center, May 7, 2014. http://www.pewresearch.org/fact-tank/2014/05/07/opting-out-about-10–of-highly-educated-moms-are-staying-at-home.

——. "Stay-at-Home Moms and Dads Account for About One-in-Five U.S. Parents." September 24, 2018. https://www.pewresearch.org/fact-tank/2018/09/24/stay-at-home-moms-and-dads-account-for-about-one-in-five-u-s-parents.

Livingston, Gretchen, and Kim Parker. "8 Facts About American Dads." Pew Research Center, June 12, 2019. https://www.pewresearch.org/fact-tank/2019/06/12/fathers-day-facts.

Lockman, Darcy. *All the Rage: Mothers, Fathers, and the Myth of Equal Partnership*. New York: HarperCollins, 2019.

Lorenz, Taylor, and Joe Pinsker. "The Slackification of the American Home: Stretched for Time, Some Households Are Starting to Operate More Like Businesses." *The Atlantic*, July 2019. https://www.theatlantic.com/family/archive/2019/07/families-slack-asana/593584.

Lupton, Deborah. "M-Health and Health Promotion: The Digital Cyborg and Surveillance Society." *Social Theory & Health* 10, no. 3 (2012): 229–244.

——. *The Quantified Self*. Cambridge, UK: Polity Press, 2016.

——. "The Quantified Self Movement: Some Sociological Perspectives." *This Sociological Life* (blog), November 4, 2012. https://simplysociology.wordpress.com/2012/11/04/the-quantitative-self-movement-some-sociological-perspectives.

Lyon, David. *Surveillance Society: Monitoring Everyday Life*. London: McGraw-Hill Education, 2001.

Lythcott-Haims, Julie. *How to Raise an Adult: Break Free of the Overparenting Trap and Prepare Your Kid for Success*. New York: Henry Holt, 2015.

Madden, Mary, et al. "Teens, Social Media, and Privacy." Pew Research Center, May 21, 2013, 2–86. http://www.pewinternet.org/2013/05/21/teens-social-media-and-privacy.

Madowitz, Michael, Alex Rowell, and Katie Hamm. "Calculating the Hidden Cost of Interrupting a Career for Child Care." *Center for American Progress*, June 21, 2016. https://www.americanprogress.org/issues/early-childhood/reports/2016/06/21/139731/calculating-the-hidden-cost-of-interrupting-a-career-for-child-care.

Magee, Anna. "Say Goodbye to Kale: The Superfood Trends for 2017—and Five New Ingredients to Watch." *The Telegraph*, January 2, 2017. https://www.telegraph.co.uk/health-fitness/nutrition/say-goodbye-kale-superfood-trends-2017–five-new-ingredients.

Marçal, Katrine. *Who Cooked Adam Smith's Dinner? A Story of Women and Economics*. New York: Pegasus Books, 2016.

Marcario, Rose. "Patagonia's CEO Explains How to Make On-Site Childcare Pay for Itself." *Fast Company*, August 15, 2016. https://www.fastcompany.com/3062792/patagonias-ceo-explains-how-to-make-onsite-child-care-pay-for-itself.

Mark, Gloria, Stephen Voida, and Armand Cardello. "'A Pace Not Dictated by Electrons': An Empirical Study of Work Without Email." *Proceedings*. SIGCHI Conference on Human Factors in Computing Systems. Austin, Texas, 2012, 555–564. https://doi.org/10.1145/2207676.2207754.

Mazmanian, Melissa. "Avoiding the Trap of Constant Connectivity: When Congruent Frames Allow for Heterogeneous Practices." *Academy of Management Journal* 56, no. 5 (2013): 1225–1250.

——. "Worker/Smartphone Hybrids: The Daily Enactments of Late Capitalism." *Management Communication Quarterly* 33, no. 1 (2019): 124–132.

Mazmanian, Melissa, and Christine M. Beckman. "'Making' Your Numbers: Engendering Organizational Control Through a Ritual of Quantification." *Organizational Science* 29, no. 3 (2018): 357–379.

Mazmanian, Melissa, Christine M. Beckman, and Ellie Harmon. "Ethnography Across the Work Boundary: Benefits and Considerations for Organizational Research." In *Handbook of Qualitative Organizational Research: Innovative Pathways and Methods*, eds. K. D. Elsbach and R. M. Kramer, 262–271. New York: Taylor & Francis, 2016.

Mazmanian, Melissa, and Ingrid Erickson. "The Product of Availability: Understanding the Economic Underpinnings of Constant Connectivity." *Proceedings*. SIGCHI Conference on Human Factors in Computing Systems, 2014, 763–772. https://dl.acm.org/citation.cfm?id=2557381.

Mazmanian, Melissa, and Simone Lanette. "'Okay, One More Episode': An Ethnography of Parenting in the Digital Age." *Proceedings*. 2017 ACM Conference on Computer Supported Cooperative Work and Social Computing. Portland, Oregon, 2017, 2273–2286. https://doi.org/10.1145/2998181.2998218.

Mazmanian, Melissa, Wanda J. Orlikowski, and JoAnne Yates. "The Autonomy Paradox: The Implications of Mobile Email Devices for Knowledge Professionals." *Organization Science* 24, no. 5 (2013): 1337–1357.

Melnick, Meredith. "Are You Among the 'Sleepless Elite'—Or Just Sleep Deprived?" *Time*, April 7, 2011. http://healthland.time.com/2011/04/07/are-you-among-the-sleepless-elite-%E2%80%94-or-just-sleep-deprived.

Messenger, Jon, et al. *Working Anytime, Anywhere: The Effects on the World of Work*. Luxemborg and Geneva: Eurofound and the International Labour Office, 2017. http://eurofound.link/ef1658EN.

Meyerson, Debra. *Tempered Radicals: How People Use Difference to Inspire Change at Work*. Stanford, CA: Stanford University Press, 2001.

Michel, Alexandra. "Transcending Socialization: A Nine-Year Ethnography of the Body's Role in Organizational Control and Knowledge Workers' Transformation." *Administrative Science Quarterly* 56, no. 3 (2012): 325–368.

Midkiff, Sarah. "Lauren Groff Gives the Perfect Response to the Work-Life Balance Question." *Refinery29*, July 19, 2018. https://www.refinery29.com/en-us/2018/07/204867/author-lauren-groff-work-life-balance-response.

Milkie, Melissa, Kei M. Nomaguchi, and Kathleen E. Denny. "Does the Amount of Time Mothers Spend with Children or Adolescents Matter?" *Journal of Marriage and Family* 77, no. 2 (2015): 355–372.

Milkie, Melissa A., Sara B. Raley, and Susan M. Bianchi. "Taking On the Second Shift: Time Allocations and Time Pressures of US Parents with Preschoolers." *Social Forces* 88, no. 2 (2009): 487–518.

Miller, Claire Cain. "How Same-Sex Couples Divide Chores, and What It Reveals About Modern Parenting." *New York Times*, May 16, 2018. https://www.nytimes.com/2018/05/16/upshot/same-sex-couples-divide-chores-much-more-evenly-until-they-become-parents.html.

———. "The Relentlessness of Modern Parenting." *New York Times*, December 25, 2018. https://www.nytimes.com/2018/12/25/upshot/the-relentlessness-of-modern-parenting.html.

———. "Women Did Everything Right. Then Work Got 'Greedy'." *New York Times*, April 26, 2019. https://www.nytimes.com/2019/04/26/upshot/women-long-hours-greedy-professions.html.

Mills, C. Wright. *The Sociological Imagination*. New York: Oxford University Press, (1959) 2000.

Mischel, Walter, Yuichi Shoda, and Philip K. Peake. "The Nature of Adolescent Competencies Predicted by Preschool Delay of Gratification." *Journal of Personality and Social Psychology* 54, no. 4 (1988): 687–696.

Moberg, Ylva. "Does the Gender Composition in Couples Matter for the Division of Labor After Childbirth?" IFAU-Institute for Evaluation of Labour Market and Education Policy Working Paper, no. 8, April 2016.

Moen, P., E. Kelly, and R. Hill. "Does Enhancing Work-Time Control and Flexibility Reduce Turnover? A Naturally Occurring Experiment." *Social Problems* 58, no. 1 (2011): 69–98.

Moore, Mignon R., and Michael Stambolis-Ruhstorfer. "LGBT Sexuality and Families at the Start of the Twenty-First Century." *Annual Review of Sociology* 39 (2013): 491–507.

Morandin, Gabriele, Marcello Russo, and Ariane Ollier-Malaterre. "Put Down That Phone! Smart Use of Smartphones for Work and Beyond." *Journal of Management Inquiry* 27, no. 3 (2018): 352–356.

Morduch, Jonathan, and Rachel Schneider. "We Tracked Every Dollar 235 U.S. Households Spent for a Year, and Found Widespread Financial Vulnerability." *Harvard Business Review*, April 12, 2017. https://hbr.org/2017/04/we-tracked-every-dollar-235-u-s-households-spent-for-a-year-and-found-widespread-financial-vulnerability.

Mosco, Vincent. *The Digital Sublime: Myth, Power, and Cyberspace*. Cambridge, MA: MIT Press, 2005.

Myrdal, Alva. *Nation and Family: The Swedish Experiment in Democratic Family and Population Policy*. New York: Harper & Brothers, 1941.

National Responsible Fatherhood Clearinghouse. "About Us." https://www.fatherhood.gov; accessed September 12, 2019.

Neighmond, Patti. "Benefits of Sports to a Child's Mind and Heart All Part of the Game." *Morning Edition*, National Public Radio, July 1, 2015. https://www.npr.org/sections/health-shots/2015/07/01/418899249/benefits-of-sports-to-a-childs-mind-and-heart-all-part-of-the-game.

Nelson, Amy. "The Myth of CEO Work-Life Balance." *Forbes*, September 4, 2018. https://www.forbes.com/sites/amynelson1/2018/09/04/the-myth-of-ceo-work-life-balance/#197739bd19ae.

Nicol, Will. "Best Parental Control Apps for Your Kids' Smartphone." *Digital Trends*, June 4, 2018. https://www.digitaltrends.com/mobile/best-parental-control-apps.

Ochs, Elinor, and Tamar Kremer-Sadlik. *Fast-Forward Family: Home, Work, and Relationships in Middle-Class America*. Berkeley: University of California Press, 2013.

O'Connor, Siobhan. "The Secret Power of Play." *Time*, September 6, 2017. http://time.com/4928925/secret-power-play.

Odgers, Candice L. "Smartphones Are Bad for Some Adolescents, not All." *Nature* 554, no. 7693 (2018): 432–434.

Office of Disease Prevention and Health Promotion. "Active Adults." U.S. Department of Health and Human Services, September 7, 2017. https://health.gov/paguidelines/guidelines/chapter4.aspx.

Ornish Lifestyle Medicine. "The Proven Lifestyle." Ornish Lifestyle Medicine, 2018. https://www.ornish.com/proven-program/#section_lifestyle.

Orzechowicz, David. "The Walk-In Closet: Between 'Gay-Friendly' and 'Post-Closeted' Work." In *Research in the Sociology of Work*. Edited by Steven Vallas, 187–213. Bingley, UK: Emerald Group, 2016.

Padavic, Irene, Robin J. Ely, and Erin M. Reid. "Explaining the Persistence of Gender Inequality: The Work-Family Narrative as a Social Defense Against the 24/7 Work Culture." *Administrative Science Quarterly*. Forthcoming; available at https://doi.org/10.1177/0001839219832310.

Paolicchi, Scarlet. "Importance of Family Dinner & The Billion Family Dinners

Challenge." *Family Focus Blog*, September 9, 2015. https://familyfocusblog. com/importance-of-family-dinners-the-billion-family-dinners-challenge.

Parker, Kim, and Eileen Patten. "The Sandwich Generation: Rising Financial Burdens for Middle-Aged Americans." Pew Research Center, January 30, 2013. https://www.pewsocialtrends.org/2013/01/30/the-sandwich-generation.

Patterson, Donald J., and Sandy Patterson. "Take Charge of Your Family's Digital Culture." *Medium*, December 31, 2014. https://medium.com/@donpatterson/ take-charge-of-your-familys-digital-culture-74e3c22e16ab.

Paul, Pamela. "Let Children Get Bored Again." *New York Times*, February 2, 2019. https://www.nytimes.com/2019/02/02/opinion/sunday/children-bored.html.

Pedulla, David S., and Sarah Thébaud. "Can We Finish the Revolution? Gender, Work-Family Ideals, and Institutional Constraint." *American Sociological Review* 80, no. 1 (2015): 116–139.

Pells, Rachael. "Giving Your Child a Smartphone Is Like Giving Them a Gram of Cocaine, Says Top Addiction Expert." *The Independent*, June 7, 2017. https:// www.independent.co.uk/news/education/education-news/child-smartphones-cocaine-addiction-expert-mandy-saligari-harley-street-charterclinic-technology-a7777941.html.

Perlow, Leslie A. "Boundary Control: The Social Ordering of Work and Family Time in a High-Tech Corporation." *Administrative Science Quarterly* 43 (1998): 328–357.

———. *Sleeping with Your Smartphone: How to Break the 24/7 Habit and Change the Way You Work*. Cambridge, MA: Harvard Business Review Press, 2012.

———. "The Time Famine: Toward a Sociology of Work Time." *Administrative Science Quarterly* 44 (1999): 57–81.

Perlow, Leslie A., and Erin L. Kelly. "Toward a Model of Work Redesign for Better Work and Better Life." *Work and Occupations* 41, no. 1 (2014): 111–134.

Perlow, Leslie A., and Jessica L. Porter. "Making Time Off Predictable—and Required." *Harvard Business Review* 87, no. 10 (2009): 102–109.

Pesche, Megan H., Alison L. Miller, Danielle P. Appugliese, Katherine L. Rosenblum, and Julie C. Lumeng. "Affective Tone of Mothers' Statements to Restrict Their Children's Eating." *Appetite* 103 (2016): 165–170.

Petriglieri, Jennifer. *Couples That Work: How Dual-Career Couples Can Thrive in Love and Work*. Cambridge, MA: Harvard Business Review Press, 2019.

Pew Research Center. "Children's Extracurricular Activities." Pew Research Center, December 15, 2017. http://www.pewsocialtrends.org/2015/12/17/5–childrens-extracurricular-activities.

———. "Mobile Fact Sheet." Pew Research Center, February 5, 2018. http://www. pewinternet.org/fact-sheet/mobile.

———. "Raising Kids and Running a Household: How Working Parents Share the

Load." Pew Research Center, November 4, 2015. http://www.pewsocialtrends. org/2015/11/04/raising-kids-and-running-a-household-how-working-parents-share-the-load.

Pfeffer, Carla A. "'Women's Work'? Women Partners of Transgender Men Doing Housework and Emotion Work." *Journal of Marriage and Family* 72, no. 1 (2010): 165–183.

Phillips, Lisa. *The Artistic Edge: 7 Skills Children Need to Succeed in an Increasingly Right Brain World.* Toronto: The Artistic Edge, 2012.

Pillemer, Julianna, and Nancy P. Rothbard. "Friends Without Benefits: Understanding the Dark Sides of Workplace Friendship." *Academy of Management Review* 43, no. 4 (2018): 635–660.

Podobnik, Bruce. "New Urbanism and the Generation of Social Capital: Evidence from Orenco Station." *National Civic Review* 91, no. 3 (2002): 245–255.

Polivy, Janet. "Psychological Consequences of Food Restriction." *Journal of the Academy of Nutrition and Dietetics* 96, no. 6 (1996): 589–592.

Porter, Gayle, and Nada K. Kakabadse. "HRM Perspectives on Addiction to Technology and Work." *Journal of Management Development* 25 (2006): 535–560.

Pugh, Allison J. *The Tumbleweed Society: Working and Caring in an Age of Insecurity.* New York: Oxford University Press, 2015.

Putnam, Robert D. *Our Kids: The American Dream in Crisis.* New York: Simon & Schuster, 2016.

Pylypa, Jen. "Power and Bodily Practice: Applying the Work of Foucault to an Anthropology of the Body." *Arizona Anthropologist* 13 (1998): 21–36.

Quadlin, Natasha. "The Mark of a Woman's Record: Gender and Academic Performance in Hiring." *American Sociological Review* 83, no. 2 (2018): 331–360.

Quantified Self: Self Knowledge Through Numbers. "What Is Quantified Self?" 2019. https://quantifiedself.com/about/what-is-quantified-self.

Quart, Alissa. *Squeezed: Why Our Families Can't Afford America.* New York: HarperCollins, 2018.

Rapoport, R., Bailyn, L., J. K. Fletcher, and B. H. Pruitt. *Beyond Work-Family Balance: Advancing Gender Equity and Workplace Performance.* San Francisco: Jossey-Bass, 2002.

Reid, Erin. "Embracing, Passing, Revealing, and the Ideal Worker Image: How People Navigate Expected and Experienced Professional Identities." *Organization Science* 26, no. 4 (2015): 997–1017.

Reynolds, Gretchen. "The Scientific 7-Minute Workout." *New York Times,* May 9, 2013. https://well.blogs.nytimes.com/2013/05/09/the-scientific-7-minute-workout/?_r=0.

Rich, Motoko. "Japan's Working Mothers: Record Responsibilities, Little Help from Dads." *New York Times,* February, 2, 2019. https://nyti.ms/2DPtFa8.

Ripley, Amanda. "The Case Against High-School Sports." *The Atlantic*, October 2013. https://www.theatlantic.com/magazine/archive/2013/10/the-case-against-high-school-sports/309447.

Rivera, Lauren, and András Tilcsik. "Class Advantage, Commitment Penalty: The Gendered Effect of Social Class Signals in an Elite Labor Market." *American Sociological Review* 81, no. 6 (2016): 1097–1131.

Robb, Michael. "Think You Know What Your Kids Are Doing Online? Think Again." Common Sense Media, December 11, 2017. https://www.commonsensemedia.org/blog/think-you-know-what-your-kids-are-doing-online-think-again.

Rodsky, Eve. *Fair Play: A Game-Changing Solution for When You Have Too Much to Do (and More Life to Live)*. New York: G.P. Putnam's Sons, 2019.

Ruddick, Sara. *Maternal Thinking: Toward a Politics of Peace*. Boston: Beacon Press, 1995.

Rudman, Laurie A., and Kris Mescher. "Penalizing Men Who Request a Family Leave: Is Flexibility Stigma a Femininity Stigma?" *Journal of Social Issues* 69, no. 2 (2013): 322–340.

Samsung, "Family Hub." Samsung, January 2018. https://www.samsung.com/us/explore/family-hub-refrigerator/overview.

Sanchez, Claudio. "Does Preschool Pay Off? Tulsa Says Yes." National Public Radio, December 12, 2017. https://www.npr.org/sections/ed/2017/12/12/568378251/does-preschool-pay-off-tulsa-says-yes.

Santos, Maricar. "When You Factor in Family Duties, the Average Working Mom Works 98 Hours a Week." *Working Mother*, July 26, 2017. https://www.workingmother.com/when-you-factor-in-family-duties-average-working-mom-works-98-hours-week.

Schiebinger, Londa, and Shannon K. Gilmartin. "Housework Is an Academic Issue." *Academe* 96, no. 1 (2010): 39–44.

Schneebaum, Alyssa. "The Economics of Same-Sex Couple Households: Essays on Work, Wages, and Poverty." PhD diss., University of Massachusetts Amherst, 2013. Open Access Dissertations, https://scholarworks.umass.edu/open_access_dissertations/818.

Schneider, Daniel, and Kristen Harknett. "Consequences of Routine Work-Schedule Instability for Worker Health and Well-Being." *American Sociological Review* 84, no. 1 (2019): 82–114.

Schor, Juliet. *The Overworked American: The Unexpected Decline of Leisure*. New York: Basic Books, 1992.

Schor, Juliet B., and William Attwood-Charles. "The 'Sharing' Economy: Labor, Inequality, and Social Connection on For-Profit Platforms." *Sociology Compass* 11, no. 8 (2017): e12493.

Schor, Juliet B., Connor Fitzmaurice, Lindsey B. Carfagna, Will Attwood-Charles, and Emilie Dubois Poteat. "Paradoxes of Openness and Distinction in the Sharing Economy." *Poetics* 54 (2016): 66–81.

Schüll, Natasha Dow. *Addiction by Design: Machine Gambling in Las Vegas.* Princeton, NJ: Princeton University Press, 2012.

Schulte, Brigid. "Making Time for Kids? Study Says Quality Trumps Quantity." *Washington Post*, March 28, 2015. https://www.washingtonpost.com/local/making-time-for-kids-study-says-quality-trumps-quantity/2015/03/28/10813192-d378-11e4-8fce-3941fc548f1c_story.html?noredirect=on&utm_term=.cfb380ed6e61.

———. *Overwhelmed: How to Work, Love, and Play When No One Has the Time.* Basingstoke, UK: Macmillan, 2015.

———. "Preventing Busyness from Becoming Burnout." *Harvard Business Review*, April 15, 2019. https://hbr.org/2019/04/preventing-busyness-from-becoming-burnout.

Scramble Family Dinner Challenge. "Take the Family Dinner Challenge." 2018. https://www.thescramble.com/family-dinner-challenge.

Sears, William, and Martha Sears. *The Attachment Parenting Book: A Commonsense Guide to Understanding and Nurturing Your Baby.* New York: Little, Brown, 2001.

Seidman, Ellen. "I Am the Person Who Notices We Are Running Out of Toilet Paper, and I Rock: A Tribute to Moms Everywhere." *Love That Max* (blog), May 5, 2016. https://www.lovethatmax.com/2016/05/mothers-day-2016.html.

Senior, Jennifer. *All Joy and No Fun: The Paradox of Modern Parenthood.* London, UK: Hachette, 2014.

Shapiro, Eliza. "Bright Spot for N.Y.'s Struggling Schools: Pre-K." *New York Times*, January 1, 2019. https://nyti.ms/2RrOn7L.

Sharma, Sarah. *In the Meantime: Temporality and Cultural Politics.* Durham, NC: Duke University Press, 2014.

Shilling, Chris. *The Body: A Very Short Introduction.* Oxford: Oxford University Press, 2016.

———. "The Rise of Body Studies and the Embodiment of Society: A Review of the Field." *Horizons in Humanities and Social Sciences: An International Refereed Journal* 2, no. 1 (2016): 1–14.

Skenazy, Lenore. *Free-Range Kids: How to Raise Safe, Self-Reliant Children (Without Going Nuts with Worry).* San Francisco: Jossey-Bass, 2009.

Slaughter, Anne-Marie. *Unfinished Business.* New York: Random House, 2015.

Small, Mario L. *Unanticipated Gains: Origins of Network Inequality in Everyday Life.* Oxford: Oxford University Press, 2009.

Smith, Kevin. "Acai The Superfruit of Marketing." *Smashbrand*, June 2, 2013. https://www.smashbrand.com/articles/acai-the-superfruit-of-marketing.

Squire, Kurt D., and Constance Steinkuehler. "The Problem with Screen Time." *Teachers College Record* 199, no. 12 (2017): 1–24.

Stack, Megan K. *Women's Work: A Reckoning with Work and Home*. New York: Doubleday, 2019.

Stone, Pamela. *Opting Out? Why Women Really Quit Careers and Head Home*. Berkeley: University of California Press, 2008.

Stone, Pamela, and Meg Lovejoy. *Opting Back In: What Really Happens When Mothers Go Back to Work*. Berkeley: University of California Press, 2019.

Strauss, Valerie. "Top 10 Skills Children Learn from the Arts." *Washington Post*, January 22, 2013. https://www.washingtonpost.com/news/answer-sheet/wp/2013/01/22/top-10–skills-children-learn-from-the-arts/?utm_term=.0533d4ea1bbf.

Sweeney, Kristin K., Abbie E. Goldberg, and Randi L. Garcia. "Not a 'Mom Thing': Predictors of Gatekeeping in Same-Sex and Heterosexual Parent Families." *Journal of Family Psychology* 31, no. 5 (2017), 521–531.

Taraday, Jeff. "The Great Egg Debate: 4 Reasons You Need to Stop Eating Eggs." *Breaking Muscle*. https://breakingmuscle.com/healthy-eating/the-great-egg-debate-4-reasons-you-need-to-stop-eating-eggs.

Thébaud, Sarah, and David S. Pedulla. "Masculinity and the Stalled Revolution: How Gender Ideologies and Norms Shape Young Men's Responses to Work-Family Policies." *Gender & Society* 30, no. 4 (2016): 590–617.

Tornello, Samantha L., Bettina N. Sonnenberg, and Charlotte J. Patterson. "Division of Labor Among Gay Fathers: Associations with Parent, Couple, and Child Adjustment." *Psychology of Sexual Orientation and Gender Diversity* 2, no. 4 (2015): 365–375.

Towers, Ian, Linda Duxbury, Christopher Higgins, and John Thomas. "Time Thieves and Space Invaders: Technology, Work and the Organization." *Journal of Organizational Change Management* 19, no. 5 (2006): 593–618.

Turco, Catherine J. "Cultural Foundations of Tokenism: Evidence from the Leveraged Buyout Industry." *American Sociological Review* 75, no. 6 (2010): 894–913.

Turkle, Sherry. *Alone Together: Why We Expect More from Technology and Less from Each Other*. London: Hachette UK, 2017.

——. "Always-On/Always-On-You: The Tethered Self." In *Handbook of Mobile Communication Studies*, ed. James E. Katz, 121–137. Cambridge, MA: MIT Press, 2008.

——. *Reclaiming Conversation: The Power of Talk in a Digital Age*. New York: Penguin Books, 2016.

Twenge, Jean M. *iGen: Why Today's Super-Connected Kids Are Growing Up Less Rebellious, More Tolerant, Less Happy—and Completely Unprepared for Adulthood—and What That Means for the Rest of Us*. New York: Simon & Schuster, 2017.

U.S. Census Bureau. "Americans Moving at Historically Low Rates, Census Bureau Reports." November 16, 2016. https://www.amazon.com/dp/B0741DXTBW?tag=bfrebecca-20&ascsubtag=4946035%2C18%2C33%2Cmobile_web%2C0%2C0&th=1.

———. "The Majority of Children Live with Two Parents, Census Bureau Reports." November 17, 2016. https://census.gov/newsroom/press-releases/2016/cb16-192.html.

Van Steenbergen, E. F., and N. Ellemers. "Is Managing the Work-Family Interface Worthwhile? Benefits for Employee Health and Performance." *Journal of Organizational Behavior* 30, no. 5 (2009): 616–642.

Village to Village Network. "Village Model," 2019. https://www.vtvnetwork.org/content.aspx?page_id=22&club_id=691012&module_id=248578#top.

Wade, Lisa. "The Invisible Workload That Drags Women Down." *Time*, December 29, 2016. http://time.com/money/4561314/women-work-home-gender-gap.

Wajcman, Judy. *Pressed for Time: The Acceleration of Life in Digital Capitalism.* Chicago: University Of Chicago Press, 2014.

Walker, Matthew. *Why We Sleep: Unlocking the Power of Sleep and Dreams.* New York: Scribner, 2017.

Walzer, Susan. *Thinking About the Baby: Gender and Transitions into Parenthood.* Philadelphia: Temple University Press, 1998.

Wang, Wendy, Kim Parker, and Paul Taylor. "Breadwinner Moms." Pew Research Center, May 29, 2013. http://www.pewsocialtrends.org/2013/05/29/breadwinner-moms/.

Weeden, Kim, Youngjoo Cha, and Mauricio Bucca. "Long Work Hours, Part-Time Work, and Trends in the Gender Gap in Pay, the Motherhood Wage Penalty, and the Fatherhood Wage Premium." *The Russell Sage Foundation Journal of the Social Sciences* 2, no. 4 (2016): 71–102.

Weeks, Kathi. *The Problem with Work: Feminism, Marxism, Antiwork Politics, and Postwork Imaginaries.* Durham, NC: Duke University Press, 2011.

Weisshaar, Katherine. "From Opt Out to Blocked Out: The Challenges for Labor Market Re-Entry After Family-Related Employment Lapses." *American Sociological Review* 83, no. 1 (2018): 34–60.

Westervelt, Amy. *Forget "Having It All": How America Messed Up Motherhood and How to Fix It.* New York: Seal Press, 2018.

———. "The Surprising Benefits of Relentlessly Auditing Your Life." *New York Times*, May 25, 2019. https://www.nytimes.com/2019/05/25/opinion/gender-marriage-spreadsheet.html.

Widdows, Heather. *Perfect Me: Beauty as an Ethical Ideal.* Princeton, NJ: Princeton University Press, 2018.

Williams, Joan C. "Deconstructing Gender." *Michigan Law Review* 87, no. 797 (1989): 797–845.

——. *Unbending Gender: Why Family and Work Conflict and What to Do About It.* Oxford: Oxford University Press, 2000.

Williams, Joan C., Jennifer L. Berdahl, and Joseph A. Vandello. "Beyond Work-Life 'Integration.'" *Annual Review of Psychology* 67 (2016): 515–539.

Williams, Joan C., and Stephanie Bornstein. "The Evolution of FReD: Family Responsibilities, Discrimination and Developments in the Law of Stereotyping and Implicit Bias." *Hastings Law Journal* 59 (2008): 1311–1358.

Williams, Simon J. "Health as Moral Performance: Ritual, Transgression and Taboo." *Health* 2, no. 4 (1998): 435–457.

Wills, Kate. "Man Who Has It All: Parody Gender Equality Twitter Account Has Hit a Nerve." *The Independent*, February 24, 2016. https://www.independent.co.uk/life-style/gadgets-and-tech/despite-his-sarky-tweets-on-gender-equality-women-just-love-themanwhohasitall-a6893921.html.

Wolf, Gary. "Know Thyself: Tracking Every Facet of Life, From Sleep to Mood to Pain, 24/7/365." *Wired*, June 22, 2009. https://www.wired.com/2009/06/lbnp-knowthyself.

Women's Bureau. "Working Mother's Issue Brief." *U.S. Department of Labor*, June 13, 2016. https://www.dol.gov/wb/resources/WB_WorkingMothers_508_FinalJune13.pdf.

WorkLife Law. "What Is FRD (Family Responsibilities Discrimination)?" University of California Hastings College of the Law, 2019. https://worklifelaw.org/get-help/what-is-frd.

World Health Organization. "Guidelines on Physical Activity, Sedentary Behavior and Sleep for Children Under 5 Years of Age." *World Health Organization*, 2019. https://apps.who.int/iris/handle/10665/311664.

Wynn, Alison T. "Misery Has Company: The Shared Emotional Consequences of Everwork Among Men and Women." *Sociological Forum* 33, no. 3 (2018): 713–734.

Wynn, Alison T., and Aliya H. Rao. "Failures of Flexibility: How Perceived Control Motivates the Individualization of Work-Life Conflict." *Industrial and Labor Relations Review*, 2019.

Yardi, Sarita, and Amy Bruckman. "Social and Technical Challenges in Parenting Teens' Social Media Use." *Proceedings.* SIGCHI Conference on Human Factors in Computing Systems, Vancouver, BC, Canada, 2011, 3237–3246. https://doi.org/10.1145/1978942.1979422.

Yavorsky, Jill E., Lisa A. Keister, Yue Qian, and Michael Nau. "Women in the One Percent: Gender Dynamics in Top Income Positions." *American Sociological Review* 84 (2019): 54–81.

Zelman, Kathleen M. "Good Eggs: For Nutrition, They're Hard to Beat." *WebMD*, 2016. https://www.webmd.com/diet/features/good-eggs-for-nutrition-theyre-hard-to-beat#1.

Zerubavel, Eviatar. "Private Time and Public Time: The Temporal Structure of Social Accessibility and Professional Commitments." *Social Forces* 58, no. 1 (September 1979), 38–58.

Ziptopia. "Don't Touch That Phone: How to Plan a Technology Detox." *Zipcar*, 2015. https://www.zipcar.com/ziptopia/around-the-bend/dont-touch-that-phone-how-to-plan-a-technology-detox.

INDEX